Communications in Computer and Information Science 506

Commenced Publication in 2007
Founding and Former Series Editors:
Alfredo Cuzzocrea, Dominik Ślęzak, and Xiaokang Yang

More information about this series at http://www.springer.com/series/7899

Slimane Hammoudi · Luís Ferreira Pires
Joaquim Filipe · Rui César das Neves (Eds.)

Model-Driven Engineering and Software Development

Second International Conference, MODELSWARD 2014
Lisbon, Portugal, January 7–9, 2014
Revised Selected Papers

Springer

Editors
Slimane Hammoudi
Université d'Angers/ESEO
Angers
France

Joaquim Filipe
INSTICC
Setúbal
Portugal

Luís Ferreira Pires
University of Twente
Enschede
The Netherlands

Rui César das Neves
Polytechnic Institute of Setúbal
Lisbon
Portugal

ISSN 1865-0929 ISSN 1865-0937 (electronic)
Communications in Computer and Information Science
ISBN 978-3-319-25155-4 ISBN 978-3-319-25156-1 (eBook)
DOI 10.1007/978-3-319-25156-1

Library of Congress Control Number: 2015950049

Springer Cham Heidelberg New York Dordrecht London

Printed on acid-free paper

Springer International Publishing AG Switzerland is part of Springer Science+Business Media (www.springer.com)

Preface

The present book includes extended and revised versions of a set of selected papers from the Second International Conference on Model-Driven Engineering and Software Development (MODELSWARD 2014), held in Lisbon, Portugal, January 7–9, 2014.

The purpose of the International Conference on Model-Driven Engineering and Software Development is to provide a platform for researchers, engineers, academicians as well as industrial professionals from all over the world to present their research results and development activities in using models and model-driven engineering techniques for software development.

MODELSWARD 2014 was sponsored by INSTICC (the Institute for Systems and Technologies of Information, Control and Communication) and held in cooperation with ACM SIGMIS – ACM Special Interest Group on Management Information Systems, ARTEMIS Project MBAT, MDE Expertise Project, The Open Group – SOA Work Group, and technically co-sponsored by the AIS Special Interest Group on Modeling and Simulation (AIS SIGMAS).

The conference received 88 paper submissions from 32 countries, covering all continents. To evaluate each submission, a double-blind paper review was performed by the Program Committee. After a stringent selection process, 15 papers were published and presented as full papers (30-min oral presentation), leading to a full-paper acceptance ratio of about 17 %, which shows our commitment of offering a high-quality forum also for forthcoming editions of this conference.

The MODELSWARD program included panels and five invited talks delivered by internationally distinguished speakers, namely: Philippe Desfray (SOFTEAM, France), Colin Atkinson (University of Mannheim, Germany), Silvia Abrahão, (Universitat Politecnica de Valencia, Spain), Kim G. Larsen (Aalborg University, Denmark), and Andreas Holzinger (Medical University Graz, Austria).

This book contains ten papers from MODELSWARD 2014 that have been selected, extended, and thoroughly revised.

We would like to thank the authors, whose research and development efforts are recorded here for future generations.

April 2015

Joaquim Filipe
Luís Ferreira Pires
Rui César das Neves
Slimane Hammoudi

Organization

Conference Co-chairs

Joaquim Filipe	Polytechnic Institute of Setúbal/INSTICC, Portugal
Rui César das Neves	Polytechnic Institute of Setúbal, Portugal

Program Co-chairs

Luis Ferreira Pires	University of Twente, The Netherlands
Slimane Hammoudi	ESEO, MODESTE, France

Organizing Committee

Helder Coelhas	INSTICC, Portugal
André Lista	INSTICC, Portugal
Andreia Moita	INSTICC, Portugal
Raquel Pedrosa	INSTICC, Portugal
Vitor Pedrosa	INSTICC, Portugal
Cláudia Pinto	INSTICC, Portugal
Susana Ribeiro	INSTICC, Portugal
Sara Santiago	INSTICC, Portugal
Mara Silva	INSTICC, Portugal
José Varela	INSTICC, Portugal
Pedro Varela	INSTICC, Portugal

Program Committee

Silvia Abrahão	Universitat Politecnica de Valencia, Spain
Fernando Brito e Abreu	ISCTE-IUL and CITI/FCT/UNL, Portugal
Hamideh Afsarmanesh	University of Amsterdam, The Netherlands
Guglielmo de Angelis	CNR – ISTI, Italy
Keijiro Araki	Kyushu University, Japan
Colin Atkinson	University of Mannheim, Germany
Paris Avgeriou	University of Groningen, The Netherlands
Elarbi Badidi	United Arab Emirates University, UAE
Doo-Hwan Bae	Korea Advanced Institute of Science and Technology (KAIST), Republic of Korea
Daniel Balasubramanian	Vanderbilt University, USA
Bernhard Bauer	University of Augsburg, Germany
Luca Berardinelli	University of L'Aquila, Italy

Alexandre Bergel	Pleiad Lab, Computer Science Department (DCC), University of Chile, Santiago, Chile
Lorenzo Bettini	Università di Torino, Italy
Paolo Bocciarelli	University of Rome Tor Vergata, Italy
Jan Bosch	Chalmers University of Technology, Sweden
Jean-Pierre Bourey	Ecole Centrale de Lille, France
Mark van den Brand	Eindhoven University of Technology, The Netherlands
Robin van den Broek	JEM-id, The Netherlands
Antonio Brogi	Università di Pisa, Italy
Manfred Broy	Technische Universität München, Germany
Achim D. Brucker	SAP Research, Germany
Philipp Brune	University of Applied Sciences Neu-Ulm, Germany
Juan Manuel Gonzalez Calleros	Universidad Autónoma de Puebla, Mexico
Cinzia Cappiello	Politecnico di Milano, Italy
Sergio de Cesare	Brunel University, UK
W.K. Chan	City University of Hong Kong, Hong Kong, SAR China
Michel Chaudron	Chalmers | Gotenborg University, Sweden
David Chen	Laboratory IMS, France
Yuting Chen	Shanghai Jiaotong University, China
Dickson Chiu	Dickson Computer Systems, Hong Kong
Antonio Cicchetti	Malardalen University, Sweden
Kevin Daimi	University of Detroit Mercy, USA
Florian Daniel	University of Trento, Italy
Leonidas Deligiannidis	Wentworth Institute of Technology, USA
Zinovy Diskin	McMaster University and University of Waterloo, Canada
Dimitris Dranidis	CITY College, University of Sheffield, Greece
Holger Eichelberger	Universität Hildesheim, Germany
Vadim Ermolayev	Zaporozhye National University, Ukraine
Maria Jose Escalona	University of Seville, Spain
Rik Eshuis	Eindhoven University of Technology, The Netherlands
Angelina Espinoza	Universidad Autónoma Metropolitana, Iztapalapa (UAM-I), Spain
Vladimir Estivill-Castro	Griffith University, Australia
João Faria	FEUP, University of Porto, Portugal
Cléver Ricardo Guareis de Farias	University of São Paulo, Brazil
Jamel Feki	University of Sfax, Tunisia
Gianluigi Ferrari	University of Parma, Italy
Paul Fishwick	University of Texas at Dallas, USA
John Fitzgerald	Newcastle University, UK
Stephan Flake	Orga Systems GmbH, Germany
Lidia Fuentes	Universidad de Málaga, Spain
Carlo A. Furia	ETH Zurich, Switzerland

Juan Garbajosa	Technical University of Madrid, UPM, Spain
Alessandro Garcia	Pontifical Catholic University of Rio de Janeiro, Brazil
Angelo Gargantini	University of Bergamo, Italy
Paola Giannini	Università del Piemonte Orientale, Italy
Stefania Gnesi	CNR, Italy
Cesar Gonzalez-Perez	Institute of Heritage Sciences (Incipit), Spanish National Research Council (CSIC), Spain
Pieter Van Gorp	Eindhoven University of Technology, The Netherlands
Michael Grimaila	Center for Cyberspace Research, USA
Slimane Hammoudi	ESEO, MODESTE, France
Klaus Havelund	Nasa/Jet Propulsion Laboratory, USA
Brian Henderson-Sellers	University of Technology, Sydney, Australia
Jose R. Hilera	University of Alcala, Spain
Marianne Huchard	Lirmm Université Montpelier 2, France
Ricardo Jardim-Gonçalves	Universidade Nova de Lisboa, UNINOVA, Portugal
Carlos Juiz	Universitat de les Illes Balears, Spain
George Kakarontzas	Technological Education Institute of Larissa, Greece
Teemu Kanstren	VTT, Finland
Georgia Kapitsaki	University of Cyprus, Cyprus
Jacek Kesik	Lublin University of Technology, Poland
Joseph Kiniry	Technical University of Denmark, Denmark
In-Young Ko	Korea Advanced Institute of Science and Technology, Republic of Korea
Grzegorz Koziel	Lublin University of Technology, Poland
Martin Kropp	University of Applied Sciences Northwestern Switzerland, Switzerland
Uirá Kulesza	Federal University of Rio Grande do Norte (UFRN), Brazil
Jochen Küster	IBM Research, Switzerland
Anna-Lena Lamprecht	Potsdam University, Germany
Kevin Lano	King's College London, UK
Doug Lea	State University of New York at Oswego, USA
Kun Chang Lee	Sungkyunkwan University, Republic of Korea
Dongxi Liu	CSIRO, Australia
Francesca Lonetti	National Research Council (CNR) Pisa, Italy
Denivaldo Lopes	Federal University of Maranhão, Brazil
Roberto Lopez-Herrejon	Johannes Kepler, University Linz, Austria
Der-Chyuan Lou	Chang Gung University, Taiwan
Eda Marchetti	ISTI-CNR, Italy
Beatriz Marin	Universidad Diego Portales, Chile
Steve McKeever	Uppsala University, Sweden
Stephen Mellor	Freeter, UK
Dragan Milicev	University of Belgrade, Serbia
Marek Milosz	Lublin University of Technology, Poland
Dugki Min	Konkuk University, Republic of Korea
Valérie Monfort	Université de Paris1 Panthéon Sorbonne, France

Sascha Mueller-Feuerstein	Ansbach University of Applied Sciences, Germany
Debajyoti Mukhopadhyay	Maharashtra Institute of Technology, India
Andrzej Niesler	Wroclaw University of Economics, Poland
Halit Oguztüzün	Middle East Technical University, Turkey
Olaf Owe	University of Oslo, Norway
Gordon Pace	University of Malta, Malta
Oscar Pastor	Universidad Politécnica de Valencia, Spain
Patrizio Pelliccione	Chalmers University of Technology and University of Gothenburg, Sweden
Dana Petcu	West University of Timisoara, Romania
Alexander Petrenko	ISPRAS, Russian Federation
Luis Ferreira Pires	University of Twente, The Netherlands
Malgorzata Plachawska-Wójcik	Lublin University of Technology, Poland
Ivan Porres	Åbo Akademi University, Finland
Elke Pulvermueller	University of Osnabrück, Germany
Wolfgang Reisig	Humboldt-Universität zu Berlin, Germany
Werner Retschitzegger	Johannes Kepler University, Austria
Laurent Rioux	THALES, France
Jose Raul Romero	University of Cordoba, Spain
Gustavo Rossi	Lifia, Argentina
Davide Di Ruscio	University of L'Aquila, Italy
Motoshi Saeki	Tokyo Institute of Technology, Japan
Francesca Saglietti	University of Erlangen-Nuremberg, Germany
Rick Salay	University of Toronto, Canada
Comai Sara	Politecnico di Milano, Italy
Petr Sauer	University of Economics, Czech Republic
Anthony Savidis	Institute of Computer Science, FORTH, Greece
Giuseppe Scanniello	University of Basilicata, Italy
Jean-Guy Schneider	Swinburne University of Technology, Australia
Wieland Schwinger	Johannes Kepler University, Austria
Peter Sestoft	IT University of Copenhagen, Denmark
Marten van Sinderen	University of Twente, The Netherlands
Stefan Sobernig	WU Vienna, Austria
Arnor Solberg	Sintef, Norway
Richard Soley	Object Management Group, Inc., USA
Stéphane Somé	University of Ottawa, Canada
Jean-Sébastier Sottet	Public Research Center Henri Tudor, Luxembourg
George Spanoudakis	City University London, UK
James Steel	University of Queensland, Australia
Alin Stefanescu	University of Pitesti, Romania
Perdita Stevens	University of Edinburgh, UK
Ragnhild Van Der Straeten	Vrije Universiteit Brussel, Belgium
A. Taleb-Bendiab	Edith Cowen University, Australia
Massimo Tivoli	University of L'Aquila, Italy
Riccardo Torlone	Università Roma Tre, Italy

Salvador Trujillo	Ikerlan, Spain
Naoyasu Ubayashi	Kyushu University, Japan
Sabrina Uhrig	Universität Bayreuth, Germany
Andreas Ulrich	Siemens AG, Germany
Gianluigi Viscusi	Università di Milano-Bicocca, Italy
Christiane Gresse von Wangenheim	UFSC - Federal University of Santa Catarina, Brazil
Viacheslav Wolfengagen	Institute JurInfoR, Russian Federation
Haiping Xu	University of Massachusetts, Dartmouth, USA
Tao Yue	Simula Research Lab, Norway
Gefei Zhang	Celonis GmbH, Germany
Heming Zhang	Tsinghua University, China
Haiyan Zhao	Peking University, China
Olaf Zimmermann	HSR Hochschule für Technik Rapperswil, Switzerland
Elena Zucca	University of Genova, Italy

Additional Reviewers

Laura Belli	Università degli Studi di Parma, Italy
Xabier de Carlos	Ikerlan, Spain
Federico Ciccozzi	Mälardalen University, Sweden
Ferruccio Damiani	Università Degli Studi di Torino, Italy
Jessica Diaz Fernandez	Universidad Politécnica de Madrid, Spain
Alessio Ferrari	CNR, Italy
Christian Gierds	Humboldt-Universität zu Berlin, Germany
Beatriz Gomez	University of the Balearic Islands, Spain
Isaac Lera	University of the Balearic Islands, Spain
Aitor Murguzur	IK4-IKERLAN, Spain
Hajer Saada	LIRMM, France
Giorgio Oronzo Spagnolo	ISTI CNR ITALY, Italy
Volker Stolz	Universitetet i Oslo, Norway
Jan Sürmeli	Humboldt-Universität zu Berlin, Germany
Anjelika Votintseva	Siemens AG, Germany
Gil Zohav	BGU, Israel

Invited Speakers

Philippe Desfray	SOFTEAM, France
Colin Atkinson	University of Mannheim, Germany
Silvia Abrahão	Universitat Politecnica de Valencia, Spain
Kim G. Larsen	Aalborg University, Denmark
Andreas Holzinger	Medical University Graz, Austria

Contents

Invited Papers

World Wide Modeling: The Agility of the Web Applied to Model Repositories

Philippe Desfray(✉)

SOFTEAM, Paris, France
philippe.desfray@softeam.fr

Abstract. In today's era of data sharing, immediate communication and world-wide distribution of participants, at a time when teams are asked to be ever more agile, the traditional approach of model repositories no longer meets expectations. Centralized organization has become inconsistent with the way in which the world and its companies function.

In today's world, it is virtually impossible to set up a model repository for different enterprise entities, large-scale systems or projects, which can be accessed by all participants (readers, contributors, partners, and so on). Standard techniques based on a centralized repository with a designated manager come up against a vast variety of situations, with participants who neither want nor are able to conform to uniform rules and management.

This does not allow model-based knowledge management at an enterprise or global level. It inhibits agility and open team cooperation. We believe that this is a major hurdle to the dissemination of model-based approaches; the reality of heavy-weight model management hinders the most appealing of model-based approaches.

Based on the latest technologies and research for model repositories, this talk will explain why current model repository technologies are a major drawback and will present a way of supporting highly decentralized organizations, and agile and open team cooperation. Scaling up and widening the scope of model repositories will enable modeling support to be applied to the "extended enterprise", which incorporates its eco-system (providers, partners, and so on).

Keywords: Model repositories · World wide modeling · Pervasive modeling · Model distribution · Model teamwork · Model organization · MDA · Model fragment · Model governance · Models ecosystems

1 Overview

In today's era of data sharing, immediate communication and world-wide distribution of participants, at a time when teams are asked to be ever more agile, the traditional approach of model repositories no longer meets expectations. Centralized organization has become inconsistent with the way in which the world and its companies function.

Consequently, a new repository approach is emerging through the "Constellation" repository technology provided by the upcoming version 3 of the Modelio modeling tool[1]. This is a major change in concept, based on recent approaches and technologies

[1] Modelio comes in an open source distribution available on www.modelio.org and in a commercial distribution available on www.modeliosoft.com.

S. Hammoudi et al. (Eds.): MODELSWARD 2014, CCIS 506, pp. 3–11, 2015.
DOI: 10.1007/978-3-319-25156-1_1

that are better adapted to today's world: Models have to be distributed and shared in as vast and immediate a way as the web. Agile cooperation modes, such as those used in open source projects, also have to be supported at model level (Fig. 1).

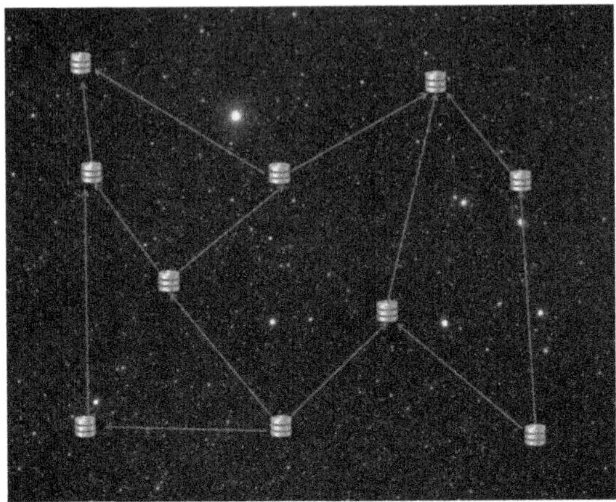

Fig. 1. Constellation of repositories.

The existence of the open source distribution of Modelio will enable increased repository accessibility, by removing cost and subscription-related barriers.

This white paper presents this new approach, and shows how different organization modes can best use it.

This work is part of our continuous efforts for globalizing the MDA [1] approach, in order to maximize the distribution and the ROI of the model driven technologies [2]. Getting a technology for easily distributing models, added to other model related techniques such as the usage of viewpoints [3] and of techniques for packaging know-how in model driven development [4] are means for having a broader access to models and model driven technologies, and for improving the ROI from models [5].

2 Model Repository Centralization: The Limitations of the Standard Model

In today's world, it is virtually impossible to set up a model repository for different enterprise entities, large-scale systems or projects, which can be accessed by all participants (readers, contributors, partners, and so on). Standard techniques based on a centralized repository with a designated manager come up against a vast variety of situations, with participants who neither want nor are able to conform to uniform rules and management (Fig. 2).

This traditional centralization imposes:

- A need for centralized declaration of users and configurations.
- A mandatory organization of repository models.

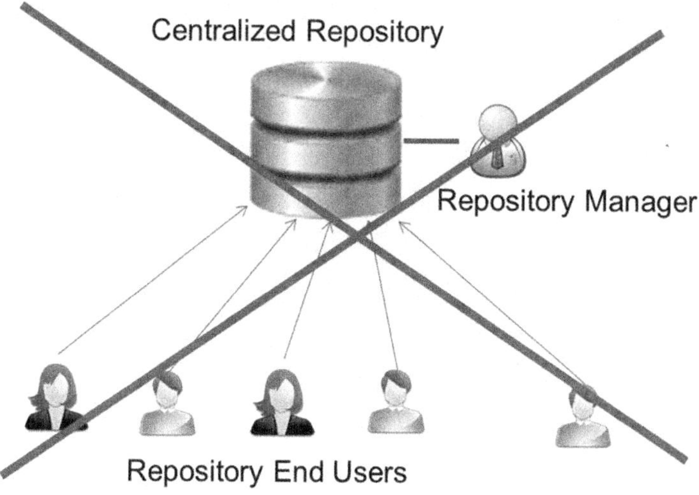

Fig. 2. Centralized organization: A model which has reached its limits.

- A limited repository storage and access mode, which goes against the need for ubiquity and nomadic mode autonomy.
- A costly approach, requiring "server" licenses for each participant.

This kind of approach clearly hinders team agility, as well as team and model distribution. For example, it cannot be considered for contributory open source projects, or for systems and projects involving several partners. As a result, it cannot be used by large companies, whose different departments are often autonomous. This is a real obstacle to model-based knowledge management within organizations.

The use of a centralized repository does present a number of advantages, and has proven its worth over the years. However, it has reached its limits for the adoption and sharing of models, and goes against openness and agility. After presenting a totally decentralized architecture, we will demonstrate how the two approaches can be combined, so as to benefit from the advantages of both.

3 Taking Inspiration from the Web, a Widely Used and Tested Approach for Information Publication

Modelio's new "Constellation" repository technology is based upon two widespread approaches supporting cooperation and information and contribution sharing:

- The web, whose omnipresence and flexibility are required by everyone.
- The distribution of models through "libraries". This approach is widely used for code in open source projects and software development, which are a major source of sharing and re-use.

Like the web, there is no "central server" with Constellation. The organization is highly decentralized, which allows the most open and agile cooperation modes. In its own way, the Modelio modeling tool plays the role of an internet browser. Its open source distribution, which also includes "Constellation", provides open access to the repository (Fig. 3).

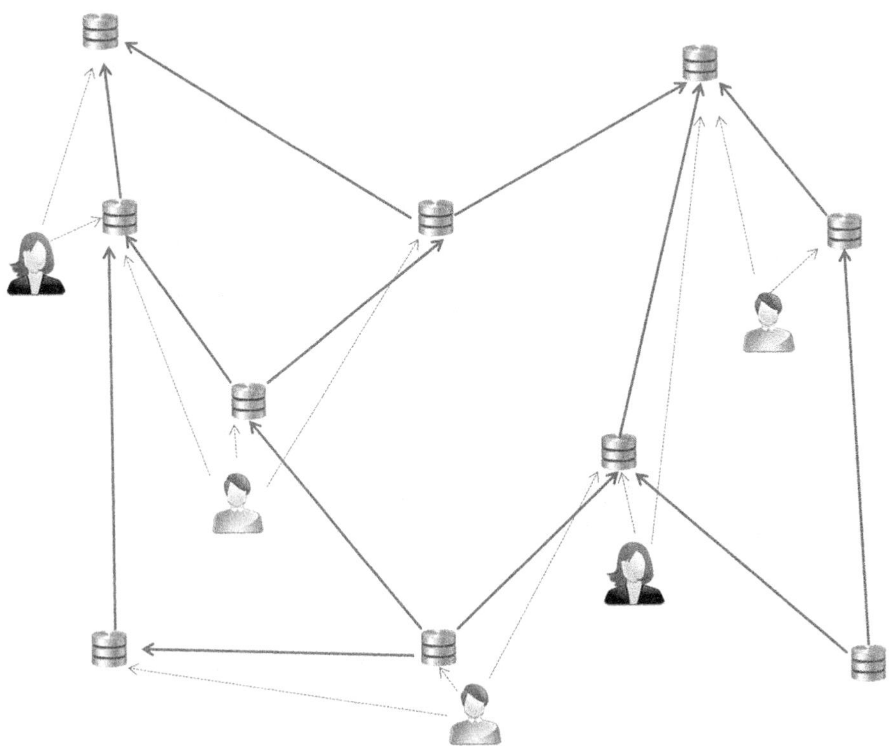

Fig. 3. Decentralized organization: Distribution of users and model fragments.

Constellation is a network (or web) of "model fragments", which constitute autonomous groups of model elements. Each model fragment has its own independent storage, and can have several access modes (local, shared, versioned and configured, library, web, secure web). The model elements in a fragment can be linked to other model elements from different fragments (Fig. 4), and the "model" then has a range which includes several distributed fragments.

A "model" groups fragments together in order to meet a specific goal. For example, this can be a project, a system, architecture, and so on.

Using the Modelio modeling tool, which acts as a sort of fragment and model browser, the user therefore edits a model which is a set of fragments whose components are interlinked. These fragments can be transparently local or remote via the web or any other network. The user edits or browses a model of unlimited size, without having to worry about the actual location of the elements handled, which are scattered across different fragments in the Constellation.

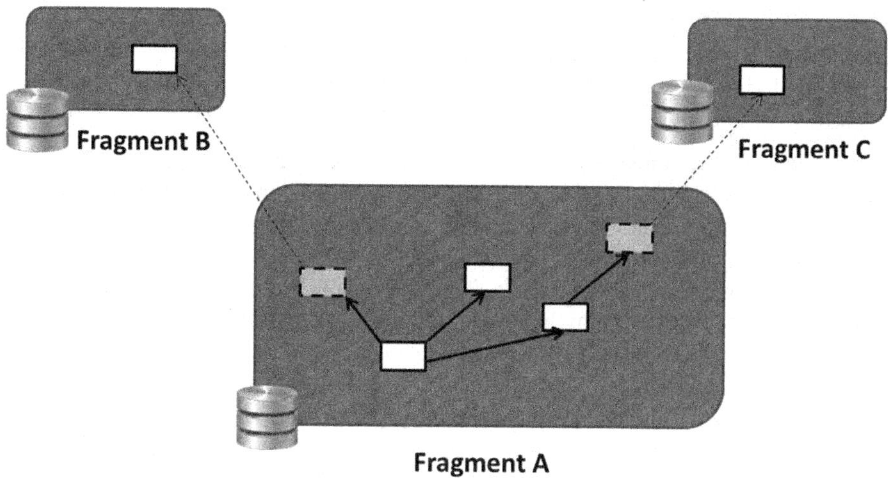

Fig. 4. Transparent referencing between fragments.

4 Defining a Model and Its Components in a Constellation

A model is an abstract representation in the form of images and text. It represents something (a system, a problem, a solution, concepts, procedures, …) for a particular community of participants (designers, developers, business analysts, users, …), and has a clearly defined objective (pedagogical example, business view, design, analysis, implementation, …).

The images and texts that a model presents are views of the model elements which constitute it. Model elements break a model down into elementary information, for example a class, an attribute, an attribute's type, an operation's parameter, an association end, and so on.

Handling an individual model element rarely makes sense for a user, who will usually work with a more macroscopic agglomerated element. The following model element aggregation structures can therefore be identified:

- *Configuration Units* are Groups of Model Elements which are Individually Managed by the User. Their definition can vary, but in practice they constitute a management unit for the user, who handles them and manages their version and configuration. They typically correspond to a Class, a Use Case, a Component, a Process or a Package. A configuration unit can also be locked to control and avoid concurrent access to it: it is a user's work unit.
- *Model Fragments* are Groups of Higher Level Model Elements. Materialized as packages, they group configuration units. Model designers attribute logical consistency to model fragments, but their primary function is to autonomously store a part of a model. Their components can be linked to model elements belonging to other model fragments. A model element is also not definitively linked to a fragment. It can be moved to other fragments, according to the organizational needs of the designers.

- *Models* are Groups of Model Fragments with a Defined Goal (the Model of an Application, of System Architecture, of a Particular Problem, and so on). Models identify the fragments which compose it and group them in a specific context. Fragments exist independently of models, and can be referenced by several models.

When a model is edited, the location of fragments is transparent: they can be local to a machine, on a local company network, or published on the web. Decisions on breakdown into fragments, physical location and accessibility are driven by participants' organizational, cooperation and accessibility needs.

As with internet browsers, access to other fragments via the web cannot be guaranteed. The remote element may be absent, the internet connection can be interrupted, and so on. The architecture of Constellation guarantees that links from origin elements to remote elements remain visible, and that reconnection with absent elements happens transparently, as with broken links and absent pages in internet browsers.

In Fig. 5, a model has been defined, targeting the software development of a Java application made up of several fragments:

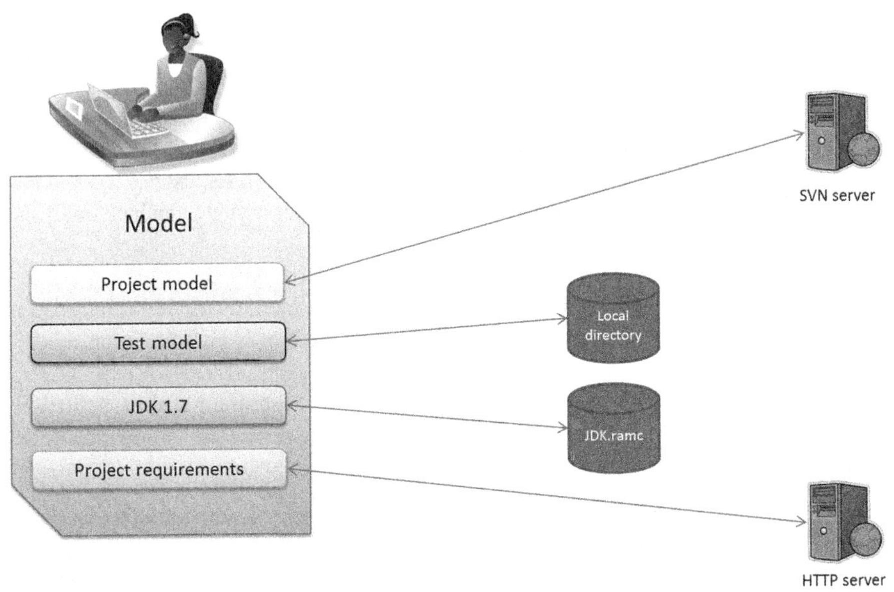

Fig. 5. Example of model configuration.

- The Model Developed during the Project. This model is shared by all project participants. Access to the model is controlled by SVN, which manages versions, configuration and concurrent access.
- A Local Test Model. This fragment is only visible to the current user, who stores it locally on his/her workstation.
- The JDK (Java) Library Model: This reversed model is distributed in the form of a "model component" (or model library), and is accessible in read-only mode.

- The Requirements Model Resulting from Business Analysis. This model can be accessed in read-only mode via http. It is used to trace the application model to requirements and to run impact analyses.

This example shows us that a model (dedicated here to a project) is configured by assembling fragments which can have different statuses and access modes (remote and managed in teamwork mode and in configuration, local to a workstation, in the form of a library, in open access mode via the internet).

5 Modelio Servers: Governing Modeling for a System or Organization

Like the web, the Constellation technology is naturally distributed and has no centralizing element. This characteristic ensures openness for participants.

To combine the advantages of the openness of decentralization and the control afforded by a centralized repository approach, servers must be put in place.

In a “Constellation” architecture, model servers provide a central access point to a set of distributed model fragments. A server defines a community that will use a set of fragments and takes care of making sure that access rights, conventions and rules are respected. In a constellation of model fragments, an unlimited number of servers can exist, with each model fragment accessible by zero or several servers.

The function of the model server (Modeliosoft solution) is therefore to organize the repository, govern access to it, assist teams in a particular cooperation mode and manage model and project portfolios. Servers also manage project configuration, by updating and maintaining the consistency of all participant configurations (versions of Modelio “plug in” extensions or “modules”, fragments and libraries)[2]. A server is used to define user communities, which share organization rules and conventions. The server presents its users with a portfolio of models (or projects). In a typical model Constellation, several servers co-exist and share model fragments, by governing and controlling the models accessible to the community. This co-existence of several servers which share model fragments is the most important new development with regard to standard server schemas. It enables openness and sharing between the different “worlds” that each server represents within a “universe” which is the Constellation architecture.

The fragments managed by a server can be accessible from other servers or in the absence of servers, which allows the most openness and the widest sharing. Conversely, they can be visible to only a restricted community, in accordance with strict rules and security and confidentiality constraints.

The use of Modelio servers with the Constellation technology thus enables the combination of the agility and openness required by certain cooperation modes with the organization rules dedicated to certain groups of participants (Fig. 6).

[2] Here we find traditional server services, already provided in the current version of Modelio.

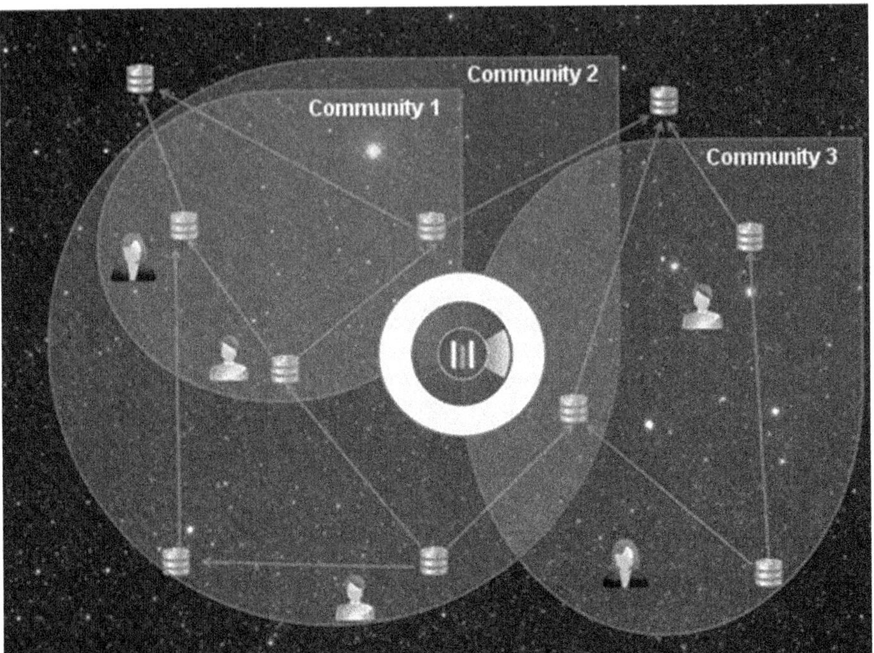

Fig. 6. Servers organize different communities in a constellation of model fragments.

6 Conclusion

This new approach to organizing repositories removes the obstacles of the current centralized view, both in terms of the organization and distribution of participants and date, and in terms of the volume of data handled.

It provides repositories with great agility, and enables the use of organization modes which are in tune with current cooperation modes.

This approach provides large-scale organizations with a means of building a real, universally accessible model repository, while retaining the means of governing and sharing conventions within participant communities. In this way, it supports the diversity of entities which exist within an organization, and their autonomy, while facilitating sharing and cooperation. This widening enables modeling support to be applied to the "extended enterprise", which incorporates its eco-system (providers, partners, and so on).

This approach also provides a solution to tool limitations with regard to the support of large-scale models (due to the size and number of concurrent accesses), by breaking them down into fragments and allowing "load balancing" strategies and data replication/synchronization strategies between servers.

Finally, it allows a more lightweight, more flexible organization for all sorts of communities: open source, small to medium-sized companies, and so on.

The new technical and functional capabilities are recognized, and the time has come for organizations to take ownership of this approach, in order to put in place open and distributed cooperation modes which correspond to their goals.

References

1. MDA Guide Version 1.0.1, OMG 2003. www.omg.org/news/meetings/…Manual/00-2_MDA_Guide_v1.0.1.pdf
2. Desfray, P.: Modelio: globalizing MDA. In: Proceedings of the Tools and Consultancy Track of the Fifth European Conference on Model-Driven Architecture Foundations and Applications (ECMDA-FA 2009). University of Twente, Enschede, The Netherlands, June 2009
3. Fischer, K., Panfilenko, D., Krumeich, J., Born, M., Desfray, P.: Viewpoint-based modeling—towards defining the viewpoint concept and implications for supporting modeling tools. In: EMISA (2012)
4. Bendraou, R., Desfray, P., Gervais, M.P., Muller, A.: MDA tool components: a proposal for packaging know-how in model driven development. Software System Modeling **7**(3), 329–343 (2008)
5. Hartman, A., Schieferdecker. I.: Model Driven Architecture–Foundations and Applications (2008)

Models in Software Architecture Derivation and Evaluation: Challenges and Opportunities

Javier Gonzalez-Huerta, Emilio Insfran, and Silvia Abrahão(✉)

ISSI Research Group, Universitat Politècnica de València,
Camino de Vera, s/n, 46022 Valencia, Spain
{jagonzalez, einsfran, sabrahao}@dsic.upv.es

Abstract. Software architecture derivation and evaluation are complex and error prone activities that still represent an open problem with many challenges and opportunities where model-driven software development can play a leading role. In software product line development, the use of model-driven principles could help by providing a richer semantic representation of a product line and by capturing the architectural design decisions and its impact on the product quality attributes. In this chapter, we analyze the main challenges and opportunities surrounding the product architecture derivation and evaluation and introduce QuaDAI, a method for the derivation, evaluation, and improvement of product architectures in model-driven software product line development environments. The method comprises a multimodel, which represents the different viewpoints of a software product line, and a process conducted by model transformations that automate the derivation, evaluation, and improvement of product architectures.

Keywords: Software architectures · Software product lines · Model-driven development · Quality assurance

1 Introduction

Software architecture derivation and evaluation in Software Product Line (SPL) development environments is a complex and error-prone process [1] that still represents an open problem with many challenges and opportunities where Model-Driven Software Development (MDSD) can play a leading role. MDSD advocates the use of models not only to document the software development lifecycle but also to obtain the final product as a result of a model transformation chain. MDSD has been traditionally applied in the development of SPLs, especially for solving the configuration and product architecture derivation problem. A SPL is a set of software-intensive systems sharing a common, managed set of features that satisfy the specific needs of a particular market segment or mission and that are developed from a common set of core assets in a prescribed way [2]. SPLs emerged as a promising approach to improve software development processes so as to reduce costs and enhance productivity and product quality.

Quality assurance is a crucial activity for the success of any software development effort, but is even more important in SPL development since a defect in a core asset may impact negatively on the quality of the whole set of products within the product line. This fact is especially relevant when dealing with the software architecture. Software architecture is a key asset in SPL development and plays a dual role: on the

S. Hammoudi et al. (Eds.): MODELSWARD 2014, CCIS 506, pp. 12–31, 2015.
DOI: 10.1007/978-3-319-25156-1_2

one hand, the product line architecture (PLA) should provide variation mechanisms that help to achieve a set of explicitly allowed variations and, on the other hand, the product architecture (PA) is derived from the PLA by exercising its built-in architectural variation points [2]. Software architectures are the means for the attainment of the non-functional requirements (NFRs) of the products that will be derived from the product line, and thus assuring the achievement of those NFRs during the architecture derivation process is a critical activity in the development process.

In the last few years, MDSD has been applied in several research works to face the product architecture derivation problem in SPL environments (e.g., [3–17]) although the majority of these approaches do not properly integrate NFRs in the derivation process. It is surprising that being quality one of the main reasons for the adoption of the SPL approach, it has been often neglected in such a critical and complex process [18]. In addition, in those cases in which the derived PA is evaluated after its derivation, this evaluation is carried out by using software architecture evaluation methods that have not been specially defined for SPLs (e.g., ATAM [19], SAAM [20]). We believe that the use of model-driven principles could help by providing a richer semantic representation of a software product line and by capturing the architectural design decisions and its impact on the product quality attributes.

In this chapter, we first discuss the challenges identified in the area of architecture derivation and evaluation in Model-Driven Software Product Line Engineering (MD-SPLE), and then introduce QuaDAI [21, 22], an integrated method for the derivation, evaluation, and improvement of product architectures in MD-SPLE environments. The method comprises a multimodel, which represents the different viewpoints of the software product line, and a process conducted by model transformations that automate the derivation, evaluation, and improvement of product architectures.

The remainder of the chapter is structured as follows. Section 2 discusses existing approaches that deal with the derivation and evaluation of architectures in SPL development. Section 3 introduces QuaDAI, a method to support the derivation, evaluation and improvement of product architectures in MD-SPLE environments. Finally, Sect. 4 provides our conclusions and final remarks.

2 Existing Approaches for Architecture Derivation and Evaluation in MD-SPLE

In this section, we analyze the approaches that support the derivation and quality evaluation of product architectures in MD-SPLE. Section 2.1 analyzes existing approaches for product architecture derivation in MD-SPLE. Section 2.2 analyzes existing software architecture evaluation methods that allow the quality evaluation and analysis of product architectures in SPL development. Finally, Sect. 2.3 summarizes the main findings.

2.1 Product Architecture Derivation in MD-SPLE

Despite the huge number of research work dealing with architecture derivation in SPL development, the introduction of quality concerns in this process has not received a proper coverage. In Table 2, we show a summary of the classification of these approaches by applying an extension of the classification criteria defined by Rabiser et al. [1] (see Table 1).

Table 1. Architecture derivation classification criteria.

Criteria	Description
C1*	Non-functional requirements (NFRs) support
C2*	Explicit representation of NFRs/quality attributes and their relationships with the features (SPL external variability) or the architectural variants
C3**	Configuration support
C4**	Automated derivation support
C5***	Adaptability and extensibility (i.e., metamodel support, extension points for the integration of domain specific generators)
C6***	Flexible and user-specific visualizations of variability (filtering, classification and ordering support based on tasks, users, roles etc.)
C7	Explicit representation of architectural variability
C8	Architectural views support
C9	ADL/Modeling language support
C10	Configuration consistency checking

*C1 and C2: Adapted from the "Application requirements management support" criterion described in [1]
**C3 and C4: Adapted from the "Automated and interactive variability resolution" criterion described in [1]
***C5 and C6: Proposed at the systematic review by Rabiser et al. [1]

Given a set of architectural variation points for a product line architecture one of the main challenges is how to decide which variation points should be selected and which ones should not taking into account not only functional but also non-functional requirements. For these reason, we have suggested the criteria on Table 1.

The analysis show that there is a lack of approaches that: (i) can be applied regardless the architectural description language or architectural viewpoint; (ii) allow the explicitly representation of the architectural variability; (iii) allow the explicit representation of the NFRs as well as the relationships among the NFRs and the features that represent the SPL external variability but also the architectural variants that realize this external variability; (iv) allow to configure the product by considering both the features and the NFRs that the product must satisfy; (v) solve the architectural variability automatically by using model transformations.

2.2 Architecture Evaluation in MD-SPLE

Over the last years, several approaches that allow the quality evaluation and assessment of SPL product architectures have been proposed (e.g., [19, 23, 25–37]). In Table 4, we show the summary of the classification of these approaches by applying the classification criteria shown in Table 3.

Table 2. Classification of architecture derivation approaches.

Approach	C1	C2	C3	C4	C5	C6	C7	C8	C9	C10
Koalish [4]	−	−	+	−	+	−	+	C&C	Own	−
Cabello et al. [6]	−	−	+	+	+	−	+	+	Own	+
Botterweck et al. [5]	−	−	+	+	+	−	+ (FM/C)	C&C	+	+ (FM/C)
Duran-Limon et al. [8]	−	−	+	+	−	−	+ (OWL and FM)	C&C	+	+ (FM)
Guana and Correal [23]	+	−	+	+	+	−	+	C&C	+	−
Czarnecki and Antkiewicz [9]	−	−	+	+	+	−	+	+	+	+ (FM)
Ziadi and Jézéquel [10]	+	−	+	+	+	−	Model	+	UML	+
PLUS-EE [11]	−	−	+	+	−	−	Model	Multiple viewpoints	UML	+
Perrouin et al. [12]	−	−	+	+	+	−	+	−	UML	+
Schaefer et al. [13]	−	−	+	+	+	−	+	CoBoxes	CoBoxes	−
Tawhid and Petriu [14]	−	−	−	+	−	−	Model	Structure	Marte	−
Sánchez et al. [15]	−	−	−	+	+	−	+	+	+	−
FeatureMapper [16]	−	−	+	+	+	−	+ (FM and Model)	+	+	+
Haugen et al. [24]	−	−	+	+	+	−	+	+	+	+

Legend: FM: Feature Model; **C&C:** Component and Connector; **FM/C:** Feature Model and Component Model; +: Supported; −: Not Supported; ± Partially Supported

Table 3. Architecture evaluation classification criteria.

Criteria	Description
C1	Defined for evaluating product architectures (PA)
C2	Multi-attribute support
C3	Objective evaluation (e.g., metric-based evaluation)/Subjective evaluation (e.g., scenario-based evaluation)
C4	Multi-architectural viewpoint/Multi-architectural description language
C5	Derivation-time evaluation

An analysis of these approaches reveals that the majority of them have not been proposed specifically for SPL development and only few of them provide coverage to the evaluation of product architecture at derivation-time (e.g., [23, 33–37]). The majority

Table 4. Classification of architecture evaluation approaches.

Method	C1	C2	C3	C4	C5
ATAM [19]	–	+	–	+	–
FAAM [25]	–	+	–	+	–
D-SAAM [26]	–	+	–	+	–
ALMA [27]	–	– (Modifiability)	–	+	–
AQA [28]	–	+	–	+	–
Alves et al. [29]	–	+	+	+	–
Gannod and Lutz [30]	–	+	–	+	–
Maccari [31]	–	– (Evolution)	–	+	–
Riva and Rosso [32]	–	– (Evolution)	+	+	–
Tawhid and Petriu [33]	+	– (Performance)	+	–	+
Alonso et al. [34]	+	– (Performance)	+	+	+
Guana and Correal [20]	+	+	–	+	+
E-ATAM [35]	+ (PLA/PA)	+	–	+	+
HoPLAA [36]	+ (PLA/PA)	+	–	+	+
CaLiPro [37]	+ (PLA/PA)	+	–	+	+

only provide scenario-based subjective evaluation (e.g., [19, 23, 25–28, 30, 31, 35–37]) and only few of them provide software metrics that allow to perform an objective evaluation of the derived product architecture through measurement processes (e.g., [29, 32–34]). However, these approaches only cover performance metrics (e.g., [32–34]) or do not cover the evaluation of product architectures (e.g., [29]). None of the approaches allow the explicit representation of design decisions and their impact on the product quality attributes.

The main finding of this analysis is that the architecture evaluation in MD-SPLE is not sufficiently covered by methods that allow the evaluation of product architectures regardless the set of quality attributes or the nature of the architecture being evaluated. In addition, we observed a lack of metric-based product architecture evaluation methods that can be applied at derivation time. In SPLE development, variability in quality attribute levels is also possible and thus the application of metric-based evaluation methods at derivation-time will allow us to analyze whether the measured values for a specific configuration are within the limits established for the product line or not. The evaluation of quality attributes after the derivation (or during derivation time) allows us the early detection of potential problems, reducing costs and enhancing productivity and product quality.

2.3 Discussion

The main finding of the analysis of existing works in the field is that there is lack of methods that support the derivation, evaluation and improvement of product architectures in an integrated manner, by means of evaluation mechanisms that allow us to ensure the fulfillment of the desired quality attribute levels at derivation and evaluation time.

A lot of effort have been spent in obtaining optimal solutions for the configuration problem [38–40], but these efforts are meaningless if the product obtained after the derivation do not fulfill the quality attribute levels that it is supposed to have. Furthermore, in many occasions the evaluations do not take into account the unpredictability of certain quality attributes [41] which makes that certain properties could not be modeled as the sum of the properties of their parts. This introduces a degree of uncertainty that can only be solved through the measurement of the actual values of these properties once the software artifacts have been obtained. Finally, the majority of the approaches have been tailored for a specific modeling language or architectural description language, or for a specific architectural viewpoint.

All the problems described above is what has motivated us to define QuaDAI as an integrated product architecture derivation, evaluation and improvement method that is applicable regardless the quality attributes to be evaluated or the architectural description languages used to specify the architecture or the architectural viewpoints of interest. We have also faced the problem of empirically validate the usefulness of the method through a family of experiments reported in [22].

3 A Multimodel Approach for the Derivation, Evaluation and Improvement of Product Architectures

QuaDAI is a generic, integrated method for the derivation, evaluation and improvement of product architectures regardless the architectural description language in which they are expressed or the domain. It is based in a multimodel [42]) that represents the different SPL viewpoints and a process consisting of a set of activities conducted by model transformations.

The approach is supported by a prototype[1] that gives support to the configuration, consistency checking and generation of the product architecture. The prototype allows to import feature models and specifications defined using third party tools and to establish the relationships among them so as to automate the product architecture derivation.

The rest of the section is structured as follows: Sect. 3.1 introduces the example we use to illustrate the method; Sect. 3.2 presents the multimodel for representing SPLs; Sect. 3.3 introduces the main activities of the QuaDAI process; Sect. 3.4 describes the details of the product architecture derivation; and finally, Sect. 3.5 describes the product architecture derivation and improvement activities.

3.1 An Illustrative Example

The different activities of the approach are illustrated through the use of a running example: a SPL from the automotive domain that comprises the safety critical embedded software systems responsible for controlling a car. This SPL comprises

[1] The prototype is available for download at: http://users.dsic.upv.es/~jagonzalez/CarCarSPL/index.html.

several features such as Antilock Braking System, Traction Control System, Stability Control System or Cruise Control System[2].

The Cruise Control System feature incorporates variability. This variability is resolved depending on other selections made on a feature model (i.e., the selection of the cruise control together with the park assistant implies the positive resolution of an extended version of the cruise control). Figure 1 shows an excerpt of the feature model that represents the SPL external variability.

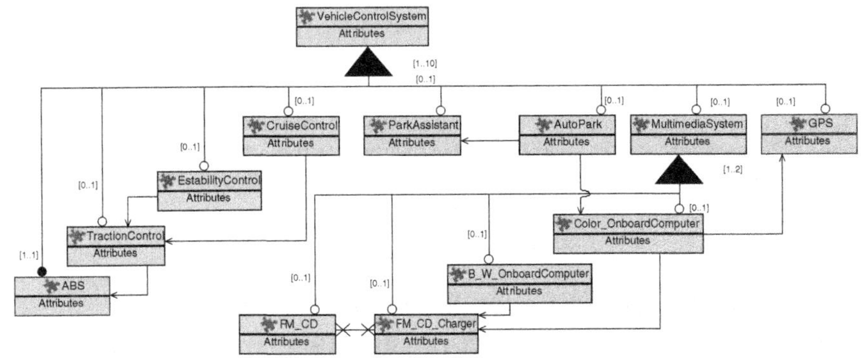

Fig. 1. Feature model representing the SPL external variability.

3.2 A Multimodel for Specifying SPLs

Traditional product line development process are based on: (1) the reuse of software assets (e.g., components, web services) that have been previously developed and stored; and (2) the realization of a production plan addressed to a product family which share a common functionality (product line architecture) but that vary in some features (variants). This approach can only be realized by assuming that we have a limited amount of variants, perfectly defined, and by assuming that these variants can be captured as instances of a feature model. However this is not realistic: variants go beyond the monotonic addition/removal of functionality grains from the product line architecture. For instance, changes in the structure or behavior of the application that is being produced can impact its quality, even for the same functionality, thus making the product unfeasible. Moreover, different properties of the application domain, design decisions, usability and user requirements, etc. are difficult to capture by means of only one feature model. This leads to the fact that only one feature model is not sufficient to define a software product line, but different views are needed.

Our approach is based on the existence of several models or system views (e.g., functionality, features, quality) with relationships among them. This approach implies the parameterization of the software production process by means of a multimodel

---

[2] The whole specification of the example is available at http://users.dsic.upv.es/~jagonzalez/CarCarSPL/links.html.

which is able to explicitly represent the different views of the products within the product line and the relationships among them.

A multimodel can be defined as a set of interrelated models that represent the different viewpoints of a particular system. A viewpoint is an abstraction that yields the specification of the whole system restricted to a particular set of concerns, and it is created with a specific purpose in mind. In any given viewpoint it is possible to produce a model of the system that contains only the objects that are visible from that viewpoint [43]. Such a model is known as a viewpoint model, or view of the system from that viewpoint. The multimodel permits the definition of relationships among model elements in those viewpoints, capturing the missing information that the separation of concerns could lead to [42].

The multimodel used to specify SPLs in order to support the derivation, evaluation and improvement of product architectures is composed of (at least) four interrelated viewpoints:

- **Variability Viewpoint,** which represents the SPL external variability expressing the commonalities and variability within the product line. Its main element is the feature, which is a user-visible aspect or characteristic of a system [44]. It is expressed in the multimodel by means of a variant [45] of the cardinality-based feature model (see Fig. 1).
- **Architectural Viewpoint,** which represents the architectural variability of the product line architecture that realizes the external variability of the SPL expressed in the variability viewpoint. It is expressed in the multimodel by means of the Common Variability Language (CVL) and its main element is the Variability Specification (VSpec). We only represent in the multimodel the architectural variability of the product line architecture. The PLA itself is represented in a base model, which is referenced by the CVL specification. A base model, under the CVL terminology, is a model on which variability is defined using CVL [46]. The base model is not part of CVL and can be an instance of any metamodel defined via MOF [46].
- **Quality Viewpoint,** which represents the hierarchical decomposition of quality into sub-characteristics, quality attributes, metrics and the impacts and constraints among quality attributes. It is expressed in the multimodel by means of a quality model for software product lines [47], which extends the ISO/IEC 25010 (SQuaRE) [48] and allows the definition of NFRs as constraints affecting characteristics, sub-characteristics and quality attributes.
- **Transformation Viewpoint** [49] that contains the explicit representation of the design decisions realized by the different model transformation processes that integrate the production plan for the model-driven development of SPLs. Alternatives may appear in a model transformation process when a set of constructs in the source model admits different representations in the target model. The application of each alternative transformation could generate alternative target models that may have the same functionality but might differ in their quality attributes. In this work, we focus on architectural patterns [50, 51]. Architectural patterns specify solutions to recurrent problems that occur in specific contexts [52]. They also specify how the system will deal with one aspect of its functionality, impacting directly on the product quality

attributes. Architectural patterns can be represented as architectural transformations, as a means to ensure the quality attributes attained by the product architectures. Figure 2 shows an excerpt of the transformation viewpoint of the multimodel, containing one design decision in which we have three alternative architectural patterns that can be applied by means of their own transformation rules.

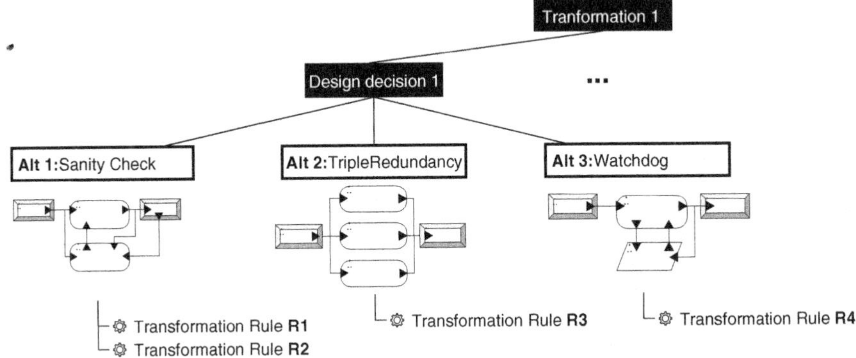

Fig. 2. Transformation viewpoint excerpt.

The multimodel also represents the relationships among elements of each viewpoint with different semantics as *is_realized_by* [53] or *impact* relationships [42]. An excerpt of these relationships is shown in Fig. 3. Through these relationships we can describe in the multimodel:

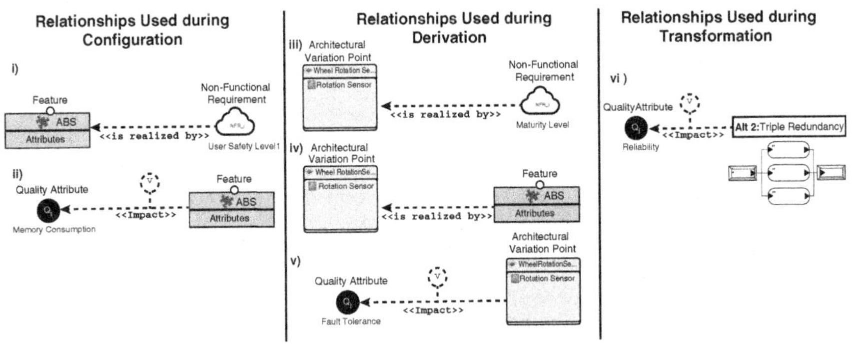

Fig. 3. Multimodel relationships.

(i) How the UserSafetyLevel1 NFR *is_realized_by* a set of features (e.g., the ABS or the Stability Control).
(ii) How the selection of a given feature *impacts* positive or negatively on a quality attribute.

(iii) How the MaturityLevel NFR *is_realized_by* a set of VSpecs (e.g., the WheelRotationSensor).
(iv) How the ABS feature *is_realized_by* a set of VSpecs (e.g., the WheelRotationSensor).
(v) How the positive resolution of a given VSpec (e.g. WheelRotationSensor) *impacts* positive or negatively on a quality attribute (e.g., FaultTolerance).
(vi) How the selection of a given architectural transformation *impacts* positive or negatively on a quality attribute.

These relationships are used to check the consistency of the product configuration in order to decide which variation points should be resolved positively in the CVL resolution model driving the product architecture derivation. The relationships are also used to select and apply the architectural transformations that best fit the prioritized quality attributes driving the transformation activity. All these activities are further described in the following subsections.

3.3 Overview of the QuaDAI Process

The process consists of a set of activities conducted by model transformations that take as input the multimodel viewpoints and the relationships defined among their elements. Figure 4 shows a summary of this process that comprises four main activities:

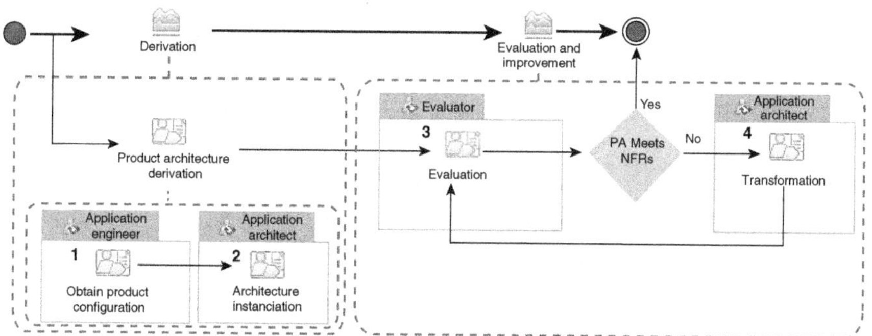

Fig. 4. QuaDAI main activities.

- **Obtain Product Configuration** in which the application engineer defines the configuration of the product under development by selecting the features, NFRs and by establishing the priority of each quality attribute[3].

[3] NFRs are defined in the quality viewpoint as constraints affecting the quality attributes whereas the prioritization of the quality attributes allows expressing the relative importance of each quality attribute.

- **Product Architecture Instantiation** in which the application architect obtains the first version of the product architecture based on the product configuration by resolving the architectural variability of the PLA.
- **Evaluation** in which the evaluator measures the derived product architecture in order to assess the degree of fulfillment of the NFRs.
- **Transformation** in which the architect applies architectural transformations so as to improve certain quality attributes when the architectural variability is not sufficient to achieve the required NFRs for the product.

3.4 Product Architecture Derivation

The derivation process for obtaining a first version of the product architecture comprises two main activities: the *Product configuration* and the *Architecture instantiation*. Figure 5 shows an excerpt of this process with its main inputs and outputs. In the *product configuration* activity, the application engineer configures the product by selecting the features and the NFRs that the product must fulfill and establishes the quality attributes priorities in the *Obtain product configuration* task. These quality attributes priorities will be used during the derivation phase to choose from a set of architectural variants that having the same functionality differ in their quality attribute levels, and in the evaluation and improvement phases to select the architectural transformations to the applied to the architecture.

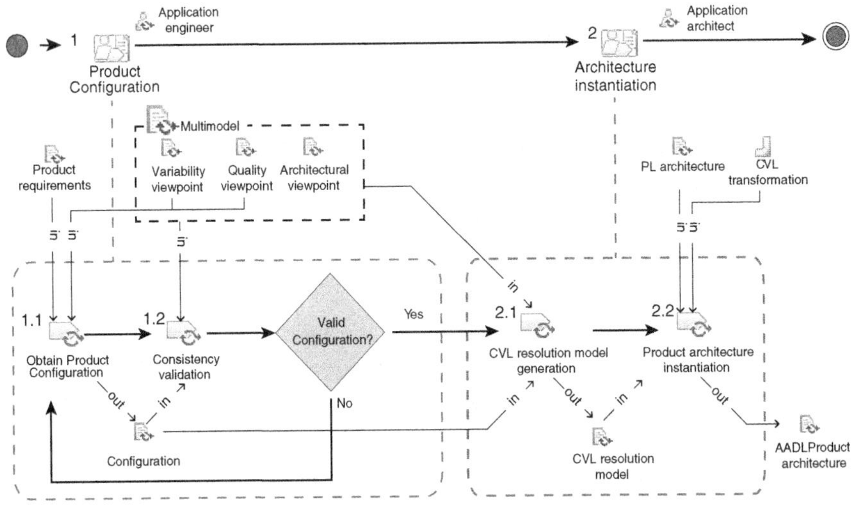

Fig. 5. Excerpt of the derivation process.

Once the product has been configured, we can check the product consistency (*Consistency validation* task). Our approach supports the intra (e.g., consistence of the feature model, consistence of the quality model) and inter-model consistency (e.g., relationships between the feature and the quality models).

Figure 6 shows the flow of steps to obtain a valid product configuration using QuaDAI. In the *Variability viewpoint validation,* we check whether the selection of features fulfills the constraints defined in the feature model. In *the Quality viewpoint validation* we check whether the priorities of the quality attributes defined in the configuration satisfy the *impact* relationships and constraints among them defined in the quality viewpoint. In the *Features-NFRs validation* we check whether the configuration satisfies the *is_realized_by* relationships defined among features and NFRs defined in the multimodel. Finally, in the *Features-attributes validation* we check whether the features selected and the prioritized quality attributes do not violate the *impact* relationships among features and quality attributes defined in the multimodel. The variability viewpoint consistency validation has been operationalized by using the FAMA [54] validator. We transform the cardinality-based feature model into the FAMA metamodel through a QVT model transformation and we project the selection of features by using a model to text transformation. The quality viewpoint and the inter-viewpoint consistency checking are carried out through OCL constraints checked at runtime by the OCLTools validator [55].

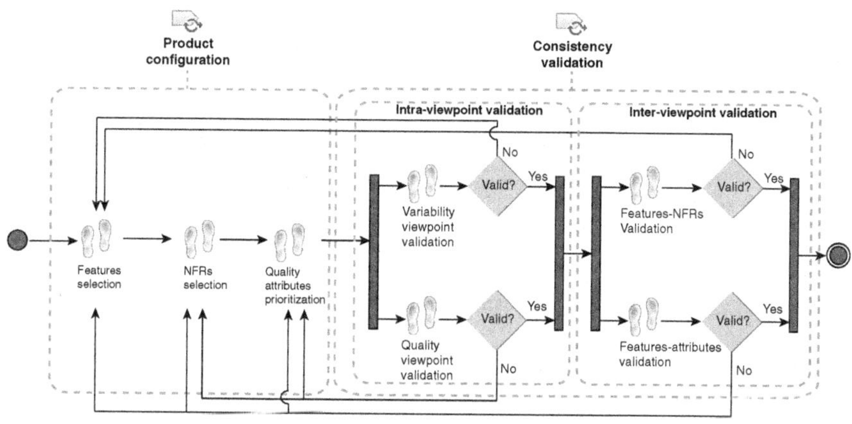

Fig. 6. Configuration and consistency checking process.

In the *architecture instantiation* activity, the application architect generates the product architecture by means of two model transformation activities. The first transformation, *CVL resolution model generation* task, takes as input a valid product configuration and the multimodel (i.e., the relationships between the architectural viewpoint with the variability and the quality viewpoints) and, through a QVT model transformation, generates a CVL resolution model. With the multimodel relationships, the QVT transformation decides which architectural variants have to be positively resolved in each variation point.

Finally, the *product architecture instantiation* task, through a CVL transformation, takes as input the CVL resolution model and generates the product architecture. This product architecture represents the resolution of the PLA architectural variability taking into account not only the functional requirements but also the NFRs and the quality attributes priorities defined in the configuration.

Figure 7 shows the outline of the Product architecture instantiation in which the product architecture is generated after the resolution of the PLA architectural variability through the CVL resolution model generation. The product architecture shown in Fig. 7 has been generated by the *product architecture instantiation* for the automotive example when the application engineer selects only the *ABS* feature (see Fig. 1) and introduces the product specific NFRs, which come from the system's requirements, demanding a fault tolerance of the ABS greater than 99.5 % and restricting the ABS latency time to 5 ms.

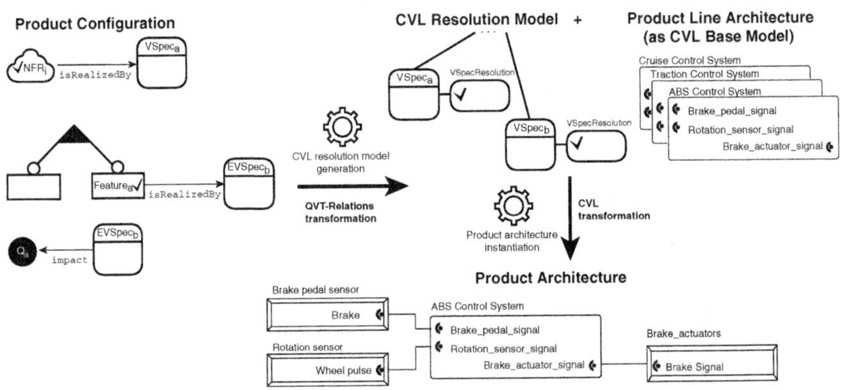

Fig. 7. Product architecture instantiation.

3.5 Product Architecture Evaluation and Improvement

After obtaining the product architecture during the product architecture instantiation, it should be evaluated to assess the degree of fulfillment of the product's NFRs and, in those cases in which the NFRs cannot be achieved by exercising the architectural variability mechanisms of the product line architecture pattern-based architectural transformations can be applied to the product architecture in order to improve its quality. This process comprises two main activities: *Evaluation* and *Transformation*. Figure 8 shows an excerpt of this process with its main inputs and outputs.

In the *Product architecture evaluation task* the evaluator applies the software measures from the quality viewpoint of the multimodel to the product architecture in order to evaluate whether or not it satisfies the desired NFRs. This can be done by means of various measurement methods:

- Measurement through model transformation processes: metrics that require more complex processing can be implemented as model transformations.
- Measurement through architectural modeling tools: in those cases in which some architectural modeling tools have mechanisms to perform the measurement, this will be delegated to such architectural modeling tools.

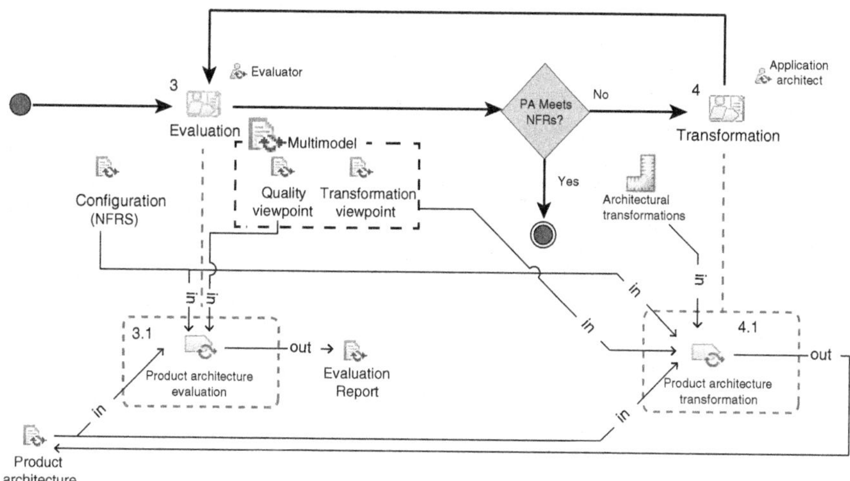

Fig. 8. Excerpt of the evaluation and improvement process.

- Measurement through OCL restrictions: in those cases where the metrics can be operationalized in this language, architectural models can be measured by using OCL constraints defined directly on the models at M1 level by means of the OCL Tools. These constraints can be used as a consistency validation for the obtained architectural models (e.g., to validate the memory consumption of all the components that combine the architecture using derived attributes).

Once the measurement process has been carried out by applying the measurement method selected in each case, the multimodel allows us to validate the degree in which the NFRs are fulfilled, using the measurement results. We have developed a tool that gives support to the creation and use of multimodels and which allows, on one hand, to specify the NFRs for both the SPL and the product under development and, on the other hand, to enter the measurement result in the multimodel and to perform the validation of the OCL constraints at runtime by using the OCLTools validator.

The evaluation for the example architecture shown in Fig. 7 may conclude that the architecture meets the latency NFR but that the fault tolerance NFR is not achieved, and architectural transformations may thus be required. In those cases in which the NFRs cannot be achieved by exercising the architectural variation mechanisms, in the second activity, *Product Architecture Transformation*, we can apply pattern-based architectural transformations to the product architecture. This transformation uses the impact relationships among architectural transformations and quality attributes to determine which architectural transformation must be applied to the product line architecture in order to achieve the desired quality attribute levels. In particular, the architectural patterns that we used for the automotive example are: homogeneous redundancy pattern [50] and triple modular redundancy pattern [50] whose details are briefly introduced in Table 5.

Table 5. Architectural transformations description.

Name	Rationale	Left-hand side	Right-hand side
T1: Triple Modular Redundancy (TMR)	Only detects random faults. Since the channels are homogeneous, any systematic fault in one channel must be present in both of the others.		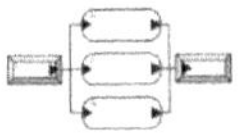
T2: Sanity Check Pattern (SC)	Detects gross deviations from the controlled value to the actuator value. Provides minimal coverage against faults.		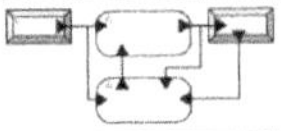

To define the corresponding impact relationships among architectural patterns and quality attributes, the domain architect must rank each architectural transformation with regard to the Q quality attributes in a trade-off analysis using the AHP technique. For each quality attribute Q_a, s/he compares the N potential architectural transformation in a pairwise comparison. To determine how an architectural transformation *Ax* supports the quality attribute Q_a, in comparison to the pattern *Ay*, a weight is assigned (1 for equally important, 3 for moderately more important, 5 for strongly more important, 7 for very strongly more important, and 9 for extremely more important). For example, the domain expert defines that TMR is strongly more important (a weight of 5) than HR with regard to fault tolerance, and that HR is moderately more important (a weight of 3) than TMR with regard to latency.

The result of this comparison is an N x Q matrix that shows the relative support of the different architectural patterns to the quality attributes as shown in Table 6(a). Then, these values are normalized by applying the formula (1) to (a) to produce Table 6(b), and finally, the impact that an architectural pattern has on a quality attribute Qa is calculated by applying the formula (2) to produce Table 6(c). This result is stored in the multimodel in the *impact* relationships among architectural transformations and quality attributes (see Fig. 3 in Sect. 3.2) and is valid for all the products in the product line.

$$NormQ_a[i,j] = \frac{Q_a[i,j]}{\sum_{k=1}^{n} Q[k,j]} \tag{1}$$

$$I[i] = \frac{\sum_{k=1}^{n} NormQ_a[i,k]}{n} \tag{2}$$

$$R_j = \sum_{i=0}^{k-1} Qi * Iij \tag{3}$$

In the automotive example, if the architect selects both the latency and the fault tolerance as being of equal importance (i.e., with a weight of 0.5 for each one) the transformation process will select the TMR pattern by applying the formula (3) to the values shown in Table 6(c) (TMR: 0.5 * 0.83 + 0.5 * 0.24 > HR: 0.5 * 0.17 + 0.5 * 0.76). Figure 9 shows the resulting product architecture after the application of the TMR pattern to the product architecture shown in Fig. 7.

The process iterates until the NFRs are achieved or when the architect detects that it is not possible to build the product with the set of NFRs selected in the configuration.

Table 6. Architectural patterns and quality attributes trade-off analysis.

(a)

	Fault Tolerance		Latency	
	TMR	HR	TMR	HR
TMR	1	5	1	1/3
HR	1/5	1	3	1
Sum	1.2	6	4	1.3

(b)

	Fault Tolerance		Latency	
	TMR	HR	TMR	HR
TMR	1 / 1.2	5 / 6	1 / 4	1/3 / 1.3
HR	1/5 / 1.2	1 / 6	3 / 4	1 / 1.3

(c)

	Impacts	
	Fault Tolerance	Latency
TMR	0.83	0.24
HR	0.17	0.76

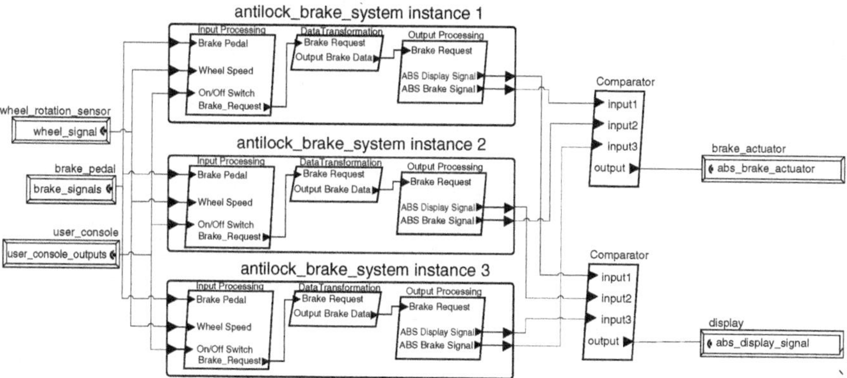

Fig. 9. Product architecture after applying the TMR pattern.

The evaluation process may result also in a renegotiation of the NFRs with the customer. In this case, the product architecture should be re-evaluated to check the conformance with the new NFRs. Finally, in some cases the architect should vary some architectural variation points to modify the candidate product architecture. For instance, in some cases the first candidate architecture may imply the positive resolution of a set of architectural variation points that may lead to quality attribute levels that are far above of a given NFR. Considering another combination of architectural variation points may also imply the fulfillment of that specific NFR but also other that were previously unfulfilled.

4 Conclusions and Final Remarks

Although in the last few years model-driven software development have been applied to address the problem of software architecture derivation and evaluation in SPL development, it still presents some drawbacks and opportunities. In general, quality assurance has not received proper coverage in existing approaches for product architecture derivation and there is a lack of generic methods that support the derivation and evaluation of product architectures regardless the quality attributes to be evaluated, the architectural description languages used to specify the architecture or the architectural viewpoints of interest. We believe that the use of model-driven principles would provide a richer semantic representation of a SPL and may be used to relate the different activities that should be performed during the derivation and evaluation of product architectures (e.g., the impact that SPL external variability has on the non-functional requirements or how the architectural design decisions impact on the quality attributes).

We have also introduced QuaDAI as an integrated, generic method for supporting the derivation, evaluation an improvement of product architectures in MD-SPLE. In this method, the product derivation and the architectural transformations are guided by the relationships and constraints established in a multimodel. The multimodel provides a sufficiently formal interrelated model that can be supported by tools capable of automating portions of the product line production planning. The approach explore model-driven concepts and techniques to make explicit the knowledge and rationale used for architectural design by capturing and representing architectural design decisions during the architecting process necessary for reducing architectural knowledge evaporation.

The multimodel is a solution for documenting design decisions and their impact on the product quality attributes. The multimodel can also be used to analyze the cost/benefit of having core assets with certain qualities (impact on quality and cost). As further work, we plan to improve the configuration and consistency validation mechanisms, to provide recommendation mechanisms based on previous selections, and to implement consistency validation for individual entities of the multimodel. In addition, we want to improve the impact specification mechanism and to analyze other multi-objective optimization methods. We also plan to perform replications of the experiments conducted to evaluate the effectiveness of QuADAI with practitioners.

References

1. Rabiser, R., Grünbacher, P., Dhungana, D.: Requirements for product derivation support: results from a systematic literature review and an expert survey. Inf. Softw. Technol. **52**, 324–346 (2010)
2. Clements, P., Northrop, L.: Software Product Lines: Practices and Patterns. Addison-Wesley Professional, Boston (2001)
3. Atkinson, C., Bayer, J., Muthig, D.: Component-based product line development: the KobrA approach. In: 1st International Conference on Software Product Lines, pp. 289–309, Denver, Colorado (2000)
4. Asikainen, T., Soininen, T., Männistö, T.: A Koala-based approach for modelling and deploying configurable software product families. In: 5th International Workshop on Product-Family Engineering, pp. 225–249, Sienna, Italy (2003)
5. Botterweck, G., Lee, K., Thiel, S.: Automating product derivation in software product line engineering. In: Software Engineering Conference, pp. 177–182, Kaiserslautern, Germany (2009)
6. Cabello, M.E.: Baseline-Oriented Modeling: una Aproximación Mda Basada en Líneas de Productos Software para el Desarrollo de Aplicaciones. PhD thesis, Departamento de Sistemas Informáticos y Computación, Universitat Poltècnica de València (2008)

7. Rossel, P.O., Perovich, D., Bastarrica, M.C.: Reuse of architectural knowledge in SPL development. In: Edwards, S.H., Kulczycki, G. (eds.) 11th International Conference on Software Reuse, pp. 191–200, Falls Church, VA, USA (2009)
8. Duran-Limon, H.A., Castillo-Barrera, F.E., Lopez-Herrejon, R.E.: Towards an ontology-based approach for deriving product architectures. In: 15th International Software Product Line Conference, vol. 2, Munich, Germany (2011)
9. Czarnecki, K., Antkiewicz, M.: Mapping features to models: a template approach based on superimposed variants. In: Glück, R., Lowry, M. (eds.) GPCE 2005. LNCS, vol. 3676, pp. 422–437. Springer, Heidelberg (2005)
10. Ziadi, T., Jézéquel, J.: Software product line engineering with the UML: deriving products. In: 10th Software Product Lines Conference, pp. 557–588, Baltimore, Maryland, USA (2006)
11. Gomaa, H., Shin, M.E.: Automated software product line engineering. In: 40th Annual Hawaii International Conference on System Science, pp. 1–10, Hawaii, USA (2007)
12. Perrouin, G., Klein, J., Guelfi, N., Jézéquel, J.M.: Reconciling automation and flexibility in product derivation. In: 12th Software Product Line Conference, pp. 339–348, Limerick, Ireland (2008)
13. Schaefer, I., Worret, A., Poetzsch-Heffter, A.: A model-based framework for automated product derivation. In: 1st International Workshop on Model-Driven Approaches in Software Product Line Engineering, pp. 14–21, San Francisco, California, USA (2009)
14. Tawhid, R., Petriu, D.C.: Product model derivation by model transformation in software product lines. In: 14th IEEE International Symposium on Object/Component/Service-Oriented Real-Time Distributed Computing Workshops, pp. 72–79, Newport Beach, Canada (2011)
15. Sánchez, P., Loughran, N., Fuentes, L., Garcia, A.: Engineering languages for specifying product-derivation processes in software product lines. In: Software Language Engineering, pp. 188–208, Toulousse, France (2008)
16. Heidenreich, F., Kopcsek, J., Wende, C.: FeatureMapper: mapping features to models. In: Companion of the 30th International Conference on Software Engineering, pp. 943–944, Vancouver, Canada (2008)
17. Haugen, Ø., Moller-Pedersen, B., Olsen, G.K., Svendsen, A., Fleurey, F., Zhang, X.: Consolidated CVL language and tool. MoSiS Project, D.2.1.4., SINTEF, Univeristy of Oslo (2010)
18. Montagud, S., Abrahão, S.: Gathering current knowledge about quality evaluation in software product lines. In: 13th Software Product Line Conference, pp. 91–100, San Francisco, USA (2009)
19. Kazman, R., Klein, M., Clements, P.: ATAM: method for architecture evaluation. CMU/SEI-2000-TR-004, ESC-TR-2000-004, Software Engineering Institute, Carnegie Mellon University (2000)
20. Kazman, R., Bass, L., Abowd, G., Webb, M.: SAAM: a method for analyzing the properties of software architectures. In: 16th International Conference on Software Engineering, pp. 81–90, Sorrento, Italy (1994)
21. González-Huerta, J., Insfrán, E., Abrahão, S.: Defining and validating a multimodel approach for product architecture derivation and improvement. In: 16th International Conference on Model-Driven Engineering Languages and Systems, pp. 388–404, Miami, USA (2013)
22. Gonzalez-Huerta, J., Insfran, E., Abrahão, S., Scanniello, G.: Validating a model-driven software architecture evaluation and improvement method: a family of experiments. Inf. Softw. Technol. **57**, 405–429 (2015)

23. Guana, V., Correal, D.: Improving software product line configuration: a quality attribute-driven approach. Inf. Softw. Technol. **55**, 541–562 (2013)
24. Fleurey, F., Haugen, Ø., Møller-Pedersen, B.: A Generic Language and Tool for Variability Modeling. SINTEF, Oslo (2009)
25. Dolan, T.J.: Architecture Assessment of Information-System Families: a Practical Perspective. PhD thesis, Technische Universiteit Eindhoven (2001)
26. Graaf, B., van Dijk, H., van Deursen, A.: Evaluating an embedded software reference architecture—industrial experience report—. In: 9th European Conference on Software Maintenance and Reengineering, Manchester, United Kingdom (2005)
27. Bengtsson, P., Lassing, N., Bosch, J., van Vliet, H.: Architecture-level modifiability analysis (ALMA). J. Syst. Softw. **69**, 129–147 (2004)
28. Matinlassi, M., Niemelä, E., Dobrica, L.: Quality-driven architecture design and quality analysis method. VTT Publications 456, VTT Technical Research Centre of Finland, Oulu, Finland (2002)
29. Alves, E., Junior, D.O., Gimenes, I.M.S.: A metric suite to support software product line architecture evaluation. In: XXIV Conferencia Latinoamericana de Informática, pp. 489–498, Santa Fé, Argentina (2008)
30. Gannod, G., Lutz, R.: An approach to architectural analysis of product lines. In: 22nd International Conference on Software Engineering, pp. 548–557, Limerick, Ireland (2000)
31. Maccari, A.: Experiences in assessing product family software architecture for evolution. In: 24th International Conference on Software Engineering, pp. 585–592, Orlando, Florida (2002)
32. Riva, C., Rosso, C.D.: Experiences with software product family evolution. In: 6th International Workshop on Principles of Software Evolution, Helsinki, Finland (2003)
33. Tawhid, R., Petriu, D.C.: Automatic derivation of a product performance model from a software product line model. In: 15th International Software Product Line Conference, pp. 80–89. IEEE, Munich, Germany (2011)
34. Alonso, A., García-Valls, M., Puente, J.: Assessment of timing properties of family products. In: ESPRIT-ATES Workshop, pp. 161–169, Las palmas de Gran Canaria, Spain (1998)
35. Kim, T., Ko, I.Y, Kang, S.W., Lee, D.H.: Extending ATAM to assess product line architecture. In: 2008 8th IEEE International Conference on Computer and Information Technology, pp. 790–797, Khulna, Bangladesh (2008)
36. Olumofin, F.G., Misic, V.B.: A holistic architecture assessment method for software product lines. Inf. Softw. Technol. **49**, 309–323 (2007)
37. Etxeberria, L.: Evaluación de atributos de calidad en líneas de productos software de forma efectiva en costes. PhD thesis, Departamento de Electonica e Informatica, Modragon Unibesitatea (2008)
38. Roos-Frantz, F., Benavides, D., Ruiz-Cortés, A., Heuer, A., Lauenroth, K.: Quality-aware analysis in product line engineering with the orthogonal variability model. Softw. Qual. J. **20**, 519–565 (2011)
39. Soltani, S., Asadi, M., Gašević, D., Simon, M.H., Bagheri, E.: Automated planning for feature model configuration based on functional and non-functional requirements. In: Proceedings of the 16th International Software Product Line Conference, vol. 1, pp. 56–65, New York, NY, USA (2012)
40. Ghezzi, C., Sharifloo, A.M.: Verifying non-functional properties of software product lines: towards an efficient approach using parametric model checking. In: 15th International Software Product Line Conference, pp. 170–174. IEEE, Munich, Germany (2011)
41. Crnkovic, I., Larsson, M., Preiss, O.: Concerning predictability in dependable component-based systems: classification of quality attributes. In: ICSE 2004 Workshops on Software Architectures for Dependable Systems, pp. 257–278, Edinburgh, Scotland, UK (2004)

42. González-Huerta, J., Insfran, E., Abrahão, S.: A multimodel for integrating quality assessment in model-driven engineering. In: 8th International Conference on the Quality of Information and Communications Technology, pp. 251–254, Lisbon, Portugal (2012)
43. Barkmeyer, E.J., Feeney, A.B., Denno, P., Flater, D.W., Libes, D.E., Steves, M.P., Wallace, E.K.: Concepts for Automating Systems Integration. NISTIR 6928, U.S. Department of Commerce (2003)
44. Kang, K.C., Cohen, S.G., Hess, J.A., Novak, W.E., Peterson, A.S.: Feature-Oriented Domain Analysis (FODA) Feasibility Study. CMU/SEI-90-TR-21 ESD-90-TR-222, Software Engineering Institute, Carnegie Melon University (1990)
45. Gómez, A., Ramos, I.: Cardinality-based feature modeling and model-driven engineering: fitting them together. In: International Workshop on Variability Modelling of Software-Intensive Systems, pp. 61–68. Linz, Austria (2010)
46. Object Management Group: Common Variability Language (CVL) OMG Revised Submission (2012)
47. González-Huerta, J., Insfran, E., Abrahão, S., McGregor, J.D.: Non-functional requirements in model-driven software product line engineering. In: Proceedings of the Fourth International Workshop on Nonfunctional System Properties in Domain Specific Modeling Languages, pp. 1–6. Innsbruck, Austria (2012)
48. ISO/IEC: ISO/IEC 25000:2005 Software Engineering - Software product Quality Requirements and Evaluation (SQuaRE) - Guide to SQuaRE (2005)
49. González-huerta, J., Insfran, E., Abrahão, S., Mcgregor, J.D.: Architecture derivation in product line development through model transformations. In: 22nd International Conference on Information Systems Development, Seville, Spain (2013)
50. Douglass, B.P.: Real-Time Design Patterns: Robust Scalable Architecture for Real-Time Systems. Addison Wesley, Boston (2002)
51. Kruchten, P.: The Rational Unified Process, an Introduction. Addison Wesley, Boston (1999)
52. Buschmann, F., Meunier, R., Rohnert, H., Sommerlad, P., Stal, M.: Pattern-Oriented Software Architecture: a System of Patterns, vol. 1. Wiley, Chichester (1996)
53. Janota, M., Botterweck, G.: Formal approach to integrating feature and architecture models. In: 11th Conference on Fundamental Approaches to Software Engineering, pp. 31–45, Budapest, Hungary (2008)
54. ISA Research Group: Fama Tool Suite. http://www.isa.us.es/fama/
55. Eclipse: Eclipse OCL. http://projects.eclipse.org/projects/modeling.mdt.ocl

Modeling Languages, Tools and Architectures

Using Patterns to Map OCL Constraints to JML Specifications

Ali Hamie(✉)

School of Computing, Engineering and Mathematics,
University of Brighton, Brighton, UK
a.a.hamie@brighton.ac.uk

Abstract. OCL is a formal notation to specify constraints on UML models that cannot otherwise be expressed using diagrammatic notations such as class diagrams. The type of constraints that can be expressed using OCL include class invariants and operation preconditions and post-conditions. Constraint patterns can be used to simplify the development of consistent constraints for UML/OCL models. This paper investigates an approach based on constraint patterns to developing JML specifications for Java implementations from OCL constraints. This would enable the checking of OCL constraints at runtime since they can be translated to JML executable assertions. The approach involves mapping each OCL constraint pattern to a corresponding JML pattern. This results in a library of JML constraint patterns that provides a seamless transition from UML/OCL designs to Java implementations.

Keywords: Constraints · Patterns · OCL · JML

1 Introduction

The Object Constraint Language (OCL) [1,2] is an integral part of the Unified Modelling Language (UML) [3], and was introduced to express additional constraints on models that diagrams cannot convey by themselves. Building class models is essential for modelling applications, however the UML class diagram cannot express all the relevant constraints about the application being modelled. Therefore class models must typically be refined with textual constraints written in OCL. Typical constraints include invariants on classes, and preconditions and postconditions of operations. The use of OCL in modelling is essential for the development of precise and abstract models. However, developing constraint specifications is not an easy task. Among other things, one important aspect needs to be taken into account: class diagrams can express complicated relationships, including subtyping, reflexive relations, or potentially infinitely large instances, and constraining such facts requires dealing with this complexity. In order to facilitate and simplify the development of constraints, the concept of specification patterns has been introduced as *constraint patterns* in MDE [4–10]. A constraint pattern captures and generalizes frequently used logical expressions.

S. Hammoudi et al. (Eds.): MODELSWARD 2014, CCIS 506, pp. 35–48, 2015.
DOI: 10.1007/978-3-319-25156-1_3

It is a parameterizable constraint expression that can be instantiated to solve a class of specification problems. At a more formal level, a constraint pattern with respect to a meta-model can be defined as a function that maps a set of meta-model elements to a constraint.

As a design notation, however, OCL is not executable and OCL constraints are not reified to implementation artifacts. This could lead to development and maintenance problems of constraints such as inconsistency. These problems can be overcome by mapping OCL constraints to source code in a form that can be executed and checked at runtime. Hamie [11–13] has defined rules for translating OCL expressions and constraints to JML expressions and assertions. This translation was refined and implemented in [14] by providing a JML class library for OCL collection types that simplifies the translation. JML is a behavioural interface specification language that can be used to specify Java classes and interfaces [15], and a significant subset of it can be checked at runtime [16]. JML is very specific to the programming language Java and thus handles many low-level details. What makes JML suitable for the translation is that it supports several language and tool features, in particular, specification only variables called *model* variables [17] and specification refinements.

This paper proposes an approach for translating OCL constraints expressed in terms of patterns to JML constraints. This approach is based on translating OCL patterns to JML specification patterns described as JML templates. That is each OCL pattern will have a corresponding JML pattern. The use of constraint patterns makes the translation intuitive and traceable. It is also expected that the use of patterns facilitate automation of the translation. In addition, the JML constraint patterns are useful for simplifying the development of assertions for Java classes and interfaces. This is important since assertions are recognised as a practical programming tool and are said to be more effective when derived from formal specifications such as OCL constraints.

The remainder of the paper is organised as follows. In Sect. 2 we briefly review OCL and JML through a small example that will be used throughout the paper. In Sect. 3 we look at constraint patterns in OCL. In Sect. 4 we describe a way for translating an OCL constraint pattern to a JML pattern. In Sect. 5 we compare our work with other works for mapping OCL to JML. Section 6 provides the conclusion and future work.

2 Background

2.1 Object Constraint Language

The Object Constraint Language (OCL) [1,2] is a textual, declarative notation that can be used to specify constraints or rules that apply to UML models. OCL can play an important role in model driven software engineering because UML class diagrams are not precise enough to enable the transformation of a UML model to complete code. In fact, it is an important component of OMG's standard for model transformation for the model-driven architecture [18].

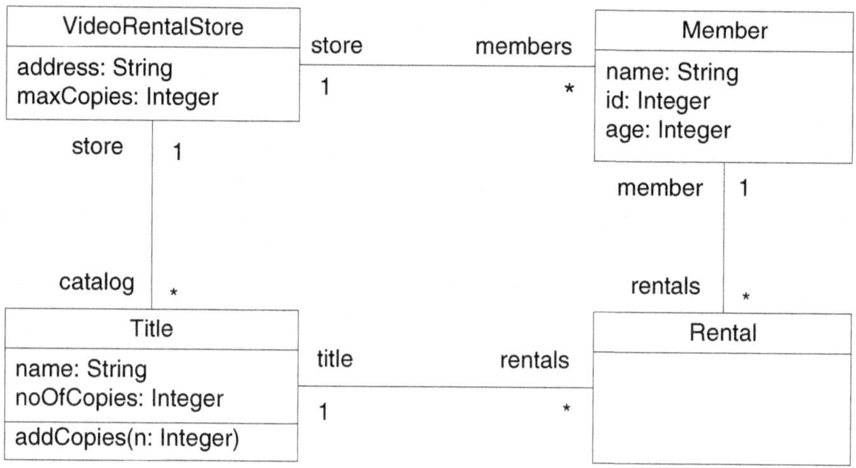

Fig. 1. A partial class model for video rental store.

A UML class diagram alone cannot express all relevant constraints about an application. The diagram in Fig. 1, for example, is a UML class diagram modelling a video rental store. There are various additional constraints on the model that cannot be expressed diagrammatically. For example, a member can only rent one copy of a video title at one particular time or the number of copies of a title is greater than zero. It is very likely that a system based only on diagrams alone will be incorrect. Such additional constraints can be precisely described using the OCL which is based on predicate logic and mathematical set theory. For example a simple constraint stating that the number of copies of a title is greater than zero can be expressed as follows.

---

context Title
inv copiesGreaterZero : **self**.noOfCopies > 0

This constraint, called an *invariant*, states a fact that should be always true in the model. The actual invariant is represented as an OCL boolean expression using the variable self that refers to an object of class Title. copiesGreaterZero is the name of the invariant.

It is also possible to use OCL in order to specify the behaviour of an operation. For example, the following OCL constraints specify the behaviour of an operation Title::addCopies(n : Integer) using a pair of predicates describing a precondition and a postcondition.

---

context Title::addCopies(n: Integer)
pre : n > 0
post : noOfCopies = noOfCopies@pre + n

The pre and postconditions state that if invoked with parameter n greater than zero the operation sets the new number of copies of the title by adding n to the previous number of copies. In the postcondition, the @pre annotation denotes the value of a property at the precondition time.

OCL supports several primitive types such as Integer, Real, Boolean, and String and collection types such as Collection, Set, OrderedSet, Bag, and Sequence [1,2]. These types are equipped with various operations that can be used for writing OCL constraints. For example the collection operation size returns the number of elements contained in a collection, and the forAll operation checks whether an expression is true for all objects in a given collection.

2.2 Java Contracts in JML

The Java Modeling Language (JML) [15] is a formal specification language that can be used to specify Java classes and interfaces. As such JML provides an extended Design-by-Contract concept to the programming language Java. The Design-by-Contract (DBC) concept includes conventional clauses for preconditions and postconditions of methods as well as class invariants. JML specifications or assertions can be added directly to source code as a special kind of comments called *annotation comments*, or they can live in separate specification files. These assertions are usually written in a form that can be compiled, so that their violations can be detected at runtime. In addition, JML provides clauses for specifying exceptions, and its extensions include model and ghost variables which describe specifications only data and therefore allow the modelling of abstract state space. The relationship between the concrete state space and the abstract one is achieved by the use of 'represents' clauses in the concrete classes and thus formulate a data refinement relation.

```
// File: Title.java
public class Title {
   /*@ spec_public @*/ private int noOfCopies;
   //@ public invariant  this.noOfCopies >= 0;

   /*@ requires  n >= 0;
     @ assignable noOfCopies;
     @ ensures noOfCopies == \old(noOfCopies) + n;
     @*/

   public void addCopies(int n) {}

   // the rest of definition
}
```

Fig. 2. Sample Java code with JML annotations.

Figure 2 shows a sample Java code annotated with JML specification written in a Java source (.java) file. The annotation comments in the source code are indicated by //@ and /*@ ... @*/. It describes the behaviour of class `Title`. The JML keyword *spec−public* states that the private field `noOfCopies` is treated as public for specification purpose; e.g., it can be used in the specifications of public methods such as `addCopies`. The example also shows the specification of the method `addCopies`. A method specification precedes the declaration of the method. The *requires* clause specifies the precondition, the *assignable* clause specifies the frame condition, and the *ensures* clause specifies the postcondition. The JML keyword *old* in the postcondition denotes the pre-state value of its expression; it is mainly used in the specification of a method such as `addCopies` that changes the state of an object.

JML is widely accepted and supported by a range of tools covering the different levels of program verification from runtime checking (Iowa State JML tools, via [19]) to static checking (ESC/Java2, [20]) to 'real' interactive verification (Loop project, [21]). Typically JML extensions are encapsulated in specially formatted Java comments, so that any Java tool can still handle the source code.

3 Constraint Patterns in OCL

Besides augmenting models with textual constraints, models can be refined by applying patterns. A *constraint pattern* can be regarded as a parameterisable constraint expression that can be instantiated to solve a class of specification problems. Common constraint expressions are generalised and captured as constraint patterns. These patterns can then be instantiated in specific contexts to generate the concrete constraints. The concept of constraint patterns has been introduced for UML/OCL in order to simplify and speed up the development of constraints and to ensure their consistency [4–10].

The semantics of constraint patterns can be captured as an OCL template, i.e. a parameterisable OCL expression [8]. These templates are used as macros because patterns are untyped. The syntax of an OCL template starts with the keyword pattern followed by the name of the pattern and a set of typed parameters in brackets. This is followed by an equals sign and an arbitrary OCL expression in which the name of the formal parameters can be used. The Singleton design pattern can be defined using the template as follows.

```
pattern Singleton(element: Class) =
   element.allInstances()->size() = 1
```

Instantiating the pattern involves replacing the formal parameters by the values of the actual parameters. As an example, we instantiate the Singleton pattern to constrain the number of video stores in a model state to one. Note that in the following the constraints *oneStore1* and *oneStore2* are semantically equivalent.

```
context VideoRentalStore
inv oneStore1: Singleton(VideoRentalStore)
inv oneStore2: VideoRentalStore.allInstances()->size() = 1
```

The above example shows that constraint patterns are a concise means of hiding the syntactic and semantic complexity of OCL expressions and offering a unique name and uniform interface to the model developer.

In [8,10] an extensible library of *elementary* constraint patterns was presented for OCL modelling. The idea of elementary constraint patterns is to identify a relevant set of atomic constraints that covers frequently occurring restrictions on a model, e.g. restrictions on attribute values or on relations between objects. In addition to elementary constraint patterns, *composite* constraint patterns were introduced in order to express complex properties by combining an arbitrary number of other constraints. The identified composite patterns include Negation, If-Then-Else, Exists, Or, and And. Tool support for specification patterns is provided in the form of a set of plug-ins for the MDE tool IBM Rational Software Architect (RSA) that enable consistency-preserving refinement of UML class models with constraint patterns [8–10].

4 Mapping OCL Patterns to JML Patterns

In this section, we consider a subset of elementary constraint patterns and how they can be mapped to JML patterns. These elementary patterns are identified from a relevant set of elementary constraints that covers frequently occurring restrictions on a model. The general form of an OCL constraint pattern is given by the following template.

pattern patternName($p_1 : Type_1, ..., p_n : Type_n$) = patternBody

patternName stands for the name of the pattern, $p_1, ..., p_n$ is the list of parameters for the pattern of types $Type_1, ..., Type_n$ respectively, and patternBody is the body of the pattern represented as an OCL expression built using the parameters and OCL operations. The types of parameters $Type_1, ..., Type_n$ are types from the UML/OCL metamodel.

We use a template similar to that of OCL to capture the semantics of the JML patterns. The corresponding JML pattern is obtained from the OCL pattern by mapping the types of parameters to types in the JML metamodel, and by translating the body of the pattern into a JML expression. If $Type_i$ is mapped to $jmlType_i$ $(i = 1, .., n)$ and patternBody is mapped to jmlpatternBody then the JML pattern is given as follows.

pattern oclPatternName($p_1 : jmlType_1, ..., p_n : jmlType_n$) = jmlpatternBody

$$\begin{array}{ccc} \textit{OCL-Pattern} & \xrightarrow{\phi} & \textit{JML-Pattern} \\ {\scriptstyle instantiate}\downarrow & & \downarrow{\scriptstyle instantiate} \\ \textit{OCL-Constraint} & \xrightarrow{\mu} & \textit{JML-Constraint} \end{array}$$

Fig. 3. Constraint pattern mapping diagram.

Translating the body of the OCL pattern to a body for the corresponding JML pattern can be achieved by using the translation rules defined in [13,14]. That is if μ is the mapping that maps OCL expressions to JML expressions then we have $\mu(patternBody) = jmlPatternBody$. The mapping μ is defined recursively over the structure of OCL expressions. This process can be applied to each OCL constraint pattern. The diagram in Fig. 3 can be interpreted as saying that there are two ways to obtain a JML assertion from an OCL constraint. The starting point is applying an OCL constraint pattern. Unfolding the definition of the pattern we obtain the OCL constraint which can be mapped to a JML assertion using the mapping defined in [13]. This does not require the introduction of patterns in JML. The other way is not to unfold the OCL pattern but to use the corresponding JML pattern to do the mapping. Then the JML assertion can be obtained by unfolding the definition of the JML pattern. Assuming appropriate mappings have been used, the two ways should lead to semantically equivalent JML assertions. Since constraint patterns can be used in OCL for the development of constraints, it makes sense to introduce them in JML so that the mapping of a pattern instantiation will be done in a natural and direct way. This also has the advantage of expressing JML constraints concisely using patterns.

4.1 Restricting Attribute Values

In this subsection we consider constraints that express relations between properties. There are three patterns that restrict the values of attributes namely *Attribute Sum Restriction*, *Attribute Relation*, and *Attribute Value Restriction*. In the following we deal with the first two patterns since the last one was considered in [22].

Attribute Sum Restriction. The *Attribute Sum Restriction* pattern has three parameters. Besides the parameter *navigation*, which denotes a path expression to a related class, this pattern has two parameters. Parameter *summation* refers to the property in the context class that denotes the value that must not be exceeded, and *summand* refers to the property in the related class that is accumulated.

```
pattern AttributeSumRestriction (navigation: Sequence(Property),
                                 summand: Property, summation: Property) =
  self.navigation.summand->sum() <= summation
```

This pattern can be used to capture the constraint that the number of copies in the video store cannot exceed the maximum number of copies. This constraint is given as follows.

```
context VideoRentalStore
inv copiesRestriction : self.catalog.noOfCopies->sum() <= maxCopies
```

Using this constraint pattern with the actual parameters catalog, noOfCopies, and maxCopies, we can express the constraint *copiesRestriction* as follows.

```
context VideoRentalStore
inv copiesRestriction: AttributeSumRestriction(catalog, noOfCopies, maxCopies)
```

The corresponding JML pattern can be given as follows. Each parameter of the OCL pattern is mapped to a parameter of the same name, and the type Property is mapped to type *Field*.

```
pattern oclAttributeSumRestriction(navigation: List<Field>,
                                   summand: Field, summation: Field) =
this.navigation.collect(x->x.summand).sum() <= summation
```

The OCL expression c.p where c is a collection and p is a property is a shorthand notation for c−>collect(p). The OCL defines a set of iterator operations such as select, reject, collect, forAll, and exists that take an OCL expression as a parameter. These operations are harder to implement in Java without the support of higher order methods. This problem can be solved since Java 8 supports higher order methods through lambda expressions [23]. For this pattern, we introduce the JML methods *collect* and *sum* that implement OCL's operations collect and sum respectively. The *collect* method takes a lambda expression as a parameter.

Let us illustrate the approach by mapping the *copiesRestriction* constraint to a JML assertion. The class VideoRentalStore has an association named catalog, representing the set of titles in the video store (see Fig. 1). As shown in Fig. 4 below, we introduce a JML model variable for this association. The model variable has the same name as that of the association and is of type *OclSet*. The *OclSet* class is part of JML library and implements OCL's set [14]. The JML invariant obtained by unfolding the pattern definition is also included in Fig. 4 for comparison.

Attribute Relation. The *Attribute Relation* pattern can be used to relate an attribute contextAttribute to a remoteAttribute by an operator. The class containing the contextAttribute and the class containing the remoteAttribute are related by navigation. This pattern is defined as an OCL template as follows.

```
public class VideoRentalStore {
 /*@ spec_public @*/ private int maxCopies;
 //@ public model OclSet<Title> catalog;
 /*@ public invariant
     oclAttributeSumRestriction(catalog,noOfCopies,maxCopies);
   @*/
 /*@ public invariant
     this.catalog.collect(t->t.noOfCopies).sum() <= maxCopies;
   @*/
}
```

Fig. 4. JML annotations from OCL Attribute Sum Restriction pattern.

```
pattern AttributeRelation (navigation : Sequence(Property),
                           remoteAttribute: Property, operator: OclExpression,
                                             contextAttribute : Property) =
self.navigation->forAll(x | x.remoteAttribute operator contextAttribute)
```

This pattern can be used to capture the constraint that the number of copies for each title is less than the maximum number of copies of the video store. This constraint is given as follows.

```
context VideoRentalStore
inv lessMaximum : self.catalog->forAll(t | t.noOfCopies < self.maxCopies)
```

Using this constraint pattern with the actual parameters catalog, noOfCopies, < and maxCopies, we can express the constraint *lessMaximum* as follows.

```
context VideoRentalStore
inv lessMaximum: AttributeRelation(catalog, noOfCopies, <, maxCopies)
```

The corresponding JML pattern can be given as follows. The parameters of the OCL pattern are mapped to parameters with the same names and with appropriate types. The body of the pattern is mapped using the universal quantification operator in JML, namely *\forall*. The JML method *includes* implements OCL's operation includes.

```
pattern oclAttributeRelation (navigation : List<Field>,
                              remoteAttribute: Field, operator: JmlExpression,
                                                contextAttribute: Field) =
(\forall x; this.navigation.includes(x); x.remoteAttribute operator contextAt-
tribute)
```

```
public class VideoRentalStore {
/*@ spec_public @*/ private int maxCopies;
//@ public model OclSet<Title> catalog;
/*@ public invariant
      oclAttributeRelation(catalog, noOfCopies, maxCopies);
@*/
/*@ public invariant
 (\forall Title t;catalog.includes(t);noOfCopies < maxCopies);
@*/
}
```

Fig. 5. JML annotations from OCL Attribute Relation pattern.

Another way to translate the body of the OCL pattern is by introducing a higher order method *forAll* that directly implements the OCL operation forAll. In this case the structure of the OCL pattern is preserved in JML.

```
pattern oclAttributeRelation(navigation : List<Field>,
                             remoteAttribute: Field, operator: JmlExpression,
                                                   contextAttribute : Field) =
this.navigation.forAll(x->x.remoteAttribute operator contextAttribute)
```

The use of the JML pattern is illustrated in Fig. 5 above.

4.2 Unique Identification

The *Unique Identification* pattern is very frequent. For example, in the video rental model it is required that the id for members is unique. That is any members m1 and m2 should be distinguishable by their membership identities. In OCL such constraint can be expressed using the operation isUnique as follows.

```
context VideoRentalStore
inv uniqueID: self.members->isUnique(id)
```

This constraint can be generalized to composite primary keys by using the OCL tuple type.

The *Unique Identifier* pattern [10] (referred to *Semantic Key* in [6]) captures the situation where an attribute (or a group of attributes) of a class plays the role of an identifier for the class. That is the instances of the class should differ in their values for that attribute (group). The corresponding OCL template is given as follows.

```
pattern UniqueIdentifier(navigation: Sequence(Property), property : Property) =
self.navigation->isUnique(property)
```

This pattern has two parameters navigation which represents a path expression to a related class, property, which denotes a property that have to be unique for each object of the context class. The body of the pattern makes use of the OCL operation isUnique. This formulation of the pattern is different from [22] where the body of the pattern is defined in terms of the operation allInstances, which returns the set of existing instances of the class, and the operation isUnique. This pattern can be generalised to more than one property by using the OCL tuple type.

The corresponding JML pattern makes use of the JML operator $\backslash forall$ and can be defined as follows.

```
pattern oclUniqueIdentifier (navigation:List<Field>, property: Field) =
(\forall a1, a2;this.navigation.includes(a1) && this.navigation.includes(a2);
                                        a1 != a2 ==> a1.property != a2.property)
```

To make the correspondence between OCL and JML simpler it is possible to introduce a primitive quantifier `\unique` that asserts the uniqueness of a property or field. In that case the *Unique Identifier* pattern can be concisely stated as follows.

```
pattern oclUniqueIdentifier (navigation:List<Field>, property: Field) =
(\unique a;this.navigation.includes(a); property)
```

An alternative way to map this OCL pattern is to make use of lambda expressions in Java. This enables the implementation of the OCL operation isUnique to a JML method to be direct and more natural. If the JML method $isUnique$ implements the OCL operation, then the JML pattern can be stated as follows.

```
pattern oclUniqueIdentifier (navigation:List<Field>, property: Field) =
this.navigation.isUnique(x->x.property))
```

Applying the *Unique Identifier* pattern in the context of the class Member we get the following OCL invariant.

```
context Member
inv uniqueID: UniqueIdentifier(members, id)
```

Translating this invariant involves mapping the OCL expression Unique Identifier(members, id) to the corresponding JML expression oclUniqueIdentifier (members,id). The following code shows the translated invariant in JML.

```
public class VideoRentalStore {
  /*@ spec_public @*/ private int id;
  //@ public model OclSet<Member> members;
 //@ public invariant oclUniqueIdentifier(members, id);
    ...
}
```

By unfolding the above invariant we obtain:

```
public class VideoRentalStore {
/*@ spec_public @*/ private int id;
//@ public model OclSet<Member> members;

/*@ public invariant
      (\forall Member a1, a2;
             members.includes(a1) && members.includes(a2);
                        a1!=a2 ==> a1.id != a2.id);
@*/
}
```

Note that the translated JML pattern does not work when the equality test is based on value equality between objects. This is the case when the type of the field is `String` where the equality test should be based on the method `equals` rather than ==. One way to have another version of the JML pattern that uses `equals`, so that the mapping chooses the right pattern based on the type of the property. Yet another way is to use a generic equality when defining the pattern and use the tool for generating the right expression based on the type of the property. The latter approach is preferable since it allows the mapping of the pattern to be natural and more elegant.

5 Related Work

The most relevant related work on constraint patterns, on which this paper is based, is given by the approaches presented in [4–6] and [8–10]. However, the contribution of this paper is introducing specification patterns for Java/JML designs inspired from those of UML/OCL patterns and using the patterns to map OCL designs to JML designs. In addition the work presented in this paper extends and refines the work in [22].

The translation of OCL constraints to JML specifications has been addressed in numerous publications. In [13] a mapping is defined that maps OCL expressions to JML expressions. The mapping is defined recursively over the structure of expressions and provided the foundations for future implementations. The paper in [12] deals with some aspects of translating OCL into JML and proposed different strategies that would be possible to use for the mapping. The mapping in [13] was refined and implemented in [14], where a new JML library that implements the standard OCL library such as collection types was introduced. However, the current approach is based on new JML specification patterns that implement or correspond to OCL specification patterns. In addition we have used new constructs in Java [23] in order to map some OCL operations to JML methods.

6 Conclusions

In this paper, we proposed an approach to translating OCL constraints to JML assertions based on the concept of constraint pattern. The main component of our approach is a set of JML constraint patterns implementing OCL constraint patterns. That is each OCL constraint pattern is mapped to a corresponding JML specification pattern represented as a JML template. The possible benefits of this approach is enhancing the quality of the translated assertions by expressing them in a more compact way, and support automating the translation. The pattern-based approach has proven to be effective for UML/OCL constraint development [8,10], so it follows that the approach of this paper helps to decrease both the time and error rate for JML constraint development. That is the JML patterns can be used stand alone to facilitate and simplify the development of JML assertions. However, appropriate tool support is needed in order to allow model developers to effectively use the pattern-based approach. The other contribution of this paper is to enhance the mapping of OCL iterator operations to JML by using lambda expressions. This has made it possible to provide a direct and natural mapping of these operations.

Future work includes the identification and mapping of other OCL constraint patterns to JML. This will also cover patterns for preconditions and postconditions of operations. Furthermore, automating the mapping of OCL patterns and the instantiation of JML patterns need to be supported by means of an appropriate tool. We will also provide an implementation of OCL iterator operations based on using lambda expressions as supported by Java. This will form an extension of the JML library that implements the OCL standard library.

References

1. Warmer, J., Kleppe, A.: The object constraint language: getting your models ready for MDA. Addison-Wesley, Reading (2003)
2. OMG (Object Management Group): Object Constraint Language (OCL), Version 2.4 (2014)
3. OMG (Object Management Group): Unified Modeling Language Specification, Version 2.5 (2013)
4. Ackermann, J.: Frequently occurring patterns in behavioral specification of software components. In: Proceedings of the Conference on Component-Oriented Enterprise Applications (COEA), pp. 41–56 (2005)
5. Ackermann, J.: Formal description of OCL specification patterns for behavioral specification of software components. In: Workshop on Tool Support for OCL and Related Formalisms, Technical Report LGL-REPORT-2005-001, EPFL, pp. 15–29 (2005)

6. Ackermann, J., Turowski, K.: A library of OCL specification patterns for behavioral specification of software components. In: Dubois, E., Pohl, K. (eds.) CAiSE 2006. LNCS, vol. 4001, pp. 255–269. Springer, Heidelberg (2006)
7. Davis, J.P., Bonnell, R.D.: Propositional logic constraint patterns and their use in UML-based conceptual modeling and analysis. IEEE Trans. Knowl. and Data Eng. **19**, 427–440 (2007)
8. Wahler, M.: Using Patterns to Develop Consistent Design Constraints. Ph.D. thesis, ETH Zurich, Switzerland (2008)
9. Wahler, M., Basin, D., Brucker, A., Koehler, J.: Efficient analysis of pattern-based constraint specifications. Softw. Syst. Model. **9**, 225–255 (2010)
10. Wahler, M., Koehler, J., Brucker, A.D.: Model-driven constraint engineering. In: MoDELS Workshp. on OCL for (Meta-)Models in Multiple Application Domains, pp. 111–125 (2006)
11. Hamie, A.: Towards verifying java realizations of OCL-constrained design models using JML. In: Proceedings of the 6th IASTED International Conference on Software Engineering and Applications (SEA 2002). IASTED Press (2002)
12. Hamie, A.: Strategies for Translating the UML/OCL Design Models to JAVA/JML Designs. In: International Computer Symposium, Taiwan (2004)
13. Hamie, A.: Translating the object constraint language into the java modelling language. In: Proceedings of the ACM Symposium on Applied Computing, pp. 1531–1535. ACM Press (2004)
14. Avila, C., Flores, G., Cheon, Y.: A library-based approach to translating OCL constraints to JML assertions for runtime checking. In: International Conference on Software Engineering Research and Practice, pp. 403–408. CSREA Press (2008)
15. Leavens, G.T., Baker, A.L., Ruby, C.: Preliminary design of JML: a behavioral interface specification language for java. ACM SIGSOFT Softw. Eng. Not. **31**, 1–38 (2006)
16. Cheon, Y., Leavens, G.T.: A runtime assertion checker for the java modeling language (JML). In: International Conference on Software Engineering Research and Practice, pp. 322–328. CSREA Press (2002)
17. Cheon, Y., Leavens, G.T., Sitaraman, M., Edwards, S.: Model variables: cleanly supporting abstraction in design by contract. Softw.: Pract. Exp. **35**, 583–599 (2005)
18. Frankel, D.: Model Driven Architecture: Applying MDA to Enterprise Computing. Wiley, New York (2002)
19. Leavens, G.T., Cheon, Y., Clifton, C., Ruby, C., Cok, D.R.: How the design of JML accommodates both runtime assertion checking and formal verification. Sci. Comput. Program. **55**, 185–208 (2005)
20. Cok, D., Kiniry, J.: ESC/Java2: uniting ESC/Java and JML. In: Barthe, G., Burdy, L., Huisman, M., Lanet, J.L., Muntean, T. (eds.) ASSIS 2004. LNCS, vol. 3362, pp. 108–128. Springer, Heidelberg (2005)
21. Jacobs, B., Poll, E.: Java program verification at nijmegen: developments and perspective. In: Futatsugi, K., Mizoguchi, F., Yonezaki, N. (eds.) ISSS 2003. LNCS, vol. 3233, pp. 134–153. Springer, Heidelberg (2003)
22. Hamie, A.: Pattern-based mapping of OCL specifications to JML contracts. In: Proceedings of the 2nd International Conference on Model-Driven Engineering and Software Development (MODELSWARD) (2014)
23. Gosling, J., Joy, B., Steele, G., Bracha, G., Buckley, A.: The Java Language Specification, Java SE 8 Edition (Java Series). Addison-Wesley, Upper Saddle River (2014)

Transformation-Wise Design of Software Architectures

Fabian Gilson(✉) and Vincent Englebert

PReCISE Research Center, University of Namur, Namur, Belgium
{fabian.gilson,vincent.englebert}@unamur.be

Abstract. Stakeholders have to face requirements in increasing number and complexity, and the link between these requirements and design artifacts is primordial. Agile design methods and documentation techniques have emerged in the past years in order to trace the decision process and the rationale sustaining a software model. The present work proposes an integrated framework combining system requirement definitions, component-based models and model transformations. Architecturally significant requirements are explicitly linked to software architecture elements and iteratively refined or implemented by model transformations. Any transformation must be documented, even briefly, and the framework retains the transformations tree. This way, the iterative decision and design processes are completely documented for future reference or modification, i.e., designers can (i) see the mapping between a system requirement and its implementation in the architecture model, (ii) explore design alternatives or apply structural modifications without losing previous versions of the model, and finally (iii) at least understand partially the reasons why the model is how it is.

Keywords: Software architecture · Design method · Design rationale · Traceability · Model transformation

1 Introduction

Software systems become complex products where many people and constraints may intervene. They are intended to offer many functionalities that can evolve over time. Many possibilities are often available to fulfill specific needs which increase the amount of design choices. A requirement can be scattered over an architecture model so that it becomes difficult to recover architectural knowledge [24]. Without appropriate design decisions and rationale tracing mechanisms, system maintenance, evolution and redeployment may be costly and time-consuming [25].

As we explain in Sect. 2, iterative design method in component-based systems is not new. The main goal of such methods is to face requirements and constraints by integrating them step-by-step [3]. However, a tricky part resides in ordering these requirements since the early decisions taken at the architecture

This paper is an updated version of *A DSL for Stepwise Design of SA* [7].

S. Hammoudi et al. (Eds.): MODELSWARD 2014, CCIS 506, pp. 49–65, 2015.
DOI: 10.1007/978-3-319-25156-1_4

or technological levels may impact the overall design possibilities [21]. Making an early decision, like choosing a particular architectural style, limits the design possibilities for later decisions and may cause expensive rework if it was wrong.

We propose in Sect. 4, an agile-based design framework intertwining structural models, requirement definitions, design rationale documentation and model transformations. These underlying languages are presented in Sect. 3. The aim of this work is to structure the iterative design process around step-by-step refinements and model transformations [12]. On the one hand, architecturally-significant requirements are expressed regarding some guidelines. On the other hand, information systems are modeled in terms of types of constructs, concrete and interconnected instances and deployment targets. The framework traces the history of the iterative decision process with corresponding models. At any time, it is possible to go back to an earlier model, make a modification and re-apply the previously defined transformations with minor necessary rework at the architecture level. Decisions and rationale are first-class entities in the design process so that we explicitly keep the link between requirements and implementing constructs with the reasons sustaining such decisions. We do not address ordering or assessment between requirements, like the *Architecture Tradeoff Analysis Method* (ATAM) [13] or the reasoning method proposed by Tekinerdogan *et al.* [23], even if such methods can be integrated in our framework.

We challenged our approach on a comparative case study on a fictitious online book store system. In Sect. 5, we present the broad outlines of the case study and analyze some of its outcomes. We discuss how our transformation-oriented method helped designers to structure the architectural knowledge, trace design alternatives and build a documented system architecture. We will afterwards discuss the benefits and limitations of our approach in Sect. 6. We finally conclude this paper with our research perspectives and future work in Sect. 7.

2 Related Work

An increasing amount of research focuses on the relations between requirements, design decisions, design rationale and architecture model. A basis for rationale and decisions reasoning has been proposed by Kruchten *et al.* [14] and a formal language for decisions modeling was developed by Zimmermann *et al.* where they refined the notion of decision into *issues*, *alternatives* and *outcomes* [26].

Although, there is a need for embedded facilities to maintain a concrete link between decisions and rationale, and resulting architecture models [2]. *Architecture Rationale and Element Linkage* is a more complete technique that integrates model elements and the rationale behind the associated design decisions [22]. Jansen *et al.* introduce a documentation *enrichment* method, supported by a tool suite, to add formal knowledge even to existing documentation [11]. van Heesch *et al.* propose a *viewpoint-based* representation of design decisions and rationale with the possibility to record also *personalized* knowledge [8]. However, all these approaches require modelers to maintain extra models so that the workload is significantly increased with a possible *discouraging* effect. Also, the adequacy between models is rarely ensured on the long run. In our method, decisions and rationale are kept inside requirement models, concretely linked to architecture model elements in a very simple way.

A couple of transformation-centric methods have emerged. In many of these approaches, models are either transformed to integrate new requirements or non functional qualities, or represent systems from a coarse-grained picture to a fine-grained one. Matinlassi proposes a technique for quality-driven model transformations where the author focuses on automation, but only on quality properties [16]. Perovich *et al.* use a more complex representation for the system functionalities [19], in terms of, among others, information flows or policies. But, as far as we know, they currently do not provide tool support and concentrate on deployment-related decisions and rationale.

3 Modeling Languages Overview

The present method focuses on software architecture design. It relies on three languages: a component-based modeling language, a requirement language with design decisions and rationale traceability, and a transformation language. In the following sections, we present the main concepts of both modeling languages. Afterwards, we introduce our specific transformation language in more details.

3.1 Architecturally Significant Requirement Modeling

In a previous work, we defined a simple modeling language to record and trace architecturally significant requirements (ASR) [5], i.e., requirements that *have a measurable impact on the software system's architecture* [4]. We provide in Listing 1.1 a sample model of a Client-Server system. Two requirements are listed: a functional requirement identified by the name *SayHello*, and a non functional one named *FastAnswer*. They are both assigned to the `Server`.

```
package example; // model header (package name)
asrmodel clientserver with example.clientserver { // link to an architecture model
  func SayHello assigned Server { // functional requirement
    description "The Server shall print 'Hello World!' to the console.";
    realisation example.myfirsttransformation; // link to a transformation
    rationale { // rationale for this design decision
      assessment "Trivial functionality, unique service should make the trick.";
      strength "Simple implementation with unique service without parameters.";
      weakness "The printed message is fixed.";
    }
  }
  nonfunc FastAnswer assigned Server { // non functional
    description "When receiving a client request, Server shall answer in less than 1 second.";
    implements Hello; // fulfill ASR by implementing interface "Hello"
    rationale {
      assessment "Parameter-less service, server response time should be fast.";
      assumption "Because service is trivial, one server should be sufficient.";
      constraint "Should be less than 100 simultaneous requests per second";
    }
  }
}
```

Listing 1.1. Sample ASR model for a Client-Server.

The present ASR model `clientserver` is part of a package and refers to an architecture model named `example.clientserver`. Both requirements are described following the writing guidelines from Alexander and Stevens [1] and conforms to the EARS templates [17]. In short, these templates define a structured way of writing system requirements in natural language. Specific pieces of information, like events, or options, are highlighted by specific terms, respectively *when* and *where*, and are present in the description at specific places. Amongst the advantages of this approach, we particularly note its ease of learning since no new (modeling) language or concept is necessary to learn, as well as its ability to induce more completeness and conciseness in requirement descriptions.

Regarding a requirement, a number of decisions can be taken. We group them in the following categories:

Assignation the requirement is assigned to a modeling construct.

Refinement a lower-level requirement is a refinement of a higher-level one, i.e., concerns part of the scope of the higher-level requirement, but describes it more precisely.

Alternative a lower-level requirement is a possible refinement alternative for a higher-level requirement.

Selection an alternative is actually selected by the designers as the *implementation* solution.

Interface usage or implementation in order to fulfill a requirement, an existing interface is used or implemented, or in case of non functional requirements, the given interface conforms to the needed properties to achieve this requirement.

Re-assignment the requirement is reassigned to another modeling construct, i.e., the responsibility to accomplish the requirement is transferred to another model element (mainly software components).

Realisation a structural modification must be made into the component model and this will be expressed as a model transformation (cfr. Sect. 4).

When a modeler takes a decision, its type is recorded in the model. For any type of decision, a set of rationale can be added of which the *assessment* is mandatory. We briefly present here the type of rationale that can be filled in an ASR model.

Assessment the actual reason sustaining the design decision.

Assumption any assumption made on the environment or on other elements.

Strength any advantage of this decision.

Weakness any disadvantage or limitation of the decision.

Constraint any constraint or consequence related to this decision.

The proposed syntax for ASR models enforces designers to document their choices in terms of assignments of requirement to modeling constructs, and in terms of refinements of requirements. First, we explicitly trace the link between a requirement and the model element in charge of its implementation. This enhances the architectural knowledge regarding *who* is implementing *what*. Second, we keep the history of the decisions regarding a requirement (re-assignments, refinements and alternatives) for documentation purposes. Third, design decisions must be documented by at least one reason sustaining such a choice. A minimum amount of information is mandatory in order to avoid putting to much unnecessary or unwanted effort in documentation tasks. Further details, like strengths and weaknesses, can be added by the modeler at his own discretion.

3.2 Architecture Modeling

Attached to a requirement model, a structural definition of the system must be provided. For this purpose, we defined a *3-layers* component-based modeling language [6][1]. We present in the following how information systems are modeled in three inter-related stages: *definition*, *assemblage* and *deployment* (DAD).

Stage One: Definition. Roughly, in the first stage, abstract component types are connected by link types through interfaces. The model can be drawn at any level of details and component types may contain other types that are connected by inner interfaces. For instance, a first architectural representation could be composed by only one component named `System` with all requirements assigned to it. Listing 1.2 illustrates part of the *definition* stage for our Client-Server.

```
package example;
dadmodel clientserver {
  definition {
    interface Hello { sync void hello (); }
    componenttype Client { uses Hello as hello; }
    componenttype Server { implements Hello as hello; }
    connectortype One2One { mode one2one; }
    linkagetype from Client.hello to Server.hello with One2One;
  }
}
```

Listing 1.2. Definition stage for a Client-Server.

As for an ASR model, a DAD model must belong to a package. In this case, we decided to use the same names for both ASR and DAD models for convenience. We defined a simple interface `Hello` with a unique synchronous service named `hello()` without parameters. This interface is used by a type of component `Client` and a `Server`. When an interface is exposed in any way by a type of component, it becomes a facet of this component with a given polarity (*usage* or *implementation*). We also define a type of connector which is point-to-point, i.e. connecting one type of component to only one other type of component at a time. We finally link the `Client` to the `Server` with the `One2One` type of connector in a *provide-require* contract through the facets.

A set of primitive types has been defined, as *integer*, *boolean* or *string*. Architects may obviously define custom primitive types or structures. User-defined types may also be *mapped to* Java types to reuse existing definitions or clarify its semantics. In a DAD model, primitive types, structures or interfaces are all considered as generic types and can be used to type a parameter.

[1] The reader is encouraged to refer to this paper for a more complete discussion.

At this point, we defined the building blocks we can *instantiate* and concretely connect during the *assemblage* stage. The type of linkage defined from now only constrains how the type of components can be linked to each other (i) through which interface and, (ii) how many instances of a type of a component will be involved in the connection.

Stage Two: Assemblage. In Listing 1.3, we introduce a communication protocol and present the *assemblage* stage of the DAD model.

```
definition {
  /* omitting previously defined constructs */
  protocol TCP { // communication protocol for concrete binding
    layer: transport;
  }
  connectortype One2One {  // link supports TCP protocol
    mode: one2one;
    accepts TCP;
  }
}
assemblage {
  soi client[0 100] : Client { // a set of instances of type Client
    Client.hello as hello on TCP; // expose the required facet hello over TCP
  }
  soi server : Server { // a set of instances of type Server
    Server.hello[20] as hello on TCP; // expose the provided facet hello over TCP
  }
  // bind all clients to the server (individually with a point-to-point connector)
  linkage from client.hello [0 100] to server.hello with One2One;
}
```

Listing 1.3. Assemblage stage for a Client-Server.

The protocol TCP specifies with, basic properties, a communication protocol that will be used to support the connection between instances of component types. A protocol is at least defined by the communication layer, so it is possible to specify a wide range of connections from low-level protocols like Bluetooth to high-level ones like program call. In our case, we use the TCP protocol and add it to the accepted protocols of our connector type.

We create a set of instances (SoI) for each component type previously defined. SoI are declared with a minimum and a maximum cardinality that express the amount of instances of the same type that can be present in a concrete architecture. In our example, a maximum of 100 instances of the `Client` component type can be created. This SoI has one port typed by the facet `hello` on the `TCP` protocol. The `Server` is unique and has 20 ports of the type `hello` available, also over `TCP`. `Clients` SoIs are linked to the `server` according to the linkage type defined at the previous stage. At this point, we specify a concrete architecture instance with a certain amount of each component types, available ports (i.e., interface instances) and connections on specific protocols.

Stage Three: Deployment. Current design methods often omit infrastructure constraints [15]. We believe that this problem can be partially tackled by integrating the constraints as soon as they appear in the design phase. We provide basic and extensible building blocks to define the target platform. In Listing 1.4, we specify these types of blocks and illustrate the abstract *deployment* phase.

```
definition {
  /* omitting previously defined constructs */
  gatetype Ethernet {   // type of physical port
    supports TCP;
  }
  nodetype Computer gates { // type of computation node (machine)
    Ethernet eth;
  }
  mediumtype E100BaseT {  // type of concrete (physical) link
    supports TCP;
  }
}
assemblage { /* hidden for conciseness */ }
deployment {
  node computer[101] : Computer; // need 101 computers
  /* bind all client machines to the server (we do not care about the number of
   physical cables but on the media's properties) */
  plug E100BaseT from computer[0 99]::eth to computer[100]::eth;
  deploy client on computer[0 99]; // deploy clients
  deploy server on computer[100]; // deploy server
  open client.hello on computer[0 99]::eth; // need Hello by ethernet gates
  open server.hello on computer[100]::eth; // open Hello on ethernet gates
}
```

Listing 1.4. Deployment stage for a Client-Server.

Three new types of model elements are created at the *definition* stage. First, a type of gate specifies a network interface or a physical port on a computation device. Gate types support a possibly non exhaustive list of protocols. In our example, we define an `Ethernet` gate type supporting our `TCP` protocol. Second, we define a type of node that can represent any type of computation machine or platform environment. A node type can be equipped by a number of gates of certain types. Third, type of communication media, such as network cables or communication buses, are defined. A type of medium also support a list of protocols. These physical infrastructure-related constructs, as well as many others, can be more precisely defined by an extensible property mechanism out of the scope of this paper.

When we have specified types of nodes, gates and media, we can define an abstract deployment by mapping the set of instances onto these physical constructs. For this purpose, we have to create 101 nodes of type `Computer`. We do not need to specify medium instances since we are only concerned by the properties attached to a type of medium and how nodes are accessible from *outside*. so we *plug* communication medium types from all client machines to the server.

We now *deploy* our set of instances on nodes and *open* their ports (typed by interfaces) on gates. The overall communication binding, from the *definition* layer to the *deployment*, is *reified* using the communication protocol. In this example, we use a unique protocol (`TCP`), but more complex verifications with *compatible* protocols can be done, depending on user-defined properties.

Note that, in a DAD model, all stages are optional. One can isolate whatever he wants in a specific DAD model and import (using the `import` keyword in the model header) any other model element defined elsewhere. This mechanism will be further developed in Sect. 4.4 when we will talk about pattern injections.

4 Step-by-step Refinement with Model Transformations

During the creation of the architecture of a software system, architects usually start from a coarse-grained architectural style, choose one architecturally significant requirement (regardless how they prioritize them), refine it to more precise ones if necessary and *implement* it in the architecture. At some points in the design process, architects may perform some validation of the produced model(s). During this iterative process, multiple alternatives can be explored and wrong decisions can be taken so that architects have to backtrack to a previous version of the model. As pointed out in Sect. 1, this decision process and the rationale sustaining a *final* architecture are frequently lost after a while and further evolutions and bug fixes become time consuming or error-prone.

The approach used in our framework is transformation-centric: any change in an architecture model must be expressed as a model transformation. In order to test our proposal, we implemented both languages presented in Sects. 3.1 and 3.2 and the transformation language described in the following as Eclipse plugins with the Xtext framework[2]. We also implemented a transformation engine working on the abstract syntax tree of our model.

From the definition of all known requirements in an ASR model and a first, even empty, DAD model, any modification to the architecture must be expressed using one of the following transformation rules. A single file can group many transformations, related to one requirement, that will be applied all in once. A new model is then created by the transformation engine and this model can be further refined, i.e. transformed, to implement other requirements.

4.1 General Template and Creation of Constructs

We group rules related to a specific requirement in a DAD-Transformations set (DAD-T). Similarly to DAD and ASR models, a transformations set belongs to a package. A transformation is always related to a requirement, referred in the model by the keyword `concerns`, declared on top of the DAD-T file. A DAD model can also be referenced when the transformation is linked to a specific architecture model, i.e., the transformations set is not the definition of a pattern.

A creation rule is defined by the keyword `create` followed by the definition of the new construct. In Listing 1.5, we show how the `Hello` interface could have been created with related `Client` facet and port in a transformation model.

[2] Xtext is a toolset designed to build configurable textual editors for Domain Specific Languages as Eclipse plugins on top of the Eclipse Modeling Framework. See www.eclipse.org/Xtext and www.eclipse.org/modeling/emf.

```
package example;
asrmodel example.clientserver; // involved asr model (mandatory)
dadmodel example.clientserver; // involved dad model (optional)
transformationset createHello concerns SayHello { // transfo. refers to an ASR
  create interface Hello { // create interface
    sync void hello();
  }
  create facet { // create facet in Client
    uses Hello as hello;
  } in Client;
  create port { // create port in client
    Client.hello as hello on TCP;
  } in client;
}
```

Listing 1.5. Creation of the `Hello` interface.

Any construct from the *definition* stage can be created in a similar fashion. The transformation engine will inject them into the bound DAD model. Prior to a creation, the engine verifies that no name conflict occurs: names must be unique by construct type and a check is performed using fully qualified names.

4.2 Deletion of Constructs

It is indeed possible to delete constructs from an architecture model. Not only *definition* stage elements can be deleted, but also any other model elements.

The transformation engine ensures that deletions are always done *in cascade*, i.e., all related constructs or instances are deleted when a particular element is deleted[3]. For example, Listing 1.6 is the resulting DAD model after the deletion of the `Client` component type from the model illustrated in Listing 1.4.

```
definition {
  interface Hello { sync void hello (); }
  /* component type Client deleted */
  componenttype Server { implements Hello as hello; }
  /* omitting remaining of def. stage */
}
assemblage {
  // set of instance typed by Client deleted
  soi server : Server { Server.hello as hello on TCP; }
  /* linkage with the soi "client" is deleted */
}
deployment {
  node computer[101] : Computer;
  /* plus is still present since the infrastructure configuration is
  not dependent from the assemblage, but supports it */
  plug E100BaseT from computer[0 99]::eth to computer[100]::eth;
  /* deployment of the soi "client" is deleted */
  deploy server on computer[100];
  /* gate opening deleted too */
  open server.hello on computer[100]::eth;
}
```

Listing 1.6. DAD model after deletion of `Client` component type.

In this example, the related linkage type involving the `Client` component type has been removed. The transformation engine deleted the set of instances typed by the `Client`, the linkage where this set of instances appeared, as well

[3] For a complete view of the relations between model constructs, please refer to [6].

as the related deployment statements. Note that the plug clause is still present since the infrastructure configuration is meant to support the deployment of the *assemblage*, but does not depend on it. A similar behavior is always applied for all other model elements where the engine removes all constructs with a reference to the suppressed element.

4.3 Fine-Grained Alteration of Constructs

Frequently, architects need more fine-grained transformations where they can, for example, add a service to an interface, add a gate to a node or alter a data structure. For example, in Listing 1.7, we modify the `hello` interface.

```
alter interface Hello {
  // add new asynchronous service with a delay before saying HelloWorld
  add async invokeHello(int delay);
  rewrite hello { // add an input parameter to specify the message
    add in string message;
  }
}
```

Listing 1.7. Fine grained alteration of an interface.

A new asynchronous service is added into the interface with a *delay* parameter. The second alteration adds a new parameter with its access type (may be *input*, *output* or *both*) to the `hello` service to define the content of the message.

For every construct with *internal* definitions, similar transformations can be defined. Here again, name validity checks (names must be unique for their parent's scope) are performed to avoid conflicts.

4.4 Pattern Definition, Injection and Replacement

In order to enhance re-usability, design patterns can be created with DAD-T sets. They are expressed as transformation rules, as illustrated in Listing 1.8, and linked to ASR models specifying their assets (not included for brevity reason).

```
package example;
asrmodel example.observer;
transformationset observer concerns Observer {
  create interface IObserver { async notify(); }
  create interface ISubject {
    async register(IObserver o);
    async unregister(IObserver o);
  }
  create componenttype Observer {
    implements IObserver as iobserver;
    uses ISubject as isubject;
  }
  create componenttype Subject {
    implements ISubject as isubject;
    uses IObserver as iobserver;
  }
  create connectortype Simple { mode one2one; }
  create connectortype Multi { mode one2many; }
  create linkagetype from Subject.iobserver to Observer.iobserver with Multi;
  create linkagetype from Observer.isubject to Subject.isubject with Simple;
}
```

Listing 1.8. Definition of the `Observer` pattern.

The transformations set creates the `Observer` and `Subject` as well as the needed interfaces, facets and types of linkage. A pattern must be self-contained, i.e. all needed constructs are defined in the model, or it can import some external resources with the `import` keyword, similarly to DAD models.

To inject this pattern into an architecture model, assume we had a requirement asking for such a pattern, we simply need to *include* the pattern-related transformations set, then to *replace* and *merge* the target constructs, as shown in Listing 1.9. The `include` mechanism can be used for any type of reusable transformation rules. Note that if the `merge` option is not passed, a construct is totally *replaced* by another one without *merging* their definitions.

```
package example;
asrmodel example.clientserver;
dadmodel example.clientserver;
transformationset inj_observer concerns Observer {
  include example.observer; // execute pattern transformation
  replace Subject by Server merge; // merge Subject into Server
}
```

Listing 1.9. Pattern injection with merge.

The result is presented in Listing 1.10. An `Observer` construct has been created and the `Server` now implements and uses the `Subject`-related interfaces. More complex replacements with specific *overrides* can also be defined. For example, one can override a given facet by another with a compatible definition (i.e., services signatures and properties).

```
definition {
  interface IObserver {/* omitting definition */}
  interface ISubject {/* omitting definition */}
  componenttype Server {
    implements Hello as hello;
    implements ISubject as isubject;
    uses IObserver as iobserver;
  }
  componenttype Observer {
    implements IObserver as iobserver;
    uses ISubject as isubject;
  }
  linkagetype from Server.iobserver to Observer.iobserver with Multi;
  linkagetype from Observer.isubject to Server.isubject with Simple;
  // omitting remaining of model
}
```

Listing 1.10. After pattern injection.

Other types of transformations exist, such as renaming, moving elements, etc., but are not shown in the present paper for brevity reasons.

4.5 Decision and History Tracking

Coupled with the rationale and design decision tracing in ASR files, as presented in Sect. 3.1, we implemented a simple tree-based history tracing mechanism. Figure 1 shows a screen capture of our Eclipse plugin and illustrates a history tree in the package explorer (left-hand side of the picture).

Every time a model is transformed, a new model is created in a separate folder. By convention, we start from a folder named *revision1* and append *.1* after a transformation is carried on a DAD model. When backtracking to a previous model, a new branch will be created by increasing the higher sub-branch number. For example, after the model *revision 1.1.1.1*, we started back from the model at revision *1.1* so a new branch numbered *1.1.2* was created. This mechanism keeps the history of all created models and can be used to draw *revision graphs* to explore the iteration history in a more convenient way.

We intend to review the iteration process in order to define *release points* where a set of transformations are grouped to define coarse-grained evolutions or patches, which offers possibilities for software configuration management. Other avenues worth exploring would be to see how task-oriented methods, like the *MyLyn*[4] project, can be integrated into our framework, as well as collaborative model editing and versionning [20].

5 A Comparative Case Study

We experimented our approach with a comparative case study on a fictitious online book store system. We confronted our framework against SysML [18]. In brief, a web-based *online library* presents a catalog of books aggregated from registered *book stores*. When a customer purchases a book, the *library* starts an auction between the *stores* to buy the book at the cheapest price. Afterwards, the *library* contacts a *delivery system* to pick up the book at the winning *store* and to deliver it to the customer.

The case study was conducted on a group of 24 master students at the University of Namur, all familiar with UML diagrams, but not with SysML,

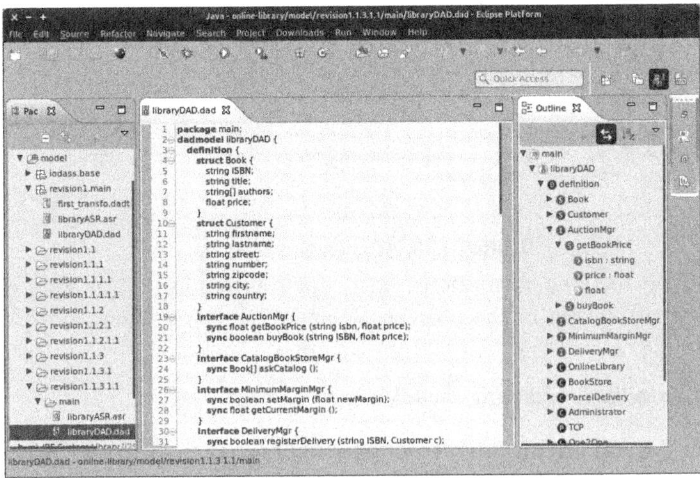

Fig. 1. Capture of the Eclipse plugin with history tracking in package explorer.

[4] www.eclipse.org/mylyn/.

neither with our framework. We organized a preliminary round to evaluate their system modeling competences. During a lecture, the students were asked to draw a class diagram based on a requirement document. Three researchers, also familiar with software modeling, classified the diagrams in four categories based on their syntactic and semantic correctness. This way, we divided the students in two groups of comparable competences and made teams of two students for the remaining of the study, the first group had to design the *online library* in SysML, the second with our framework.

We presented separately the language artifacts and the tool support to each group. Both groups also received the same description of the *system-to-be* and were asked to build it (design and code) in two phases. For the first phase, the requirements were clearly stated in the documents to let them getting familiar with the new languages. For the second phase, the descriptions were more fuzzy and were related to the evolution of the system.

After each phase, we evaluated the quality of the models and the documentation created by the students, as well as the functional correctness of the produced code. We verified to what extent they documented the decisions sustaining the produced architectures. Basically, we checked if all model elements had at least one justification explaining why they were created into the model.

Students were asked to answer anonymously to a questionnaire in classroom to evaluate the expressiveness, the documentation and evolution facilities of the languages they used. The students also formulated reviews and advices in a project report where they could express their feelings regarding the aforesaid criteria. In the questionnaire, we used a non-graduated ruler going from "fully disagree" (**0** value) to "fully agree" (**5** value) and measured the students answers. We also dissimulated redundant questions in order to double-check the given answers. On the 24 questionnaires, we discarded four of them for each group because the gaps between the answers to these control questions were too large. We present in Table 1 part of the results regarding expressiveness, evolution and documentation facilities. The second column (**S**) shows the aggregated rating for SysML and the last column for our framework (**D**).

As shown in Table 1, our framework offers a significant improvement regarding constructs expressiveness (*q.1*). Regarding documentation (*q.2*), the difference is not significant enough. Concerning model evolution (*q.3*), the results of our framework are slightly inferiors. Two aspects can explain these last values. First, our framework relies on textual models which are, by nature, less visual than graphical models. Second, during the experiment, the comments present in the DAD models were lost after a transformation, which revealed to be a significant lack at participants eyes when we analyzed their reviewing documents.

In their reviews, many students mentioned a significant improvement in the traceability of requirements, design rationale and decisions compared to their experience (mainly with UML diagrams and text-based documentation). Moreover, we noticed a higher tendency to refine requirements into sub-requirements and explore alternatives with our formalisms. The overall

Table 1. Sample questions and aggregated ratings.

Questions	S	D
1. The languages constructs allow to represent:		
a. the functionalities of the system	3.68	4.33
b. the technological and communication constraints	1.95	4.48
c. the non functional requirements	3.10	4.12
2. The written documentation allows to efficiently comprehend the system within the framework of a modification of the system	2.63	2.85
3. During the second phase:		
a. A major work was necessary to comprehend again the architectural concepts of the system	0.97	1.21
b. The modeling languages eased the structural changes linked to the new functionalities to implement	3.83	3.25

functional completeness was also slightly higher in our framework since 6 teams had a fully functional auction process against 4 teams on the SysML side.

6 Discussion and Limitations

The ASR model covers a notable part of the project backlog, as defined by Hofmeister *et al.* [10], which is a key document for system engineering. Design rationale, decisions and structured requirements are present in the model and related to the modeling constructs that implement them. This simple mechanism enhances the architectural knowledge without asking much documentation effort. By adding user-defined properties, *meta-properties* regarding the project itself, like requirement ordering methods, standards and so forth can be specified. The framework also enforces documentation of design iterations in a lightweight way and records changes in the model as explicit transformations.

The transformation inclusion mechanism offers a lightweight way to define and re-use patterns in a transformations set. Working on the concrete syntax results in more concise rules and improves the readability of such transformations comparing to general-purpose transformation languages. However, reusability of transformations is limited to concrete syntax elements and patterns injections require to write mapping rules between pattern constructs and the current model. But since patterns play an important role as a mean of documentation and communication, we believe a concrete syntax is more accurate for such a goal.

Coupled with the history mechanism, design or technological alternatives can be explored and documented. Similarly to the study conducted in [9], we observed a more systematic refinement of requirements and alternative explorations in our case study. Though, a proper graphical visualization facility should be provided to efficiently identify *deltas* between models and to navigate easily between revisions. Also, a couple of relations between design decisions will be taken into account in a future release of the language. It will be possible to identify conflicts and inter-dependencies between requirements, so that the decision-making process will be enhanced for designers.

At current point of development, models are expressed in textual syntax. Even if such representation is very expressive, the analysis and communication of textual models is often less natural for humans.

Last, a larger case study should be conducted in order to evaluate if the transformation-centric method coupled to a task-oriented approach scales to industrial cases.

7 Conclusions and Future Work

We introduced a transformation-centric design framework based on Domain Specific Languages. Architectural constructs are explicitly related to requirement specifications and implemented iteratively in the architecture with model transformations. Every decision is recorded in the requirement model with its design rationale. A tool is provided for textual models, as well as a transformation engine. We conducted a comparative case study to partially validate our proposal and evaluate its benefits.

In the future, we intend to add behavioral specifications to *definition* layer construct types with, at first, tag-based properties and *first order predicate logic* statements. Such behavioral properties will help designers to ensure a transformation does not break behavioral aspects of an existing architecture. Additionally, coupled with the extended requirements modeling language, mechanisms will be provided to record *personalized* knowledge too.

A visual representation of the history tree with model *deltas* should be integrated in the tool to facilitate further references to transformations outcomes, design alternatives and system evolutions. Ideally, a final goal would be to synchronize a graphical representation on textual architecture models to benefit from the advantages of both textual and graphical visualizations.

References

1. Alexander, I.F., Stevens, R.: Writing Better Requirements. Addison-Wesley (2002)
2. de Boer, R.C., van Vliet, H.: On the similarity between requirements and architecture. J. Syst. Softw. **82**(3), 544–550 (2009)
3. Bosch, J., Molin, P.: Software architecture design: Evaluation and transformation. In: IEEE International Conference on the Engineering of Computer-Based Systems, p. 410 (1999)
4. Chen, L., Ali Babar, M., Nuseibeh, B.: Characterizing architecturally significant requirements. Softw. IEEE **30**(2), 38–45 (2013)
5. Gilson, F., Englebert, V.: Rationale, decisions and alternatives traceability for architecture design. In: Proceeding of the 5th European Conference on Software Architecture, Companion volume, p. 4. ACM (2011)
6. Gilson, F., Englebert, V.: Towards handling architecture design, variability and evolution with model transformations. In: Proceeding of the 5th Workshop on Variability Modeling of Software-Intensive Systems, pp. 39–48. ACM (2011)

7. Gilson, F., Englebert, V.: A domain specific language for stepwise design of software architectures. In: Proceeding of the 2nd International Conference on Model-Driven Engineering and Software Development (MODELSWARD 2014), pp. 67–78. SciTePress (2014)
8. van Heesch, U., Avgeriou, P., Hilliard, R.: A documentation framework for architecture decisions. J. Syst. Softw. **85**(4), 795–820 (2012)
9. van Heesch, U., Avgeriou, P., Tang, A.: Does decision documentation help junior designers rationalize their decisions? a comparative multiple-case study. J. Syst. Softw. **86**(6), 1545–1565 (2013)
10. Hofmeister, C., Kruchten, P., Nord, R.L., Obbink, H., Ran, A., America, P.: A general model of software architecture design derived from five industrial approaches. J. Syst. Softw. **80**(1), 106–126 (2007)
11. Jansen, A., Avgeriou, P., van der Ven, J.S.: Enriching software architecture documentation. J. Syst. Softw. **82**, 1232–1248 (2009)
12. Jansen, A., Bosch, J.: Software architecture as a set of architectural design decisions. In: Proceeding of the 5th Working IEEE/IFIP Conference on Software Architecture, pp. 109–120. IEEE Computer Society, Washington, DC (2005)
13. Kazman, R., Klein, M., Clements, P.: ATAM: method for architecture evaluation. Technical report CMU/SEI-2000-TR-004, SEI, Carnegie Mellon University (2000)
14. Kruchten, P., Lago, P., van Vliet, H.: Building up and reasoning about architectural knowledge. In: Hofmeister, C., Crnković, I., Reussner, R. (eds.) QoSA 2006. LNCS, vol. 4214, pp. 43–58. Springer, Heidelberg (2006)
15. Malek, S., Medvidovic, N., Mikic-Rakic, M.: An extensible framework for improving a distributed software system's deployment architecture. IEEE Trans. Softw. Eng. **38**(1), 73–100 (2012)
16. Matinlassi, M.: Quality-driven software architecture model transformation: Towards automation. Ph.D. thesis, ESPOO: VTT technical Research Centre of Finland, vTT Publications 608 (2006)
17. Mavin, A., Wilkinson, P.: Big ears (the return of "easy approach to requirements engineering"). In: Proceeding of the 18th IEEE International Requirements Engineering Conference, pp. 277–282 (2010)
18. Object Management Group: OMG Systems Modeling Language (OMG SysMLTM), version 1.3, June 2012. oMG Formal document number: formal/2012-06-01
19. Perovich, D., Bastarríca, M.C., Rojas, C.: Model-driven approach to software architecture design. In: ICSE Workshop on Sharing and Reusing Architectural Knowledge, pp. 1–8 (2009)
20. Rutle, A., Rossini, A., Lamo, Y., Wolter, U.: A category-theoretical approach to the formalisation of version control in MDE. In: Chechik, M., Wirsing, M. (eds.) FASE 2009. LNCS, vol. 5503, pp. 64–78. Springer, Heidelberg (2009)
21. Tang, A., Ali Babar, M., Gorton, I., Han, J.: A survey of architecture design rationale. J. Syst. Softw. **79**(12), 1792–1804 (2006)
22. Tang, A., Jin, Y., Han, J.: A rationale-based architecture model for design traceability and reasoning. J. Syst. Softw. **80**(6), 918–934 (2007)
23. Tekinerdogan, B., Özturk, K., Dogru, A.: Modeling and reasoning about design alternatives of software as a service architectures. In: Proceeding of the 9th Working IEEE/IFIP Conference on Software Architecture, pp. 312–319 (2011)
24. Tyree, J., Akerman, A.: Architecture decisions: demystifying architecture. IEEE Softw. **22**, 19–27 (2005)

25. Watkins, R., Neal, M.: Why and How of requirements tracing. IEEE Softw. **11**, 104–106 (1994)
26. Zimmermann, O., Koehler, J., Leymann, F., Polley, R., Schuster, N.: Managing architectural decision models with dependency relations, integrity constraints, and production rules. J. Syst. Softw. **82**(8), 1249–1267 (2009)

What Are the Used UML Diagram Constructs? A Document and Tool Analysis Study Covering Activity and Use Case Diagrams

Gianna Reggio, Maurizio Leotta(✉), Filippo Ricca, and Diego Clerissi

DIBRIS, Università di Genova, Genova, Italy
{gianna.reggio,maurizio.leotta,filippo.ricca}@unige.it,
diego.clerissi@gmail.com

Abstract. UML offers a very large set of constructs for each of its diagram types, however many of them seem scarcely used or even their existence is not known. Here, we decided to present a precise view of the usage levels of the constructs of activity and use case diagrams by means of a document and tool analysis study, covering preliminarily: books, courses, tutorials, and tools about UML. Results of the study show that, among the 47 activity diagrams constructs, a large majority of them seem to be scarcely used, while, only nine result widely used, whereas only two of the nine constructs of the use case diagrams seem scarcely used. This work is part of a larger project aimed at investigating the usage level of the UML diagrams and their constructs, also by means of a personal opinion survey intended for UML users.

Keywords: UML usage · Survey · Empirical study

1 Introduction

UML is a truly large notation offering many different diagrams, 14 in the last approved version [1], and for each diagram it provides a large set of constructs covering any possible need of any modeller for any possible task. As a result, the UML specification is a huge book, the UML metamodel is large and quite complex, and the definition and the understanding of its static and dynamic semantics is a truly difficult task, with also the consequence to make difficult to teach it both at the school/university level or in the industry [2]. Moreover, the large number of constructs and the consequent very large metamodel make complex and time consuming developing transformations of UML models and building tools for the UML. Clearly, these UML features have a negative impact on how the UML is perceived by the modellers hindering its adoption [3], and leading in some cases to replace the UML by ad-hoc Domain Specific Languages (DSLs).

On the other hand, users naturally tend to consider and use only a portion of its diagrams/constructs, and forgetting about some other ones. On his blog I. Jacobson states "For 80 % of all software only 20 % of UML is needed" [4].

S. Hammoudi et al. (Eds.): MODELSWARD 2014, CCIS 506, pp. 66–83, 2015.
DOI: 10.1007/978-3-319-25156-1_5

Furthermore, few people try to learn the UML by reading its specification [1], instead the large majority of the users rely on books and courses/tutorials or just start to use some tools for drawing UML diagrams that in general do not cover the whole UML. For this reason, in many cases, the UML users will never become aware of the existence of many specific constructs (e.g., how many of you do know the existence of the "Parameter Set" for activities or has even used this construct?).

We would like to asses by means of a document and tool analysis study which parts of the UML (diagrams and constructs) are the most used in practice and which are the less ones (and thus also indirectly which part of the UML is really known), using again the words of Jacobson trying to see if an "essential UML" [4] emerges. To discover how much a UML diagram/construct is used, we chose to preliminarily investigate objective sources: (1) the books about the UML, (2) the IT University courses covering also the UML, (3) the tutorials presenting the UML to the practitioners, and (4) the tools for producing UML models. Moreover, similarly to [2,5], we are conducting a personal opinion survey [6] asking to UML users of different kinds (e.g., industrial practitioners and academics) which parts of the UML they know and which they have never used.

For a given UML diagram/construct, we have proceeded as follows. We have investigated the books to discover if they were citing such diagram/construct, and if they were giving an example of it. Similarly for the courses/tutorials, whereas for the tools we have tried to produce a model containing such diagram/construct (notice that we speak of a model not of a diagram, since there are several UML constructs that cannot be shown in a diagram). Finally, we have computed descriptive statistics to present the results. In this study, we analysed 30 books, 20 tools, 22 courses, and 18 tutorials.

The dimension of the UML prevented us to investigate the usage level of the constructs of all the 14 diagram types (for example a personal survey covering all diagrams would require at least one hour to be filled), thus we considered only the constructs of activity and use case diagrams, chosen because both are quite known and used, and the former has a large number of constructs, whereas the latter has only few constructs.

The results of this document and tool analysis study, and of the future personal opinion survey should be of help to many different categories of people:

- **Teachers and Instructors:** allowing to offer courses and/or tutorials concentrating only a smaller language made out of the most used UML diagrams/constructs;
- **Tool Builders/Users:** obvious advantages since the tools covering the most used diagrams/constructs will be simpler to implement/use;
- **Notation Designers:** interested in discovering scarcely used constructs, and understanding for which reasons they have been added to the language. Moreover, other interesting questions arise: are the scarcely used constructs derived[1] or primitive? Can the scarcely used constructs be applied only in specific cases?

[1] A derived construct may be replaced by a combination of other constructs.

It will be interesting to investigate whether the metamodel (and subsequently the UML specification book) may be easily simplified to cover only the most used constructs.

In our opinion, handling a notation with a large set of constructs where a portion of them are scarcely used, if not almost unknown, is problematic because it can cause a waste of effort and resources by who want/must use it (e.g., there are countries where some contracts with the public administration must be accompanied by a UML model). Indeed, trivially, to print the reference document requires 700 sheets, but also understanding the metamodel/preparing for the certification/deciding what to teach to the students/reading a UML book require a large number of hours; and we do not have to forget that also maintaining the official specification and any related item requires a large amount of effort due to its size.

Also the OMG has recently recognised the need to simplify the UML with the initiative "UML Simplification" [7] which will result in the next UML version (2.5), but in this case the simplification concerns only the way UML is defined without any impact about its constructs.

In a previous phase of this document and tool analysis study [8], we analysed the usage level of the 14 types of UML diagrams; in this paper, we present the results of a following step of our work focusing on the usage level of the activity and use case diagram constructs covering books, courses/tutorials, and tools.

The remainder of the paper is organized as follows. In Sect. 2, we present related work literature regarding empirical study about the UML. In Sect. 3, we sketch the relevant aspects of the conducted document and tool analysis study such as: goals, research questions, followed process and analysis methodology. The results of the document and tool analysis study about activity and use case diagram's constructs are presented in Sect. 4, preceded by a summary of the results on the UML diagrams shown in [8], while threats to validity are discussed in Sect. 5. Finally, Sect. 6 concludes the paper.

2 Related Work

The systematic literature review by Mohagheghi et al. [9] about model-based software development states that "the UML is currently the most widely used modelling language". A similar result has also been obtained in [10] where a personal opinion survey with 155 Italian professionals has been conducted, while in [11] emerges that UML is often employed by companies in the software analysis and design phases.

Another personal opinion survey about UML (171 professionals in total), by Dobing and Parsons [5], points out another strong statement: "regular usage of UML was lower than expected". The authors of [5] suggest that the difficulty of understanding many of the notations supports the argument that the UML may be too complex. The same claim, in more or less different forms, is present in several blogs, where several proposals of UML simplification are arising[2].

[2] e.g., www.devx.com/architect/Article/45694 and blogs.msdn.com/b/sonuarora/archive/2009/11/02/simplify-uml.aspx.

Maybe, the most authoritative is the one of Ivar Jacobson entitled "Taking the temperature of UML" [4], where he wrote: "Still, UML has become complex and clumsy. For 80 % of all software only 20 % of UML is needed. However, it is not easy to find the subset of UML which we would call the 'Essential' UML. We must make UML smarter to use". The need to simplify the UML is also shown by the recently released OMG draft proposal about this topic [7]. Moreover, the complexity of the UML seems to be one of the factors that limit its diffusion and usage in the industry [3]: "UML is considered unnecessarily complex" and understanding its notation could require a considerable overhead.

In the tentative to find the "essential UML", Erickson and Siau [12] have conducted a Delphi study[3] with the goal of identifying a UML kernel for three well-known UML application areas: Real-Time, Web-based, and Enterprise systems. The participants to the study (44 experts in total) were asked to rate the relative importance of the various UML diagrams in building systems. UML overall results (i.e., non-domain specific) were: 100 % for Class and Statechart diagrams, 95.5 % for Sequence diagrams, 90.9 % for Use Case diagrams. All the others diagrams received a percentage lesser than 50 % (e.g., 27.3 % for Activity diagrams). Another personal opinion survey about UML [2] with 131 subjects confirms the results of Erickson and Siau. Results indicate that the three most important diagrams are Use Case diagrams, Class diagrams and Sequence diagrams.

The main conclusions from another systematic literature review by Budgen et al. [13] about empirical evidence of the UML are two:

- while there are many studies that use the UML in some way, including to assess other topics, there are relatively few for which the UML is itself the object of study, and hence that assess the UML in some way (e.g., UML studies of adoption and use in the field).
- there is a need to study the UML and its elements much more rigorously and to identify which features are valuable, and which could be discarded.

Our preliminary empirical work, much in the spirit of the Erickson and Siau's work but using a different approach, tries to add a small tile to the empirical knowledge about the UML as requested in the first conclusion of the Budgen's systematic literature review. We could say that our work tries to identify which UML features (diagrams and constructs) are valuable, and which could be discarded — as requested in the second point of the Budgen's work — equating the word "valuable" with "used in practice" and the concept "could be discarded" with "not used in practice".

3 Study Definition

The instrument we selected to take a snapshot of the state of the practice concerning UML usage is that of a document and tool analysis study [14]. In the work's design and execution phases we followed as much as possible the guidelines provided in [15] and used the same presentation format of [16].

[3] It attempts to form a reliable consensus of a group of experts in specialized areas.

The document and tool analysis study has been conducted through the following steps: (1) goals selection, (2) goals transformation into research questions, (3) identification of the population, sample and process, (4) data extraction, and (5) analysis of results and packaging.

We conceived and designed the document and tool analysis study with the **goal** of understanding *which are the less/most used parts of the UML in practice.*

Within the scope of this work, in this paper we aim at addressing two **research questions** related to the above described goal:

RQ1: Which UML constructs for the activity diagrams are the most/less used in practice?

RQ2: Which UML constructs for the use case diagrams are the most/less used in practice?

3.1 Population Identification

The first step to conduct a document and tool analysis study is defining a target population. The target population of our study consists of *sources* concerning UML. In particular, in this study we considered the following four kinds of objective sources: books, tools, courses and tutorials. Currently, we are conducting a personal opinion survey [6] with industrial practitioners and academics to understand which parts of the UML they know, which they use, and which they have never used.

To sample the population and select the sources to consider in our study we: (1) conducted a systematic search performed using Internet resources, Web search engines and electronic databases and (2) used non-probabilistic (convenience sampling) methods [17]. Moreover, in making decisions about whether (or not) to include a source in the study, we adopted some well-defined inclusion/exclusion criteria (see below).

Inclusion and Exclusion Criteria. The inclusion/exclusion criteria can be common for all the kind of sources or specific. For all the sources we adopted the following inclusion criterion: only sources concerning UML versions $\geq$ 2.0.

Concerning books, in case of different editions of the same book we opted (when possible) for the last one. Moreover, we excluded elements of "grey" literature, i.e., books without ISBN.

Concerning tools, we included only UML modelling tools (both commercial and non-commercial) and excluded: (1) general graphics editor (e.g., Inkscape), (2) tools providing only a specific type of diagram (e.g., class diagrams), (3) really unstable, not complete or preliminary tools (e.g., tools in beta version).

About courses, we considered only university courses concerning IT studies. We considered courses offered also in languages different from English but known or understood by the authors (e.g., French, Italian and Spanish).

Concerning tutorials, we considered only tutorials provided on Internet as written documents (either on-line or downloadable) and video (where a person gives instructions on how to do something) but we have excluded tutorials taking the form of a screen recording (screencast) and interactive tutorials. For selecting a document of this kind we used the common meaning/perception of tutorials: a tutorial is more interactive and specific than a book or a lecture; a tutorial seeks to teach by example.

3.2 The Process

The process followed to conduct a document and tool analysis study should be as much as possible well defined in order to ensure that such a study can be objective and repeatable. For each category of sources, we followed a different process to collect them.

Books. We started by the Amazon website and used the search form to find UML related books. We selected the "Computers & Technology" category in the books section. Then, we experimented with several different search criteria using different combinations of strings. Finally, the one that retrieved the highest number of useful items was the simple string "UML 2". Starting from this long list of books ordered by relevance (2.726 books on July 20, 2013) we filtered out books not satisfying the inclusion criteria explained above. Then, we tried to

	Title	Edition	Author(s)	Year	Publisher
UML Notation Guides	UML 2.0 in a Nutshell	1st	Pilone, Pitman	2005	O'Reilly Media Inc.
	The Elements of UML 2.0 Style	1st	Ambler	2005	Cambridge University Press
	Sams Teach Yourself UML in 24 Hours	3rd	Schmuller	2004	Sams Publishing
	UML 2 Certification Guide: Fundamental & Intermediate Exams	1st	Welkiens, Oestereich	2006	Morgan Kaufmann Publishers
	UML Distilled: A Brief Guide to the Standard Object Modeling Language	3rd	Fowler	2003	Addison-Wesley
	Learning UML 2.0	1st	Miles, Hamilton	2006	O'Reilly Media Inc.
	UML 2 for Dummies	1st	Chonoles, Schardt	2003	Wiley Publishing Inc.
	UML 2 Toolkit	2nd	Eriksson, Penker, Lyons, Fado	2004	Wiley Publishing Inc.
	UML 2.0 in Action	1st	Grassle, Baumann, Baumann	2005	Packt Publishing Ltd
	UML Bible	1st	Pender	2003	Wiley Publishing Inc.
	UML Demystified	1st	Kimmel	2005	McGraw-Hill
	UML for the IT Business Analyst	1st	Podeswa	2005	Muska & Lipman Pub
	Verification and Validation for Quality of UML 2.0 Models	1st	Unhelkar	2005	John Wiley & Sons
	The Unified Modeling Language Reference Manual	2nd	Rumbaugh, Jacobson, Booch	2005	Addison-Wesley
	The Unified Modeling Language User Guide	2nd	Booch, Rumbaugh, Jacobson	2005	Addison-Wesley
Software Engineering books based on UML	Object-Oriented Software Engineering Using UML, Patterns and Java	3rd	Bruegge, Dutoit	2010	Prentice Hall
	System Analysis & Design with UML version 2.0: An Object-Oriented Approach	3rd	Dennis, Wixom, Tegarden	2009	John Wiley & Sons
	UML 2 and the Unified Process: Practical Object-Oriented Analysis & Design	2nd	Arlow, Neustadt	2005	Addison-Wesley
	UML 2 Semantics and Applications	1st	Lano	2009	John Wiley & Sons
	Object-Oriented Analysis & Design: Understanding System Development with UML 2.0	1st	O'Docherty	2005	John Wiley & Sons
	Using UML: Software Engineering with Objects and Components	2nd	Stevens, Pooley	2006	Addison-Wesley
	UML 2 Pour les bases de donnees	1st	Soutou	2007	Éditions Eyrolles
	Fast Track UML 2.0	1st	Scott	2004	Apress Media LLC
	Model-Driven Development with Executable UML	1st	Milicev	2009	Wiley Publishing Inc.
	Professional Application Lifecycle Management with Visual Studio 2010	1st	Gousset, Keller, Krishnamoorthy, Woodward	2010	Wiley Publishing Inc.
	Software Modeling and Design	1st	Gomaa	2011	Cambridge University Press
	Systems Engineering with SysML UML: Modeling, Analysis, Design	1st	Weilkiens	2006	Morgan Kaufmann Publishers
	Use Case Driven Object Modeling with UML: Theory and Practice	1st	Rosenberg, Stephens	2007	Apress Media LLC
	Management of The Object-Oriented Development Process	1st	Liu, Roussev	2006	Idea Group Inc.
	Real-Time Object Uniform Design Methodology with UML	1st	Duc	2007	Springer

Fig. 1. UML books considered.

recover them using the electronic facilities provided by our library. Finally, we collected and analysed 30 books. Note that, 18 of them are in the top 24 books ordering the Amazon list by relevance. The list of the selected books is shown in Fig. 1. More in detail, we have selected two kinds of books. UML guides (*UML Notation Guides*) and books using UML as a notation, i.e. books where UML is not the primary subject (*Software Engineering books based on UML*).

Tools. We started by the "List of Unified Modeling Language tools" Wikipedia page[4] containing 49 UML tools. Then, we considered also the UML-tools website[5]. A full Internet search was also carried out using Google. Also in this case, we experimented with several different search criteria using different combinations of strings to provide to Google ("UML tools", "UML tools list" and "UML free tools").

For each tool of our list, we found the official website and checked whether it was satisfying the inclusion criteria explained above. Then, we downloaded and installed the most recent version of all the selected tools. In case of commercial tools, we selected a "free for not commercial use" version or a version with university licence or a trial version. At the end, we collected and analysed 20 different tools. The complete list of tools is shown in Fig. 2. Finally, we tried to produce a model containing the diagrams and constructs of interest for our study (for each tool we produced the same model with the same diagrams and the same UML constructs). Notice that Argo UML, one of the most known UML tool, was not included in our document and tool analysis study since it does support UML 1.x only.

Courses. We started carrying out a search using Google. The combinations of strings used were: "UML course", "UML lecture" and "UML university course". We found several university courses satisfying the inclusion criteria stated above,

Name	Release	Year	Licence	Web Site
Altova Umodel		2012	Commercial (Enterprise – Trial)	www.altova.com/umodel.html
Artisan Studio	7.4	2012	Commercial (Trial)	www.atego.com/products/artisan-studio/
Astah	6.6	2012	Commercial (Community Edition)	astah.net/
Borland Together	12.0	2012	Commercial (Trial)	www.borland.com/products/together/
BOUML	6.4.3	2013	Commercial (Viewer - Limited)	www.bouml.fr/
Enterprise Architect	10	2013	Commercial (Trial 30 days)	www.sparxsystems.eu/enterprisearchitect/
IBM Rational Rhapsody Modeler	7.5	2009	Free	www-01.ibm.com/software/awdtools/modeler/
IBM Rational SW Architect	8.5.1	2012	Commercial (Trial 30 days)	www-01.ibm.com/software/awdtools/swarchitect/
MagicDraw	17.0.3	2012	Commercial (Enterprise – Trial)	https://www.magicdraw.com/
Metamill	6.1	2012	Commercial (Trial)	www.metamill.com/
Modelio	2.2.1	2012	Free	sourceforge.net/projects/modeliouml/
Open Modelsphere	3.2	2012	Free	www.modelsphere.org/
Papyrus	0.9.1	2012	Free (Eclipse Plug in)	www.eclipse.org/papyrus/
Poseidon for UML	8	2009	Commercial (Community Edition)	www.gentleware.com/
Power Designer	16.1	2012	Commercial (Trial)	www.sybase.com/products/
RedKoda	3.0.7	2012	Commercial (Community Edition)	www.redkoda.com/
Software Ideas Modeler	5.82	2013	Free	www.softwareideas.net/
StarUML	5.0.2.1570	2006	Free	staruml.sourceforge.net/
Violet	0.21.1	2007	Free	sourceforge.net/projects/violet/
Visual Paradigm	10.1	2013	Commercial (Community Edition)	www.visual-paradigm.com/product/vpuml/

Fig. 2. UML tools considered.

[4] en.wikipedia.org/wiki/List_of_Unified_Modeling_Language_tools.

[5] www.uml-tools.com.

Lecturer	Country	Title	Year
Afsarmanesh	Netherlands	Project Analysis	2012
De Angelis	Italy	Lab. Ingegneria del SW	2012/13
Ciancarini, Iorio	Italy	Lab. Ingegneria del SW	2012/13
Vincent	Australia	System Analysis and Modeling	2012/13
Casalicchio	Italy	Progettazione SW	2009/10
Gérard	France	UML	
Prié	France	Systèmes d'information méthodes avancées	2011/12
Felici	UK	Software Engineering with Objects and Components	2011/12
Siebers	UK	Object Oriented Systems	2012/13
Varrò	Hungary	Modellalapú szoftvertervezés	2012
Lehre	Germany	Softwaretechnik	2012/13
Rumpe	Germany	Modellbasierte Softwareentwicklung	2011/12
Correo, Rossi	Argentina	Uml Basico	
Brambilla	Italy	Ingegneria del SW	2012/13
Alkan	Turkey	Object Oriented Software Engineering	2012/13
Farrow	UK	Software Engineering	2012/13
Easterbrook	Canada	Engineering Large SW Systems	2012
Negre	France	Ingéniérie des Systèmes d'Information	2012/13
Sellares	Spain	Enginyeria del Software	2008/09
Jezequel	France	Approche objet pour le développement de logiciels par objets avec UML	
Turgut	US	Software Engineering I	2009
Cheng	US	Advanced Software Engineering	2013

Fig. 3. UML courses considered.

Author / Source	Title	Web Site
Allen Holub	Allen Holub's UML Quick Reference	www.holub.com/goodies/uml/index.html
Analisi-disegno	Introduzione a UML	www.analisi-disegno.com/uml/uml.htm
Crag Systems	A UML Tutorial Introduction	www.cragsystems.co.uk/uml_tutorial/index.htm
devmentor	UML Guide v2.1	devmentor.org/references/uml/uml.php
Dumke	UML Tutorial	www-ivs.cs.uni-magdeburg.de/~dumke/UML/index.htm
Embarcadero	Practical UML: A Hands-On Introduction for Developers	edn.embarcadero.com/article/31863
HTML.it	Guida UML	www.html.it/guide/guida-uml/
John Deacon	Developer's Guide to UML 2: A UML Tutorial	www.johndeacon.net/UML/UML_Appendix/Generated/UML_Appendix.asp
lemiffe	Reference Guide for UML 2.0	www.lemiffe.com/wp-content/uploads/2008/12/uml2.pdf
New Think Tank	Video Tutorials	www.newthinktank.com/2012/11/
Online Teach	UML Training	www.online-teach.com/u-m-l.php
Parlezuml	UML Tutorial	www.codemanship.co.uk/parlezuml/
Richard Botting	A Beginners Guide to The Unified Modeling Language (UML)	www.csci.csusb.edu/dick/cs201/uml.html
SmartDraw	What is UML?	www.smartdraw.com/resources/tutorials/uml-diagrams/
Sparx Systems	UML 2 Tutorial	www.sparxsystems.com.au/resources/uml2_tutorial/index.html
Storrle & Knapp	Unified Modeling Language 2.0	www.pst.ifi.lmu.de/veroeffentlichungen/UML-2.0-Tutorial.pdf
Uml.free	UML, le langage de modélisation objet unifié	uml.free.fr/index-cours.html
uml-diagrams	UML 2.5 Diagrams Overview	www.uml-diagrams.org/uml-25-diagrams.html

Fig. 4. UML tutorials considered.

but in several cases it was difficult, if not impossible, to recover the slides of the lectures, and in general the material. Often, the material was not publicly available; only the content of the lessons was present on the website. For this reason, we resort also to convenience sampling, asking to our colleagues the slides of UML courses they teach. At the end, we collected and analysed 22 different University courses. The complete list of lectures is shown in Fig. 3. Convenience sampling was also useful to balance a little the geographic origin of the UML courses (e.g., before convenience sampling we had three courses from France and zero from USA).

Tutorials. We started with the tutorial lists present in three websites[6]. Then, we integrated the obtained results with other tutorials recovered using Google (the research was conducted using the strings: "UML tutorials" and "UML guide"). Finally, we collected and analysed 18 tutorials. The complete list of tutorials is shown in Fig. 4.

4 Results of the Document and Tool Analysis Study

After having collected the sources, we extracted the data of interest for our research questions and finally we performed the analysis. Given the nature of this document and tool analysis study, that is mainly descriptive (it describes some condition or factor found in a population in terms of its frequency and impact) and exploratory, we mainly applied descriptive statistics and showed our findings by means of charts.

We preliminarily decided to interpret the results of our survey assuming that a diagram/construct is *widely used* if it is present in the 60 % or more of the sources, similarly it is *scarcely used* if it is present in the 40 % or less of the sources, having also some non-defined cases (*grey zone*). In the following subsections we briefly summarize the results concerning UML diagrams, see [8] for the details, and present the ones for the activity and the use case diagram constructs.

4.1 Level of Usage of the UML Diagrams

The level of usage of the various UML diagrams in books, courses, tutorials, tools, and in the totality of the sources respectively is summarized in Fig. 5.

If we consider the totality of the sources, disregarding their kind, we have that the scarcely used diagrams are timing, interaction overview and profile, listed starting from the most used; all of them were not present in UML 1.x, and the profile diagram appeared only in version 2.2. The last position of the profile diagram is not very surprising due both to the late appearance and to the fact that this kind of diagram has a very restrict scope (indeed it is used only to present a profile) and that, it is essentially a variant of the package diagram. Also timing diagrams have a restrict scope, and UML offers other ways to model time related aspects (e.g., timed events may be used in state machines and activity diagrams; durations and time intervals may appear in sequence diagrams), and this may be the motivation for their low usage. Finally, interaction overview diagrams are quite complex and in many cases may be replaced by sequence diagrams and/or a combination of sequence and activity diagrams, and perhaps this is the reason for not being so considered.

The widely used diagrams, when considering the totality of the sources, are instead, listed again starting from the most used ones, class (100 % in any kind of sources), activity, sequence, state machine, use cases, communication, deployment, component, object and package diagrams. The first position of class diagrams is not surprising; it is indeed the main building block of the UML, while

[6] www.uml.org/#Links-Tutorials, http://stackoverflow.com/questions/1661961/recommended-uml-tutorials, and www.jeckle.de/umllinks.htm#tutorials.

UML Diagram	Book Guide	Book Spec	Book Tot	Tool	Course	Tutorial	All Sources
Class	100%	100%	100%	100%	100%	100%	**100%**
Activity	100%	93%	97%	100%	95%	100%	**98%**
Sequence	100%	93%	97%	100%	100%	89%	**97%**
Use Case	100%	93%	97%	100%	95%	89%	**96%**
State Machine	100%	93%	97%	100%	95%	89%	**96%**
Communication	100%	80%	90%	90%	59%	89%	**82%**
Component	93%	80%	87%	85%	59%	89%	**80%**
Deployment	93%	80%	87%	90%	55%	89%	**80%**
Object	93%	80%	87%	70%	55%	67%	**71%**
Package	100%	79%	89%	65%	52%	67%	**70%**
Composite Structure	87%	60%	73%	80%	14%	33%	**52%**
Timing	87%	53%	70%	40%	5%	33%	**40%**
Interaction Overview	80%	53%	67%	45%	5%	28%	**39%**
Profile	7%	13%	10%	30%	0%	6%	**11%**

Book Guide = UML Notation Guides, Book Spec = Software Engineering books based on UML, Book Tot = All books Dashed lines represent the 40% and 60% thresholds

Fig. 5. Usage levels of UML diagrams.

the fact that activity diagrams are the second is relevant and is due, in our opinion, to the fact that they are used also for business process modelling [18] and for describing SOA based systems [19,20]. All the widely used diagrams, except the package diagram, were already present in the UML 1.x versions (although the communication diagrams were before called collaboration diagrams).

The only diagram in the grey area (i.e., above 40 % and below 60 %) is the composite structure, which allows to represent both structured classes and collaborations; again it is a new diagram appearing in the UML 2.0 and this may be a reason for its low usage. However, the result is surprising because structured classes were completely absent in UML 1.x, and this was a perceived problem, and the new collaborations are truly useful (see for example the big role that they have in representing service oriented architectures in the SoaML OMG standard profile [21]). For a more complete analysis of the results on UML diagrams and a deeper discussion see [8].

4.2 Level of Usage of the Activity Diagram Constructs

The number of available constructs in activity diagrams is 47, a truly large number, and as it is shown in Fig. 8 a lot of them are scarcely used (their description and some examples may be found in the UML specification [1]).

If we consider the totality of our sources disregarding the fact that they are of different kind, we have that the widely used constructs are only nine, precisely Action and Control Flow Edge (both 100 %), Initial and Final Node (99 %), Decision/Merge Nodes (98 %), Fork/Join Nodes (95 %), Activity Partition, i.e., swimlanes (83 %), Object Node (80 %), and Object Flow Edge (76 %)[7].

[7] This surprising result, since it is not possible to connect an object node to other nodes without using the object flow, is due to the fact that in some courses the classification of the arcs in activity diagrams in control and object flow was not mentioned.

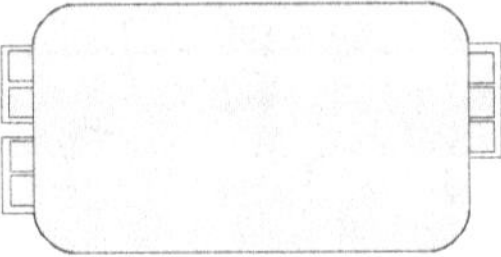

Fig. 6. Activity parameter set, usage level 10 % in the totality of the sources.

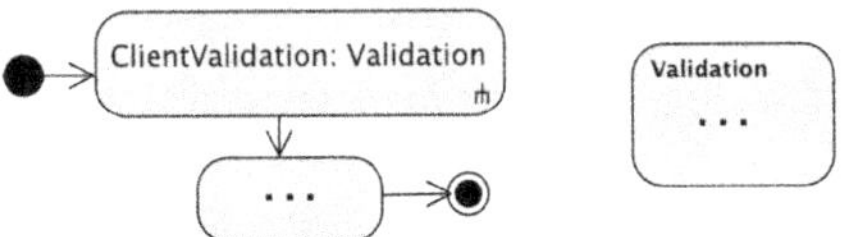

(The first action of the activity diagram on the left is a call to the behaviour defined elsewhere by the activity Validation)

Fig. 7. Call Behaviour Action (Rake) construct, usage level 39 % in the totality of the sources.

Those scarcely used, i.e., with a percentage less than 40 % are **31**, and in 8 cases the percentage is lower than 10 %. One of the least used constructs Parameter Set is shown in Fig. 6, it is used to provide alternative sets of inputs or outputs that a behaviour, and thus an activity, may use.

The fact that Activity is in the grey area is a little surprising since Activity is the construct that, together with Call Behaviour Action (rake), allows to structure complex activity diagrams, also if we suspect that in some cases Activity is considered but not precisely indicated with its proper name. See an example of Call Behaviour Action (rake) in Fig. 7.

We briefly discuss two of the least used constructs (resulting used only in 3 % of the sources): Input and Output Effects for Object Node and Decision Node with Input Flow. The semantics of the first one is not very clear "*Specifying the effect that the behaviour of actions has on the objects passed in and out of their parameters can be represented by placing the effect in braces near the edge leading to or from the pin for the parameter*" see [1]. Indeed, it may be interpreted as a kind of constraint (the preceding/following action should be such that to produce the depicted effects) and so it is not clear the difference with the local pre-post conditions. Otherwise, it may be considered as a kind of comment making explicit some effects already defined by the behaviour of the preceding/following action. In the latter case it may be replaced by a comment. Also the semantics of Decision Node with Input Flow is quite complex, see [1][371–372], but this construct may be considered as derived (it may be replaced by combining the normal and the extra input tokens of the decision node by means of a new data structure). We think that however in these two cases one of the reasons of the fact that they are neglected is the complexity of their definition.

One of the possible reasons, for the quite surprising result summarized in Fig. 8, is that in UML 1.x there were few constructs for the activity diagrams, more or less those resulting widely used in our document and tool analysis study,

Activity Diagram Construct	Book Guide	Book Spec	Book Tot	Tool	Course	Tutorial	All Sources
Action	100%	100%	100%	100%	100%	100%	**100%**
Control Flow Edge	100%	100%	100%	100%	100%	100%	**100%**
Final Node	100%	100%	100%	100%	100%	94%	**99%**
Initial Node	100%	100%	100%	100%	100%	94%	**99%**
Decision/Merge Nodes	100%	93%	97%	100%	100%	94%	**98%**
Fork/Join Nodes	100%	100%	100%	100%	100%	78%	**95%**
Activity Partition	100%	71%	86%	85%	81%	78%	**83%**
Object Node	100%	79%	90%	95%	67%	61%	**80%**
Object Flow Edge	100%	64%	83%	95%	62%	61%	**76%**
Accept Event Action	60%	43%	52%	95%	38%	28%	**53%**
Activity	93%	64%	79%	55%	38%	28%	**53%**
Flow Final Node	80%	43%	62%	85%	29%	28%	**52%**
Send Signal Node	60%	50%	55%	95%	33%	17%	**51%**
Action Pin	67%	43%	55%	75%	19%	28%	**45%**
Named Activity Edge	27%	21%	24%	95%	33%	28%	**43%**
Object Node for Objects in Specific States	53%	29%	41%	50%	38%	39%	**42%**
Call Behaviour Action (rake)	33%	43%	38%	65%	29%	22%	**39%**
Activity Parameters	67%	36%	52%	50%	19%	22%	**38%**
Accept Timed Event	53%	29%	41%	55%	24%	11%	**34%**
Expansion Region	53%	36%	45%	50%	10%	22%	**33%**
Exception Handler	47%	29%	38%	50%	10%	22%	**31%**
Interruptible Activity Region	33%	29%	31%	50%	14%	22%	**30%**
Activity Edge Connector	73%	29%	52%	10%	14%	22%	**27%**
Data Store	33%	14%	24%	55%	5%	17%	**25%**
Central Buffer Node	27%	21%	24%	55%	5%	6%	**23%**
Behaviour Specification for Object Flows	33%	14%	24%	40%	10%	11%	**22%**
Local Pre-Post Condition	53%	21%	38%	30%	0%	11%	**22%**
Weighted Activity Edge	20%	14%	17%	55%	5%	11%	**22%**
Decision Node with Behaviour	33%	29%	31%	25%	5%	6%	**18%**
Object Node Ordering Kind	13%	14%	14%	55%	0%	6%	**18%**
Structured Nodes/Activities	27%	21%	24%	40%	5%	0%	**18%**
Activity Partition Textually Presented	47%	14%	31%	0%	19%	11%	**17%**
Object Node with a Limited Upper Bound	13%	21%	17%	45%	0%	6%	**17%**
Exception Pin	27%	14%	21%	20%	5%	11%	**15%**
Selection Specification for Object Flow	13%	7%	10%	35%	5%	6%	**14%**
Join Specification	20%	7%	14%	30%	5%	0%	**13%**
Stream Pin	20%	21%	21%	15%	0%	11%	**13%**
Value Pin	13%	7%	10%	40%	0%	0%	**13%**
Parameter Set (Activity Parameters)	33%	14%	24%	5%	0%	6%	**10%**
Selection Specification for Object Node	7%	7%	7%	30%	0%	0%	**9%**
Object Node for Tokens with Signal as Type	33%	14%	24%	0%	0%	0%	**8%**
Parameter Effect Kind	7%	7%	7%	20%	0%	0%	**7%**
Activity Exception Parameters	13%	0%	7%	15%	0%	0%	**6%**
Activity Stream Parameters	7%	7%	7%	15%	0%	0%	**6%**
Stream Edge	13%	7%	10%	5%	0%	0%	**5%**
Decision Node with Input Flow	0%	0%	0%	15%	0%	0%	**3%**
Input and Output Effects for Object Node	0%	7%	3%	10%	0%	0%	**3%**

Book Guide = UML Notation Guides, Book Spec = Software Engineering books based on UML, Book Tot = All books Dashed lines represent the 40% and 60% thresholds
1 book out of 30 considers only Class Diagrams and thus it was not included in this analysis.

Fig. 8. Usage levels of activity diagram constructs.

and so those resulting scarcely used are quite new. Another reason for these constructs being so unpopular is that many of them are not depicted visually by the tools on the activity diagrams (for example, the Object Node Ordering Kind construct may be defined using the Visual Paradigm tool for an Object Node by means of the property panel but cannot be visualized).

In our opinion, some of the constructs classified by our document and tool analysis study as scarcely used or in the grey area may be useful for modelling workflows and business processes [18,19,22–24], e.g., Flow Final Node, Accept Event Action, Send Signal Node, Activity and the constructs related with exception handling; whereas many others are just a kind of derived constructs, i.e., they may be replaced by an equivalent activity diagram fragment (e.g., Value Pin).

If we examine the usage data considering separately the various kind of sources, we have that the tools and the books are "using" a greater number of constructs, whereas courses and tutorials are considering less constructs. Precisely the numbers of scarcely used/widely used constructs for the various kinds are:

- books guide: scarcely used 25 and widely used 16
- books spec: scarcely used 32 and widely used 10
- books tot (i.e., all books): scarcely used 28 and widely used 11
- tools: scarcely used 20 and widely used 15
- courses: scarcely used 38 and widely used 9
- tutorials: scarcely used 38 and widely used 9

Moreover, three constructs Accept Event Action, Action Pin and Flow Final Node result widely used for both books guide and tools. The percentages relative to courses and tutorials are really striking; the considered activity diagrams constructs are just 1/5 of those available. Finally, looking at Fig. 8, it is interesting to note that the usage levels among different sources, even if different in magnitude, have similar trends.

4.3 Level of Usage of the Use Case Diagram Constructs

Figure 9 presents the level of usage of the constructs relative to the use case diagram in the different kinds of sources. As before, we consider a construct widely used if the percentage is $\geq 60\,\%$, and scarcely used if such percentage is $\leq 40\,\%$.

Use case diagrams are quite simple, and the results are straightforward and not surprising. All constructs except Actor User Defined Icon and Extend with Condition are widely used, and Use Case and Actor have a percentage of 100 %. The use cases relationships (Include and Extend) are over 90 %, the Actor Specialization and Use Case Specialization are over 70 %, and the Subject (System) Box is over 80 %.

In this case the tools are not those providing the larger set of constructs, for Extend with Condition, User Defined Actor Icon and Subject (System) Box the percentage of tools proving them is lower than that of the books mentioning them, perhaps because they cannot be drawn reusing other visual constructs. For the courses also the Include and the Extend reach a 100 %, and the Subject (System) Box reaches 95 %.

The results seem quite clear in this case, the fundamental constructs for use case diagrams are Use Case, Actor, Extend and Include; Subject (System) Box, and

Use Case Diagram Construct	Book Guide	Book Spec	Book Tot	Tool	Course	Tutorial	All Sources
Actor	100%	100%	100%	100%	100%	100%	**100%**
Use Case	100%	100%	100%	100%	100%	100%	**100%**
Include	100%	93%	97%	100%	100%	75%	**94%**
Extend	93%	93%	93%	100%	100%	75%	**93%**
Subject (System) Box	87%	100%	93%	70%	95%	75%	**85%**
Use Case Specialization	87%	79%	83%	95%	81%	44%	**78%**
Actor Specialization	80%	71%	76%	100%	76%	38%	**74%**
Extend with Condition	53%	50%	52%	35%	38%	13%	**37%**
Actor User Defined Icon	53%	50%	52%	30%	10%	0%	**27%**

Book Guide = UML Notation Guides, Book Spec = Software Engineering books based on UML, Book Tot = All books Dashed line represents the 40% and 60% thresholds
1 book out of 30 considers only Class Diagrams and thus it was not included in this analysis.

Fig. 9. Usage levels of Use Case Diagram Constructs.

Actor/Use Case Specialization are quite useful, whereas Extend with Condition and Actor User Defined Icon are perceived as less relevant.

5 Threats to Validity

In our study a possible threat is the fact that when examining books, courses and tutorials we have decided to assume that a construct is used in that source if it is mentioned without making a deeper analysis to measure how much detailed was presented or taught. Unfortunately, it is really difficult to devise a better metric; for example, trying to distinguish if a diagram is just mentioned, shortly presented, presented, and presented with all the details may be too much depending on the personal judgement of who examines the textual sources; also counting the occurrence of the name of a construct is in our opinion too dependent on the way the texts are written, e.g., more or less verbose. We have also tried to distinguish the case of a simple mention of a construct in the text and the presence of an example of such construct, without detecting a relevant difference.

To avoid to bias the results of our document and tool analysis study, we have considered only sources concerned with the use of the UML, avoiding those with different aims, for example drawing tools suitable to produce pictures of UML diagrams, or books presenting a survey on the current visual notations have been excluded; whereas instead books covering specific use of the UML or courses about software engineering where the UML was taught were included.

Concerning the textual sources, we have considered only books/courses/tutorials presented using languages understood by the authors (i.e., English, Italian, French and Spanish). For the courses the limitation on the language is less problematic, indeed many of the courses presented using the English language are taught in countries where the English is not the mother tongue (e.g., Hungary and Turkey).

For the tools, instead, we are quite confident to have examined almost all the available ones; we think that a UML tool cannot exist without being presented somewhere on the Web. Notice that Argo UML, one of the most known UML tool was not included in our document and tool analysis study since it supports only UML 1.x.

We have considered here only four kinds of sources (books, courses, tutorials, sources) and we are aware that these are not the only ones; indeed there are also the UML users, and we are now running a personal survey to investigate which constructs they know and which they use. Instead, we do not plan to make a literature survey examining which constructs are used in scientific papers in the area of modelling or of Model Driven Development, since this will be surely biased: e.g., there are few scientific papers about class diagrams, whereas the newest and the most problematic constructs will appear in many of them. However, literature survey covering applicative areas for modelling, for example concerning SOA (Service Oriented Architecture) or requirement engineering may give valuable insights.

The various diagrams/constructs of the UML have different ages, i.e., they were introduced in the UML at different times, some appeared in the UML 1.x, others in UML 2.0 and someone is still more recent (e.g., the profile diagram appeared only in UML 2.2). To mitigate this threat we have careful considered only sources that explicitly stated that were considering at least UML 2.0. A more refined analysis made considering as a source for a given construct only those dated after the official time of appearance of the same is unfeasible, also because we have the official date of appearance of a constructs, i.e., the official approval of the OMG document presenting it, but such document was already available to the community and so the construct was already know and used.

Finally, we have decided to define widely used (scarcely used) when a construct was considered in the $\geq 60\,\%$ ($\leq 40\,\%$) of the sources, resulting also in a grey area. We think that this a sensible choice, using a threshold lower than 60 %, e.g., 50 %, should have led to have that a construct is either widely used or scarcely used without any doubt cases, and this does not sound realistic. On the other hand, a higher threshold, e.g., 80 %, should have led to a quite large number of inconclusive cases.

We have also computed the widely/scarcely used on the totality of the sources, disregarding the fact that they are of very different kinds, e.g., books and courses, and so assigning them different weights would have been more realistic. Again, we had the problem to compute these weights in an unbiased way: is it sensible to say that a book is three times more relevant than a course, or that a tool is two times more relevant than a tutorial? To avoid to make our results too dependent on our personal judgement we have preferred to assume that all the sources have the same weight.

6 Conclusions

We have investigated, by means of a document and tool analysis study, the level of usage of the UML activity and use case diagram constructs, considering in this paper four kinds of sources: books, tools, courses, and tutorials. The results of our document and tool analysis study show that, the level of usage varies considerably among the different constructs, and in some cases it is really very low. However, it is important to note that, a low level of usage of a construct does not mean that it is useless. This could be caused by different factors, for example: (1) a construct may be replaced by a combination of other constructs (i.e., it is derived), (2) its existence may be not widely known, (3) its definition could be too complex and not very clear, and thus discouraging potential users, or finally, (4) it could be useful only in very specific and rare cases.

Results show that, a large majority of the 47 activity diagrams constructs seem to be scarcely used. More precisely, 31 activity diagram constructs result scarcely used (in some cases the percentage of usage is less than 10 %), while, only nine constructs result widely used by our document and tool analysis study: Action, Control Flow Edge, Initial/Final Node, Decision/Merge Nodes, Fork/Join Nodes, Activity Partition (i.e., swimlane), Object Node, and Object Flow Edge. Instead, only two of the nine constructs of the use case diagram (Extend with Condition and Actor User Defined Icon) result scarcely used, with percentages 37 % and 27 % respectively.

In this paper, we have considered only unbiased and objective sources and examined them for checking if some UML constructs are used in an objective way (e.g., can a tool produce a model including such constructs?, is a course/ tutorial teaching the fact that UML has such constructs?). For this reason, we believe that the results of this document and tool analysis study are not biased by any personal opinion (neither ours nor of any human being taking part in the examination of the sources). We are now investigating the usage of the other UML diagrams/constructs and performing a personal survey [6] to investigate which UML diagrams/constructs are known and used by UML users trying to cover different categories of them, and different applicative fields. The combined results of this work and of the ongoing personal opinion survey should lead to finally sketch an "essential" UML.

References

1. UML Revision Task Force: OMG Unified Modeling Language (OMG UML), Superstructure, V2.4.1 (2011)
2. Grossman, M., Aronson, J.E., McCarthy, R.V.: Does UML make the grade? Insights from the software development community. Inf. Softw. Technol. **47**, 383–397 (2005)
3. Petre, M.: UML in practice. In: Proceedings of 35th International Conference on Software Engineering, ICSE 2013, pp. 722–731. IEEE (2013)
4. Jacobson, I.: Taking the temperature of UML (2009). http://blog.ivarjacobson.com/taking-the-temperature-of-uml/
5. Dobing, B., Parsons, J.: How UML is used. Commun. ACM **49**, 109–113 (2006)
6. Reggio, G., Leotta, M., Ricca, F.: Who knows/uses what of the UML: a personal opinion survey. In: Dingel, J., Schulte, W., Ramos, I., Abrahão, S., Insfran, E. (eds.) MODELS 2014. LNCS, vol. 8767, pp. 149–165. Springer, Heidelberg (2014)
7. Seidewitz, E.: UML 2.5: Specification simplification. Presented at Third Biannual Workshop on Eclipse Open Source Software and OMG Open Specifications (2012)

8. Reggio, G., Leotta, M., Ricca, F., Clerissi, D.: What are the used UML diagrams? A preliminary survey. In: Proceedings of 3rd International Workshop on Experiences and Empirical Studies in Software Modelling (EESSMod 2013), vol. 1078, pp. 3–12. CEUR Workshop Proceedings (2013)
9. Mohagheghi, P., Dehlen, V., Neple, T.: Definitions and approaches to model quality in model-based software development - a review of literature. Inf. Softw. Technol. **51**, 1646–1669 (2009)
10. Torchiano, M., Tomassetti, F., Ricca, F., Tiso, A., Reggio, G.: Relevance, benefits, and problems of software modelling and model driven techniques: a survey in the Italian industry. J. Syst. Softw. **86**, 2110–2126 (2013)
11. Scanniello, G., Gravino, C., Tortora, G.: Investigating the role of UML in the software modeling and maintenance - A preliminary industrial survey. In: Filipe, J., Cordeiro, J. (eds.) ICEIS, vol. 3, pp. 141–148. SciTePress (2010)
12. Erickson, J., Siau, K.: Can UML be simplified? Practitioner use of UML in separate domains. In: Proceedings of 12th International Workshop on Exploring Modeling Methods for Systems Analysis and Design (EMMSAD 2007), vol. 365, pp. 81–90. CEUR Workshop Proceedings (2007)
13. Budgen, D., Burn, A.J., Brereton, O.P., Kitchenham, B.A., Pretorius, R.: Empirical evidence about the UML: a systematic literature review. Softw. Pract. Exper. **41**, 363–392 (2011)
14. Prior, L.F.: Document Analysis: The Sage Encyclopedia of Qualitative Research Methods. SAGE Publications, Beverly Hills (2008)
15. Groves, R.M., Fowler, F.J.J., Couper, M.P., Lepkowski, J.M., Singer, E., Tourangeau, R.: Survey Methodology. Wiley, New York (2009)
16. Torchiano, M., Penta, M.D., Ricca, F., Lucia, A.D., Lanubile, F.: Migration of information systems in the italian industry: a state of the practice survey. Inf. Softw. Technol. **53**, 71–86 (2011)
17. Kitchenham, B., Pfleeger, S.: Personal opinion surveys. In: Shull, F., Singer, J. (eds.) Guide to Advanced Empirical Software Engineering, pp. 63–92. Springer, London (2008)
18. Reggio, G., Leotta, M., Ricca, F., Astesiano, E.: Business process modelling: five styles and a method to choose the most suitable one. In: Proceedings of 2nd International Workshop on Experiences and Empirical Studies in Software Modelling, EESSMod 2012, pp. 8:1–8:6. ACM (2012)
19. Leotta, M., Reggio, G., Ricca, F., Astesiano, E.: Towards a lightweight model driven method for developing SOA systems using existing assets. In: Proceedings of 14th International Symposium on Web Systems Evolution, WSE 2012, pp. 51–60. IEEE (2012)
20. Leotta, M., Reggio, G., Ricca, F., Astesiano, E.: Building VECM-based systems with a model driven approach: an experience report. In: Proceedings of 1st International Workshop on Experiences and Empirical Studies in Software Modelling (EESSMod 2011), vol. 785, pp. 38–47. CEUR Workshop Proceedings (2011)
21. OMG: Service oriented architecture Modeling Language (SoaML) Specification Version 1.0.1 (2012). www.omg.org/spec/SoaML/1.0.1/PDF
22. Di Cerbo, F., Dodero, G., Reggio, G., Ricca, F., Scanniello, G.: Precise vs. ultra-light activity diagrams - an experimental assessment in the context of business process modelling. In: Caivano, D., Oivo, M., Baldassarre, M.T., Visaggio, G. (eds.) PROFES 2011. LNCS, vol. 6759, pp. 291–305. Springer, Heidelberg (2011)

23. Reggio, G., Ricca, F., Scanniello, G., Di Cerbo, F., Dodero, G.: A precise style for business process modelling: results from two controlled experiments. In: Whittle, J., Clark, T., Kühne, T. (eds.) MODELS 2011. LNCS, vol. 6981, pp. 138–152. Springer, Heidelberg (2011)
24. Reggio, G., Leotta, M., Ricca, F.: Precise is better than light a document analysis study about quality of business process models. In: Proceedings of 1st International Workshop on Empirical Requirements Engineering, EmpiRE 2011, pp. 61–68. IEEE (2011)

Specialisation of Metamodels Using Metamodel Types

Henning Berg(✉) and Birger Møller-Pedersen

Department of Informatics, Faculty of Mathematics and Natural Sciences, University of Oslo, Oslo, Norway
{hennb,birger}@ifi.uio.no

Abstract. In order to be able to specialise metamodels and thereby enhance reusability of metamodels, we introduce the notions of metamodel types and subtypes. Model-driven engineering considers models and metamodels as first-class entities, however, there has not been much work on how to type models or metamodels. In this paper we discuss how a metamodel can be enclosed within a class and how this enclosing class defines the type for the metamodel. This allows us to use established object-oriented mechanisms on the metamodel level and supports specialisation of metamodels.

Keywords: Metamodelling · Typing · Subtyping · Domain-specific modelling

1 Introduction

Model-Driven Engineering (MDE) [1] is a collective term for a number of approaches and methodologies for software development in which models are first-class entities. MDE can be seen as a natural progression of object-orientation by raising the abstraction level from the class level to the model level. A model is a set of related objects, whose descriptions are formalised by a metamodel (class model). In spite of MDE's model-centric view, most MDE technologies and tools do not have native support for typing models or metamodels. This has consequences with respect to reuse of models, model transformations and interpreters. The notion of polymorphism at the metamodel level is also unclear, as the type of a metamodel is not well defined. The work of [2] motivates strongly why model substitutability is a valuable property to aim for in MDE, whereas [3] discusses using inheritance, in the form of subtype specialisations, as a basic relationship between models.

The work of [4] presents one approach to model typing in MDE. In particular, the work adresses concerns related to reuse of model transformations and interpreters, or in general, situations where external code should be applicable to a number of different models all sharing a minimum set of properties as specified by a reference model type. However, there are still many open questions on how to support cases where model types also cover behavioural aspects - in the

S. Hammoudi et al. (Eds.): MODELSWARD 2014, CCIS 506, pp. 84–99, 2015.
DOI: 10.1007/978-3-319-25156-1_6

form of functional model types. That is, model types whose definitions also cover behavioural semantics in addition to structure. Being able to address software evolution is also a motivating factor for focusing on model types.

The success of object-orientation is to a large extent a consequence of its powerful mechanisms, e.g. specialisation, polymorphism and composition (using object references). The MDE philosophy supports the idea that such mechanisms should also be available at the model and metamodel levels. Many mechanisms address these aspects of (meta)model usage and evolution, e.g. [5–10]. However, these mechanisms require the use of additional frameworks. Furthermore, composition and variability directives are described in separate resources (files) in the form of either a weaving model, pointcut model or composition/variability rules. Such additional resources complicate reuse. They also pose certain challenges in maintaining files to reflect variations of the metamodels.

The notion of *specialising* (as in subtyping) metamodels has not received the same attention as model transformations and composition. In this paper, we discuss how metamodels can be typed by nesting them within an enclosing class. We will see how the enclosing class may indeed represent the type of the enclosed metamodel. The enclosing class can be subtyped which allows us to specialise metamodels. We will focus on metamodels whose behavioural semantics is defined in methods or operations, as supported by the *Eclipse Modeling Framework (EMF)* [11], *Kermeta* [12] and the *Epsilon Object Language (EOL)* [13].

The paper is organised in five main sections. Section 2 discusses the basic mechanics of using class nesting to type metamodels, and the purpose of typing metamodels. Section 3 delves into the matter of using class nesting for defining metamodel types, whereas Sect. 4 presents related work. Section 5 concludes the paper.

2 Metamodel Types

A metamodel defined in the *Essential MetaObject Facility (EMOF)* [14] architecture comprises a set of classes contained in one or more packages. Models of the metamodel consist of objects of the classes. The classes are related by association and specialisation relationships. A metamodel can be uniquely identified by the name and namespace of its containing package. However, a package is not a semantically powerful concept [15], and can not be used as a type specification for the contained metamodel. Specifically, it is not clear how different packages relate and which operations that can globally be applied on the model objects described by the classes of the package.

A class specifies the type of its instances. The type is defined by the attributes and operations of the class. In addition, non-static nested classes (inner classes) contribute to the type, as they can be considered class-valued attributes. In this paper, we pursue the idea of defining a metamodel within an enclosing class. The enclosing class is contained in a package. The purpose of defining a metamodel within an enclosing class is that the class explicitly describes a type for the metamodel. Hence, using an enclosing class allows us to take advantage of established principles of object-orientation - at the metamodel level. The metamodel's type is that of the enclosing class. In the context of this paper, we will simply refer to a class that encloses a metamodel as a *metamodel type*. A specific instance of a metamodel type represents a specific metamodel/language, and models of this metamodel/language will be in terms of objects of the classes enclosed in the specific instance. The instances of a given metamodel type will be generated by tools, while modellers will only be concerned with making models in terms of objects of the enclosed classes.

2.1 Definitions and Example

Definition 1. *A metamodel type is an enclosing class containing an arbitrary number of non-static nested classes, attributes and operations. The nested classes constitute an EMOF-compatible metamodel. A metamodel type* τ_m *can be described as the sequence* $\langle name, c, f, o\rangle \cdot s$, *where* $c \subset \mathcal{C}$ *- a finite set of EMOF-compatible (nested) classes,* $f \subset \mathcal{F}$ *- a finite set of features (attributes and references),* $o \subset \mathcal{O}$ *- a finite set of operations and* $s \subset \mathcal{T}$ *- a finite set of super metamodel types.*

An example of a state machine metamodel type, named TStateMachine, is given below:

$$\begin{aligned}\tau_m : \langle & TStateMachine,\\ & \{\ StateMachine,\ State,\ Transition,\ Event\ \},\\ & \{\ sm : StateMachine,\ events : Event\ \},\\ & \{\ transitionTable : String\ \}\rangle \cdot nil\end{aligned}$$

Definition 2. *A metamodel type instance is an object of the class defining a metamodel type. The metamodel classes of a metamodel type can be accessed and instantiated via a metamodel type instance. Several models can be created using the same instance. A metamodel type instance may have attribute values (according to the metamodel type definition) that can be used to customise the metamodel.*

We will use Kermeta to illustrate the idea of metamodel types[1]. However, we will only use a subset of Kermeta to avoid complicating the picture. Kermeta is an object-oriented language for creating EMOF-compatible metamodels. It allows specifying the behavioural semantics of metamodels within class operations. The operations are invoked at runtime when executing a model/program. We do not discuss static semantics (OCL) in this paper.

Figure 1 gives the metamodel type TStateMachine in Kermeta syntax. The metamodel type encloses a metamodel/language for modelling of state machines. The metamodel comprises the four classes: StateMachine, State, Transition and Event. StateMachine is the top node class of the metamodel from which all other

[1] Note that the current version of EMOF/Kermeta does not support nesting of classes as discussed in this paper.

classes are reachable through relationships. There is a reference typed with this class in the enclosing TStateMachine class. This reference is used to access the current model being processed by a tool (editor, interpreter, etc.). The metamodel details are not of interest, therefore three consecutive dots are used to represent additional content.

As seen in Fig. 1, the enclosing class has a reference typed with the metamodel's top node class. It also has an operation named transitionTable() that returns a textual description of all possible state transitions of a state machine model (i.e. the model referenced by the sm reference). A step of the state machine is performed by invoking the step(...) operation in the State class. The step is carried out if the current state has a transition whose event value is equal to the operation argument.

```
package state_machine;

class TStateMachine {
  // Reference typed with the top node metamodel class
  reference sm : StateMachine[1..1]

  // Events that may occur
  attribute events : Event[1..*]

  //  Operation global to all the metamodel classes
  operation transitionTable() : String is do
    sm.states.each{ s | ... }
    ...
    result := ...
  end

  // Metamodel classes
  class StateMachine {
    attribute states : State[0..*]
    reference currentState : State[1..1]
    reference initialState : State[1..1]
    ...
  }

  class State {
    attribute name : String
    reference incoming : Transition[0..*]
    attribute outgoing : Transition[0..*]#source
    operation step( event : Event ) is do ... end
    ...
  }

  class Transition {
    reference source : State[1..1]#outgoing
    reference target : State[1..1]
    reference event : Event[1..1]
    operation trigger() is do ... end
  }

  class Event { ... }
}
```

Fig. 1. A simple metamodel type (language) for state machines.

A weighted state machine is a variant of the basic state machine that supports the description of a probabilistic aspect of events: how likely that a given transition should be triggered. This aspect can be added to the basic state machine using specialisation. A first attempt to define this special kind of state machine would be to define a subclass of StateMachine. This seems obvious, as objects of the class StateMachine represent state machine models, and as such the class StateMachine appears to be the type of all these models. However, this would not work as intended, as the addition should be in the Transition class. Hence, a next attempt would be to create a subclass of Transition (as an addition to the existing Transition class). However, this would imply that even simple state machine models might have weighted transitions. Instead, by defining the additional properties of a weighted state machine within a subclass of TStateMachine, we are able to specialise the state machine metamodel as a holistic entity and clearly differentiate the state machine variants while still being able to use tools defined according to the general variant of the state machine metamodel. (Tools e.g. editors will not be able to instantiate new classes that have been added in subtypes.) The existing models of the general state machine metamodel are still valid, as changes and added properties are given in the metamodel subtype variant. Existing tools may then invoke redefined virtual operations in the nested classes of the metamodel subtype (this requires a casting to the subtype during instantiation of the nested classes). A metamodel type for a weighted state machine is given below (the arrows indicate inheritance):

$$\begin{aligned}\tau_{mw} : \; & \langle TWeightedStateMachine, \\ & \{ \; State \uparrow State, \; Transition \uparrow Transition \; \}, \\ & \{ \; \}, \\ & \{ \; \}\rangle \cdot \{ \; TStateMachine \; \}\end{aligned}$$

Figure 2 illustrates the new metamodel type in Kermeta. Notice that TWeightedStateMachine is a specialisation of TStateMachine. The classes Transition and State are given additional properties. Figure 3 illustrates the two metamodel types, and how they relate, using a graphical notation.

```
package weighted_state_machine;
require "state_machine.kmt"

class TWeightedStateMachine inherits TStateMachine {
  class State inherits TStateMachine.State { ... }
  class Transition inherits TStateMachine.Transition {
    attribute probability : Real
  }
}
```

Fig. 2. A metamodel type for weighted state machines.

Alternatively, a state machine that supports composite states can be defined as:

$$\begin{aligned}\tau_{mc} : \; & \langle TCompositeStateMachine, \\ & \{ \; CompositeState \uparrow State \; \}, \\ & \{ \; \}, \\ & \{ \; \}\rangle \cdot \{ \; TStateMachine \; \}\end{aligned}$$

Figure 4 shows the metamodel type in Kermeta syntax.

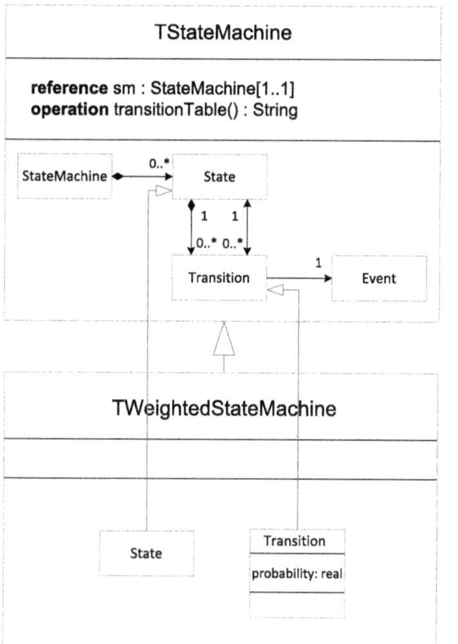

Fig. 3. Illustration of how metamodel types and classes of the metamodels relate through inheritance.

Note that this metamodel type has two classes for modelling of states: State and CompositeState (Fig. 5).

```
package composite_state_machine;
require "state_machine.kmt"

class ICompositeStateMachine inherits TStateMachine {
  class CompositeState inherits State {
    attribute stateMachine : StateMachine[0..1]
  }
}
```

Fig. 4. A state machine metamodel type with support for composite states.

2.2 Specialisation and Polymorphism

Changing an artefact of a system is not trivial since changes may impact other parts of the system, or even other systems. Changes made to artefacts at higher abstraction levels typically are more severe when it comes to impacting other parts of a software system. A metamodel is a model describing a set of models, i.e. the language of realisable models [16]. Changing a metamodel impacts all the

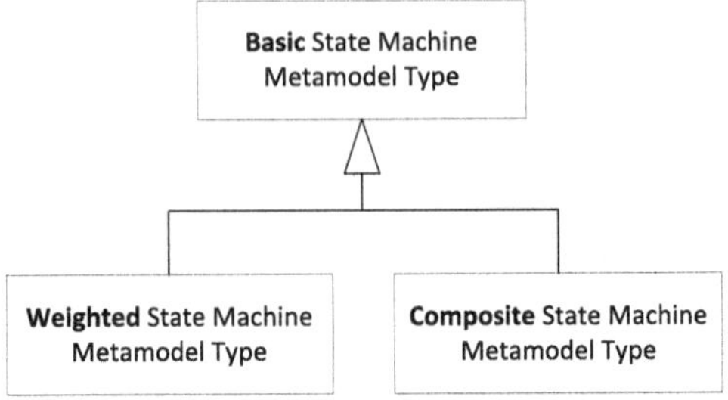

Fig. 5. The different metamodel types and how they relate.

conformant models. That is, the language of valid models that can be recognised is changed. In most cases, changing a metamodel may render its existing conformant models incompatible. This in turn requires manually changing the models or automating this process by creating a model transformation that incorporates knowledge about the changes to apply. Changes to a metamodel also impact its tools. By using specialisation based upon metamodel types it is possible to create new metamodel variations without rendering existing tools unusable. That is, the tools will still work by invoking redefined virtual operations. Hence, some of the challenges of changing software artefacts (additions) can be tackled.

One of the main contributions using metamodel types is the ability to use polymorphism. In the example, the metamodel type TWeightedStateMachine may be used as a substitute for TStateMachine. External code defined according to basic state machines can still be used with weighted state machines.

Metamodel type hierarchies may form a type system that facilitates reuse of commonly occurring metamodel structure and semantics [17]. Using an enclosing class to specify a metamodel type yields a high degree of encapsulation; a tool that is built to be compatible with the TStateMachine type can also operate on subtypes of this, e.g. TWeightedStateMachine.

So far we have discussed *concrete* metamodel types. An interesting variant is *abstract* metamodel types. Figure 6 gives an excerpt of an abstract metamodel type named TAbstractStateMachine.

```
package abstract_state_machine;

abstract class TAbstractStateMachine {
  reference sm : StateMachine[1..1]
  operation transitionTable() : String is abstract
  ...

  class StateMachine {
    attribute states : State[0..*]
    reference currentState : State[1..1]
    ...
  }
  class State {
    operation step( event : Event ) is do ... end
    ...
  }
  class Transition { ... }
}
```

Fig. 6. An abstract metamodel type.

By using an abstract metamodel type it is possible to define "a lowest common denominator" among a set of metamodels. That is, a minimal set of required structure that allows arbitrary metamodels to be equally typed (according to the abstract metamodel type). This is illustrated in Fig. 7.

The figure lists two different metamodel types AType and BType that both incorporate the structure defined by TAbstractStateMachine. The domains for the metamodels defined by the types are irrelevant. The point is that modelling of both domains requires the ability to specify behaviour in the form of state machines. For AType, the StateMachine class is specialised to contain an A1 object (A1, A2 and A3 are additional classes of the metamodel not related to state machines). Both the State and Transition classes are specialised in the definition of BType.

The resulting AType and BType are metamodels with arbitrary types of concepts (including concepts for modelling of state machines). However, they can still be typed according to a state machine viewpoint. For instance, a framework

```
package types;
require "abstract_state_machine.kmt"

class AType inherits TAbstractStateMachine {
  operation transitionTable() : String is do ... end
  ...
  class StateMachine inherits TAbstractStateMachine.StateMachine {
    attribute a1 : A1[1..1]
  }

  class A1 { ... }
  class A2 { ... }
  class A3 { ... }
}

class BType inherits TAbstractStateMachine {
  operation transitionTable() : String is do ... end
  ...
  class State inherits TAbstractStateMachine.State {
    attribute b1 : B1[0..*]
  }
  class Transition inherits TAbstractStateMachine.Transition {
    reference b2 : B2[1..*]
    reference b3 : B3[1..1]
  }

  class B1 { ... }
  class B2 { ... }
  class B3 { ... }
}
```

Fig. 7. Metamodel types incorporating common structure.

```
package interpreter;

class Interpreter {
  operation interpret( stateMachine : TAbstractStateMachine, event : Event ) is do
    stateMachine.sm.currentState.step( event )
    ...
    stateMachine.transitionTable()
    ...
  end
}
```

Fig. 8. The basic structure of an interpreter.

built around the TAbstractStateMachine can execute the behavioural semantics in the operations of the state machine classes, which may be overridden. This is possible regardless of how the AType and BType metamodel types are defined. Figure 8 illustrates how such a framework/interpreter may be constructed based on TAbstractStateMachine.

3 Implications of Metamodel Types

3.1 Interpretation and Code Generation

In Kermeta, a metamodels' behavioural semantics is defined in class operations. For instance, the semantics for stepping/triggering a new state in the state machine metamodel is defined in the step(...) and trigger() operations in the State and Transition classes. The exact definition of this semantics is not interesting. However, it is clear that the default stepping/triggering semantics will not suffice for a weighted state machine. By subtyping State and Transition, the semantics of these classes can be redefined for the new state machine type. The main point here is that a framework for interpretation of state machine models will still work by utilising the redefined semantics (as accessible through dynamic binding of step(...) and trigger()).

A typical approach for realising executable DSLs is to use code generators that work on purely structural metamodels/models. An alternative is to use the operations in the metamodel classes and in the enclosing class for implementing a code generator (where each operation contains code written in a target language). Since we allow subtyping of both the enclosing class and the inner classes of a metamodel type, we are able to redefine the code generator using virtual operations (and types).

3.2 Analysis Tools

The operations in the classes may also be used to generate information about the models. In particular the enclosing class may contain operations that work on models as a whole. We have given one such operation in the TStateMachine, namely transitionTable(). This operation contains semantics that is not part of the metamodel/language for creating state machines. Yet, it allows calculating information about a state machine that can be presented to the modeller during the modelling process. By using subtyping it is possible for analysis tools to work on metamodel variants, since the access points of the analysis tools are predefined as operations in the enclosing class.

3.3 Type Safety

In this paper, we relate variants of metamodel types using the subtyping relation [18]. Subtyping imposes certain restrictions on subtypes: the parameter types of an operation are required to be contravariant, whereas the return type needs to be covariant. What this means is that virtual operations of subtypes can be invoked type-safely in place of their supertype equivalents. As pointed out in [4], types of class properties are required to be invariant in *MetaObject Facility (MOF)* [14] metamodels. This latter requirement is difficult to fulfill, as additions of attributes and references to a class is common when creating metamodel variants. Such additions change the type of the containing class, which in turn results in a covariant redefinition of attributes and references that are typed with the class. Let us see how this affects metamodel types as presented in this paper.

There are two places where subtyping occurs in creating a metamodel type variant. First, the enclosing class is subtyped. Second, the inner classes constituting the metamodel may be subtyped selectively depending on which specialisations that are required. Recall how the Transition class needs an additional attribute probability to create a weighted state machine metamodel from the basic state machine metamodel. Let us assume that this would be the only required addition to the basic state machine metamodel. What we have now is a situation of covariant type redefinition. The attributes incoming and outgoing of the State class (see Fig. 1) are typed with Transition. The new Transition class variant contains an additional attribute. Hence, the types of the incoming reference and the outgoing attribute in the State class of the metamodel type variant (TWeightedStateMachine) are not invariant, but covariant. A potential problem would occur when related metamodel types are mixed, e.g. when a model contains instances of both state machine and weighted state machine metamodel classes. However, these situations do not occur since e.g. a model editor has to instantiate either of the metamodel types. Hence, it is not possible to instantiate the subtype of the Transition class when creating a basic state machine.

3.4 Multiple Inheritance

We have seen how metamodel types can be used to represent metamodel patterns or fragments, e.g. a state machine. We have also discussed how a metamodel can be considered and interpreted from the perspective of one specific metamodel type. Seen in the light of this, a metamodel may have several types. Put differently, a metamodel can be constructed by combining an arbitrary number of patterns. This means that a metamodel can also be considered from several perspectives depending on situation and purpose (e.g. a tool may present several viewpoints to the user, where each viewpoint corresponds to a metamodel type) (Fig. 9).

Regardless of specialisations of the inner classes, the enclosed metamodel of TMetamodel can still be considered from two perspectives/aspects: state machine and game. That is, tools defined for TAbstractStateMachine and TAbstractGame can still be used. For example, it is convenient to analyse a model conforming to the composite metamodel from the state machine perspective alone, e.g. by writing out the state transition table or similar. This is possible regardless of the added properties in specialisations of the inner classes.

```
package metamodel;
require "abstract_state_machine.kmt"
require "abstract_game.kmt"

class TMetamodel inherits TAbstractStateMachine, TAbstractGame {
  ...
```

Fig. 9. Using multiple inheritance to relate metamodel types (yielding a composite metamodel).

Using multiple inheritance may potentially require resolution of name conflicts. There are several approaches to improve the applicability of multiple inheritance, e.g. Kermeta allows the modeller to explicitly specify the operation to override in ambigious situations. We will not go into details on this subject.

An alternative to multiple inheritance is to allow references to be typed with metamodel types. This means that a class may be a consumer of e.g. a state machine. Put differently, the class may reference a metamodel type comprising constructs for modelling of state machines. Allowing references being typed with metamodel types gives interesting opportunities. However, things also get more complicated. Recall that each object of a metamodel type gives a unique metamodel. For the example this means that different objects of the state machine metamodel type (or subtypes of this) gives unique referenced state machine metamodels. Even though type-safety is still achieved, execution of the models may differ depending on the exact object of the metamodel type (or its subtypes) that is used.

3.5 Using Virtual Classes and Generic Parameters

The classes of a metamodel type can be defined as virtual and utilise generic type parameters. Let us return to our example. If the language for making metamodels (e.g. Kermeta) supports virtual classes [19], then the Transition could be defined as a virtual class and then redefined in TWeightedStateMachine (by extending the Transition class). See Fig. 3. This allows code in TStateMachine to generate Transition objects with the additional property, given that the context in which this code is executed is an object of TWeightedStateMachine. Virtual classes also allow existing tools like editors to instantiate redefined classes in metamodel subtypes. It would also be possible to define the enclosing class as virtual. See [20] for more information on using virtual classes in metamodels.

3.6 Metamodel Customisation

In its simplest form, an enclosing class does not contain other elements than the nested metamodel classes. The enclosing class may also contain attributes and operations. This adds a new dimension to metamodels. Specifically, the state of a metamodel type object can be used to customise the behavioural semantics of its encapsulated metamodel. As an example, the behavioural semantics of a metamodel (as defined in operations) may use different algorithms depending on context. These algorithms may share basic properties (attributes) whose values can be changed with the intention of tuning the behavioural semantics for a specific usage or context. Being able to adjust these properties simultaneously for all the algorithms allows customising the semantics easily without changing the actual models. The properties with their values are in the object of the enclosing class. Hence, this object's state captures an (execution) configuration for models of a given metamodel/language. Changing such values for a metamodel/language would change the meaning for all conformant models/programs. It would also be possible to maintain several objects of the enclosing class and thereby facilitate execution profiles (serialised to files). However, this will give rise to an additional level of polymorphism as different object states give different execution results.

3.7 Nesting of Metamodel Types

Metamodel types are realised using class nesting. Specifically, the enclosing class gives the enclosed metamodel a type. However, the enclosing class is only an ordinary class that takes a special role. This means that a metamodel class, i.e. a class enclosed by an outer class, may take the role as a metamodel type as well. What we achieve by this is nesting of metamodel types. In theory, there may be an arbitrary number of levels of nested metamodel types. By utilising subtyping and polymorphism this means that metamodels may be specialised at different levels. Further studies are necessary to gain insight into whether nesting of metamodel types is practical.

In [20], we discussed *generic metamodels*; a theoretical concept where class nesting is used together with type parameters for adding language constructs and customising metamodels. This work may be referred for additional details on using class nesting in metamodels.

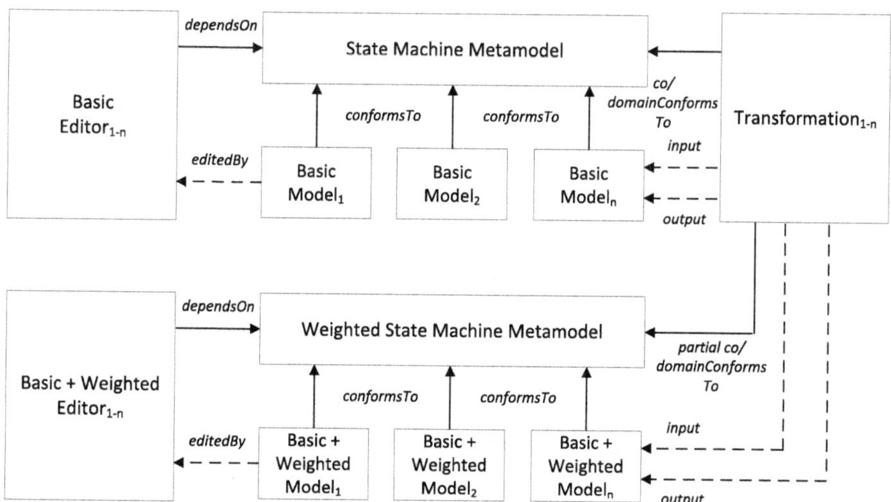

Fig. 10. Overview of how metamodels and models relate to other modelling artefacts.

3.8 Existing Tools

A key advantage with metamodel subtypes is that existing tools are not rendered invalid as new metamodel variants are created. As an example, Fig. 10 illustrates how editors and transformations interact with state machine metamodels and models.

The Basic Editors allow creating and editing model elements related to basic state machines. The Basic + Weighted Editors additionally allow modelling the probabilistic aspect of weighted state machines. The key point is that the models can still be treated as basic state machine models by the Basic Editors. A similar reasoning applies to transformations. Even though the models may include elements that model the probabilistic aspect of weighted state machines, the transformations only relate to basic state machine concepts since the transformations are defined relative to the State Machine Metamodel, i.e. the TStateMachine metamodel type.

4 Related Work

There are several mechanisms that address model composition and variability. Some of these are discussed in [21]. Common to these mechanisms is their external definition from the language used to define the models and/or metamodels. Moreover, most mechanisms use some kind of merging techniques to combine the metamodels which compromises the principle of encapsulation.

We have used Kermeta to illustrate metamodel types. Kermeta features a mechanism known as *static introduction.* This mechanism allows specifying partial class definitions using *aspects.* Several aspect definitions are combined (or woven) at runtime to form the definition of a class. The mechanism allows defining new aspects that are combined with an existing class definition. Aspects allow creating metamodel variants. However, they can not be used to type a metamodel - the resulting classes are contained in a regular package.

Model types, as described in [4] resembles the work of this paper. There are some differences and similarities that we will discuss. First, a model type can be seen as a type-safe set of an arbitrary number of model object types. The model type mechanism defines a conformance relation between model types, which allows reusing code or transformations. Specifically, code for manipulating or executing models (interpretation) can be defined according to a reference model type. All models that are typed with a model type conformant to the reference model type can be manipulated or executed by the same code. A model type is created by referring to classes of an arbitrary number of existing metamodels. This is a powerful ability, since classes defined in different packages can be "extracted" to constitute a model type.

A metamodel type, as discussed in this paper, allows typing metamodels as holistic MDE structures. We have used the notion *metamodel* type instead of *model* type because of a significant difference between the approaches. An instance of a metamodel type (object of the enclosing class) represents one particular metamodel. The object can be used to access the metamodels' classes and thereby create model objects. The object of the enclosing class also references one model whose semantics is e.g. intended to be executed at runtime. Conversely, in the work of [4], an instance of a model type can not be used to instantiate the classes of the model type. Instances of these classes are instead added to the model type instance. The model type instance acts as a filter where only objects of the model type's classes can be added to the model type instance successfully. The similarity in this respect between the approaches is that both a metamodel type instance and a model type instance can be used to reference a conformant model. The capabilities of the two model typing approaches differ. Model types are designed to simplify reuse of code from an external perspective, e.g. from the perspective of an interpreter or transformation. Conversely, metamodel types allow creating metamodel variants. By design, metamodel types are functional types. Reuse of code is achieved by creating type variants in the form of subtypes. Model types, on the other hand, are structural. They can not be combined, or be related to create variations.

The inability to use substitution in model typing is addressed by [22]. The paper discusses four subtyping mechanisms, and how these allow defining relations between model types as defined in [4]. The work differentiates between total and partial subtyping relations, that are either isomorphic (model type matching with respect to properties and operations) or non-isomorphic. According to the definitions of [22], using an enclosing class as type specification for metamodels can be seen as a total isomorphic subtyping relation that is declared explicitly. The explicitly declared subtyping relation allows reusing structure of supertypes through inheritance. And, as we have seen, the inherited classes can be redefined. Using an enclosing class supports compile-time checking of the subtyping relations between types. It is stated in [22] that it is not possible to achieve type group substitutability using object subtyping. The work on metamodel types shows that this is in fact possible when a metamodel is a property of an object - as realised using class nesting. Hence, we are able to achieve type group substitutability based upon established object subtyping principles. This includes the ability to reuse existing type checking algorithms. The drawback of our approach is that substitutability of metamodels can not be defined partially. However, as illustrated, a metamodel can be typed according to several metamodel types, which addresses this concern to some extent.

An approach for generic specification of metamodel's behaviour is discussed in [23]. The approach relies on the use of generic concepts for defining behaviour that is applicable to a family of unrelated metamodels. Concepts allow specifying details of models' structure by utilising parameters. A concept can be bound to metamodels that satisfy the concept's requirements using pattern matching. There is no dependency between a metamodel and a concept. Hence, utilising concepts is non-intrusive. Conversely, we have seen how metamodel types are related using subtyping in two levels. In other words, we utilise a typical object-oriented typing scheme that allows defining metamodel variants explicitly using subtyping.

Specialisation relationships between models are carefully discussed in [2]. The work formalises two relations for specifying forward- and backward-compatibility between models and applies these relations to, e.g. models related using subtyping. The compatibility relations are defined using a definition of conformance. Forward-compatibility is achieved if instances of a submodel conform to the supermodel, and vice versa for backward-compatibility. One important point discussed is the desire to maximise the forward-compatibility of a language since this allows reusing existing tools on new models (via redefined virtual operations). The subtyping relation ensures a high degree of forward-compatibility. Subtyping also guarantees mutator forward-compatibility. This supports a round-trip between new instances of submodels and support for these by existing tools. That is, the submodel instances appear like supermodel instances. Subtyping is the most restrictive specialisation relationship, with strict behaviour conformance of subtypes. We believe that this type of relationship is the best suited for relating metamodel types.

5 Conclusions

In this paper we have presented a novel way of typing a metamodel by defining it within an enclosing class. The enclosing class is thus the type of the metamodel. By exploiting object-oriented mechanisms we get the notion of subtyping of metamodels. Subtyping ensures substitutability between metamodel types. That is, tools defined according to a metamodel type can be reused on subtype variations of this metamodel type (possibly with redefinition of virtual operations). Another important aspect of using subtyping is the ability to maintain conformance between models and their metamodels.

An object of the enclosing class is not part of a model. It is used by tools for accessing the enclosed metamodel and for maintaining an execution configuration for the models.

References

1. Caskurlu, B.: Model driven engineering. In: Butler, M., Petre, L., Sere, K. (eds.) IFM 2002. LNCS, vol. 2335, p. 286. Springer, Heidelberg (2002)
2. Kühne, T.: An observer-based notion of model inheritance. In: Petriu, D.C., Rouquette, N., Haugen, Ø. (eds.) MODELS 2010, Part I. LNCS, vol. 6394, pp. 31–45. Springer, Heidelberg (2010)
3. Kühne, T.: Matters of (Meta-) modeling. Softw. Syst. Model. **5**(4), 387–394 (2006)
4. Steel, J., Jézéquel, J.-M.: On model typing. Softw. Syst. Model. **6**(4), 401–413 (2007)
5. Didonet Del Fabro, M., Bézivin, J., Valduriez, P.: Weaving models with the eclipse AMW plugin. In: Eclipse Modeling Symposium, Eclipse Summit Europe (2006). http://ssei.pbworks.com/f/Del+Fabro.Weaving+Models+with+the+Eclipse+AMW+plugin.pdf
6. Kolovos, D.S., Paige, R.F., Polack, F.A.C.: Merging models with the epsilon merging language (EML). In: Wang, J., Whittle, J., Harel, D., Reggio, G. (eds.) MoDELS 2006. LNCS, vol. 4199, pp. 215–229. Springer, Heidelberg (2006)

7. Groher, I., Voelter, M.: XWeave - models and aspects in concert. In: 10th International Workshop on Aspect-Oriented Modeling (AOM 2007), pp. 35–40. ACM Press (2007)
8. Fleurey, F., Baudry, B., France, R.B., Ghosh, S.: A generic approach for automatic model composition. In: Giese, H. (ed.) MODELS 2008. LNCS, vol. 5002, pp. 7–15. Springer, Heidelberg (2008)
9. Morin, B., Perrouin, G., Lahire, P., Barais, O., Vanwormhoudt, G., Jézéquel, J.-M.: Weaving variability into domain metamodels. In: Schürr, A., Selic, B. (eds.) MODELS 2009. LNCS, vol. 5795, pp. 690–705. Springer, Heidelberg (2009)
10. Morin, B., Klein, J., Barais, O.: A generic weaver for supporting product lines. In: 13th International Workshop on Early Aspects (EA 2008), pp. 11–18. ACM Press (2008)
11. The Eclipse Foundation: Eclipse Modeling Framework (EMF). http://www.eclipse.org/modeling/emf
12. Muller, P.-A., Fleurey, F., Jézéquel, J.-M.: Weaving executability into object-oriented meta-languages. In: Briand, L.C., Williams, C. (eds.) MoDELS 2005. LNCS, vol. 3713, pp. 264–278. Springer, Heidelberg (2005)
13. The Eclipse Foundation: Epsilon Object Language (EOL). http://www.eclipse.org/epsilon/doc/eol
14. Object Management Group: Meta Object Facility (MOF) Core Specification. http://www.omg.org/mof
15. Monperrus, M., Beugnard, A., Champeau, J.: A definition of abstraction level for metamodels. In: 16th Annual IEEE International Conference and Workshop on the Engineering of Computer Based Systems (ECBS 2009), pp. 315–320. IEEE Computer Society (2009)
16. Favre, J-M.: Towards a basic theory to model model driven engineering. In: 3rd International Workshop on Software Model Engineering (WISME 2004) (2004)
17. Cho, H., Gray, J.: Design patterns for metamodels. In: SPLASH 2011 Workshops Proceedings, pp. 25–32. ACM Press (2011)
18. Liskov, B.H., Wing, J.M.: A behavioral notion of subtyping. ACM Trans. Program. Lang. Syst. **16**(6), 1811–1841 (1994)
19. Madsen, O.L., Møller-Pedersen, B.: Virtual classes - a powerful mechanism in object-oriented programming. In: Proceedings of OOPSLA 1989. ACM (1989)
20. Berg, H., Møller-Pedersen, B., Krogdahl, S.: Advancing generic metamodels. In: SPLASH 2011 Workshops Proceedings, pp. 19–24. ACM Press (2011)
21. Berg, H., Møller-Pedersen, B.: Type-safe symmetric composition of metamodels using templates. In: Haugen, Ø., Reed, R., Gotzhein, R. (eds.) SAM 2012. LNCS, vol. 7744, pp. 160–178. Springer, Heidelberg (2013)
22. Guy, C., Combemale, B., Derrien, S., Steel, J.R.H., Jézéquel, J.-M.: On model subtyping. In: Vallecillo, A., Tolvanen, J.-P., Kindler, E., Störrle, H., Kolovos, D. (eds.) ECMFA 2012. LNCS, vol. 7349, pp. 400–415. Springer, Heidelberg (2012)
23. de Lara, J., Guerra, E.: From Types to Type Requirements: Genericity for Model-Driven Engineering. In: Software and Systems Modeling. Springer (2011)

Matching and Merging Scenarios Automatically with Alloy

J. Bowles[1(✉)], M. Alwanain[2], B. Bordbar[2], and Y. Chen[2]

[1] School of Computer Science, University of St Andrews,
Jack Cole Building, North Haugh, St Andrews KY16 9SX, UK
jkfb@st-andrews.ac.uk

[2] School of Computer Science, University of Birmingham,
Edgbaston, Birmingham, UK
{m.i.alwanain,b.bordbar,y.chen}@cs.bham.ac.uk

Abstract. The design of large systems often involves the creation of models that describe partial specifications. Model composition is the process of combining partial models to create a single coherent model. This paper presents an automatic composition technique for creating a sequence diagram from partial specifications captured in multiple sequence diagrams with the help of Alloy. Our contribution is twofold: a novel true-concurrent semantics for sequence diagram composition, and a model-driven transformation of sequence diagrams to Alloy that preserves the semantics of composition defined. We have created a tool *SD2Alloy* that implements the technique as follows: two given sequence diagrams are transformed into two Alloy models, and merged according to a set of syntactic logical constraints describing how their elements should be matched. These constraints are in accordance to our compositional semantics. The technique can also be used to detect problems and inconsistencies in the composition of diagrams.

Keywords: UML sequence diagrams · Model transformation · Composition · Alloy

1 Introduction

The process of developing modern systems is gradually becoming more and more complex. Due to the increase in the complexity of such software development processes, we often make use of multiple models for expressing various scenarios and viewpoints. To reduce the complexity of the design, models of the system are usually broken into partial specifications. For example, behaviour related to the interaction between parts can be captured by different sequence diagrams. However, integrating these diagrams into one to describe the whole behaviour requires *model composition* techniques. Manual model composition is error-prone, time-consuming and tedious [1]. In recent years, automated model composition has received considerable attention [2,3]. For example [2] make use of Alloy for automated composition. Nonetheless, most automated merging methods only focus on static models.

S. Hammoudi et al. (Eds.): MODELSWARD 2014, CCIS 506, pp. 100–116, 2015.
DOI: 10.1007/978-3-319-25156-1_7

In this paper we focus on the automated integration of sequence diagrams, one of UML's most popular behavioural models [4]. In particular, we focus on the composition of sequence diagrams with the help of Alloy. Our contribution is twofold: a novel true-concurrent semantics for sequence diagram composition, and a model-driven transformation of sequence diagrams to Alloy that preserves the semantics of composition.

Our automated technique follows three main steps. In the first step, multiple sequence diagrams are automatically transformed into Alloy models. For each sequence diagram a unique Alloy model is produced which if solved has as many solutions as there are possible traces of execution in the original sequence diagram. These traces have a direct correspondence to the ones obtained in the underlying semantics of sequence diagrams used, namely labelled event structures (LES) [5,6]. In the second step, the Alloy models are merged to produce a single Alloy model, which contains elements from the individual Alloy models of each sequence diagram in addition to syntactic logical constraints specifying how the elements are matched and the diagrams should be composed. The logical constraints used for the matching are syntactic and considered in our true-concurrent semantics of composition. In the third step, we use the composed model obtained, that is the conjunction of the overall logical constraints, to formally check if the sequence diagrams can be composed and obtain the composition of the diagrams automatically. These steps are fully automated in our tool *SD2Alloy* which was implemented using Model Driven Architecture (MDA) techniques [7]. Later in the paper, we justify further our choice of Alloy as a target language.

The remainder of the paper is structured as follows: Sect. 2 gives a general background of sequence diagrams, their formalisation with event structures and Alloy. Section 3 addresses model composition syntactically (at the UML level) and semantically (over labelled event structures) which guides the model transformation from sequence diagrams onto Alloy as discussed in Sect. 4. Section 5 describes model composition via Alloy, and Sect. 6 gives some details of our tool. Finally, Sect. 7 describes related work and Sect. 8 concludes the paper.

2 Background

2.1 Sequence Diagrams

UML sequence diagrams capture scenarios of execution as object (or in some cases component) interactions. Each object has a vertical dashed line called *lifeline* showing the existence of the object at a particular time. Points along the lifeline are called *locations* (a terminology borrowed from LSCs [8]) and denote the occurrence of events. The order of locations along a lifeline is significant denoting, in general, the order in which the corresponding events occur.

A *message* is a synchronous or asynchronous communication between two objects shown as an arrow connecting the respective lifelines, that is, the underlying send and receive events of the message. We only consider synchronous communication in this paper, even though both forms of communication can

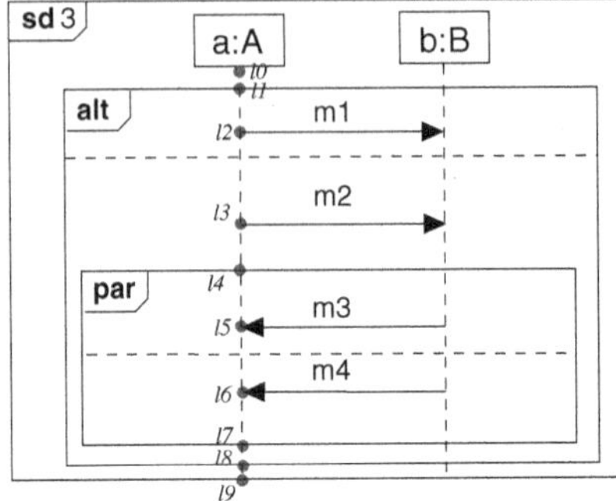

Fig. 1. A sequence diagram with nested fragments.

be addressed in our approach. An *interaction* between several objects consists of one or more messages, but may be given further structure through so-called *interaction fragments*. There are several kinds of interaction fragments including **seq** (sequential behaviour), **alt** (alternative behaviour), **par** (parallel behaviour), **neg** (forbidden behaviour), **assert** (mandatory behaviour), **loop** (iterative behaviour), and so on [4]. Depending on the operator used, an interaction fragment consists of one or more *operands*. In the case of the **alt** fragment, each operand describes a choice of behaviour. Only one of the alternative operands is executed if the guard expression (if present) evaluates to true. If more than one operand has a guard that evaluates to true, one of the operands is selected nondeterministically for execution. In the case of the **par** fragment, there is a parallel merge between the behaviours of the operands. The event occurrences of the different operands can be interleaved in any way as long as the ordering imposed by each operand as such is preserved.

Finally, interaction fragments can be nested producing expressive and complex scenarios of execution. One simple example illustrating the concepts above and with a parallel nested within an alternative fragment is given in Fig. 1. In this case, all messages (from m_1 to m_4) are sent synchronously between objects a and b. The locations along the lifeline of object a are shown explicitly. The importance of locations as well as the effect produced through the nesting of fragments (i.e., the possible traces of execution) are described in the next subsection. In particular, the distinction between the syntactic notion of a location on a sequence diagram from its semantic counterpart of an event will be clarified.

2.2 Formal Model

Several possible semantics for sequence diagrams have been defined (see [9] for an overview). In this paper we use the semantics defined in [6] which introduces a very simple and intuitive behavioural model to capture interactions, and is the only true-concurrent semantics available for sequence diagrams.

Prime event structures [5], or event structures for short, describe distributed computations as event occurrences together with binary relations for expressing causal dependency (called *causality*) and nondeterminism (called *conflict*). The causality relation implies a (partial) order among event occurrences, while the conflict relation expresses how the occurrence of certain events excludes the occurrence of others. From the two relations defined on the set of events, a further relation is derived, namely the *concurrency* relation *co*. Two events are concurrent if and only if they are completely unrelated, i.e., neither related by causality nor by conflict.

Formally, an *event structure* is a triple $E = (Ev, \rightarrow^*, \#)$ where Ev is a set of events and $\rightarrow^*, \# \subseteq Ev \times Ev$ are binary relations called *causality* and *conflict*, respectively. Causality $\rightarrow^*$ is a partial order. Conflict $\#$ is symmetric and irreflexive, and propagates over causality, i.e., $e\#e' \rightarrow^* e'' \Rightarrow e\#e''$ for all $e, e', e'' \in Ev$. Two events $e, e' \in Ev$ are *concurrent*, $e\ co\ e'$ iff $\neg(e \rightarrow^* e' \vee e' \rightarrow^* e \vee e\#e')$.

We omit further technical details on the model, but note that for the application of event structures as a semantic model for sequence diagrams we use *discrete* event structures. Discreteness imposes a finiteness constraint on the model, i.e., there are always only a finite number of causally related predecessors to an event, known as the *local configuration* of the event. A further motivation for this constraint is given by the fact that every execution has a starting point or configuration.

Event structures are enriched with a labelling function (usually a total function $\mu : Ev \rightarrow L$ that maps each event onto an element of the set L). This labelling function is necessary to establish a connection between the semantic model (event structure) and the syntactic model (here a sequence diagram).

Intuitively, each location marked along a lifeline of an object in a sequence diagram corresponds to one (possibly more) event(s) in the labelled event structure. The set of labels used could be the set of locations in a sequence diagram but is usually more concrete information on what the location represents: the initialisation of an object, sending/receiving a message, beginning/ending an interaction fragment, etc.

Consider the locations marked on Fig. 1 for object a. The events in the model shown in Fig. 2 have a direct correspondence to the locations of object a.

The graphical representation of the event structure E_a shows immediate causality between events (e.g., $e_0 \rightarrow e_1$) and direct conflict (e.g., $e_2\#e_3$). By conflict propagation we also have $e_2\#e_4$, etc. Unrelated events are concurrent (e.g., $e_5\ co\ e_6$). Intuitively, events e_1 and e_4 denote the beginning of the alternative and parallel fragments respectively. Consequently events e_5 (denoting the receipt of message m_3) and e_6 (denoting the receipt of message m_4) are concurrent. Events e_{81} and e_{82} both correspond to location l_8 denoting the end of the alternative fragment. These events must be in conflict because they represent different ways to reach the location. Note that there cannot be one end event in this case, because conflict propagates over causality and it would lead to an event in conflict with itself and hence an invalid event structure (conflict is irreflexive). Some event labels are given where (m_1, s) denotes sending message m_1, and (m_3, r) denotes receiving message m_3.

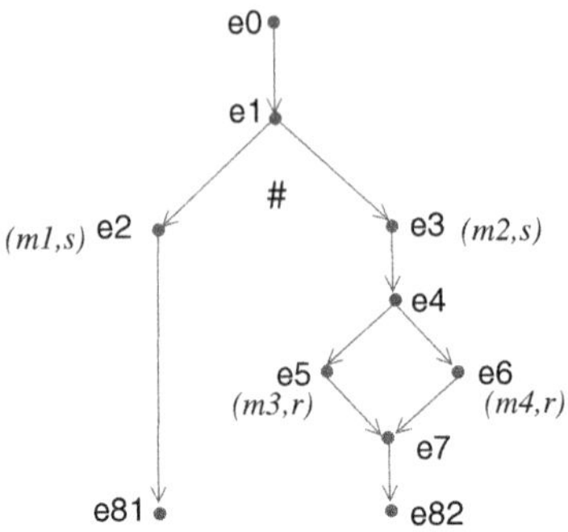

Fig. 2. Event structure for object a of Fig. 1.

Let I denote the set of objects involved in the interaction described by sequence diagram SD. A model $M_{SD} = (E, \mu)$ for a sequence diagram SD is obtained by composition of the models $M_i = (E_i, \mu_i)$ of each object instance $i \in I$. In the composed model, the set of events Ev is such that $e \in Ev$ iff there is an object $i \in I$ such that $e \in Ev_i$, or $(e_1, e_2) \in Ev$ iff there are two objects $i \neq j \in I$ with $e_1 \in Ev_i$, $e_2 \in Ev_j$, $\mu_i(e_1) = (m, s)$ and $\mu_j(e_2) = (m, r)$. In other words, shared events (e_1, e_2) correspond to message synchronisation. To keep it simple, we assume that $\mu : Ev \rightarrow Mes$ is a partial function defined over shared events only and indicating the message exchanged. I.e., $\mu(e_1, e_2) = m$ iff $\mu_i(e_1) = (m, s)$ and $\mu_j(e_2) = (m, r)$ for some $i, j \in I$. More details on the semantics of sequence diagrams using event structures can be found in [6].

2.3 Alloy

Alloy [10] is a declarative textual modelling language based on first-order relational logic. An Alloy model consists of a number of signature declarations, fields, facts and predicates. Furthermore, each signature denotes a set of atoms, which are the basic entities of Alloy. Alloy is supported by a fully automated constraint solver called Alloy Analyzer, which permits the analysis of system properties by searching for instances of the model. It is possible to check whether certain properties of the system are present. This is achieved via an automated translation of the model into a Boolean expression, which is then analysed by SAT solvers such as SAT4J [11] embedded within the Alloy Analyzer. The Alloy Analyzer has been used in various applications including the composition of static models [2].

In this paper, Alloy is used as part of an automated tool to compose sequence diagrams. The composition is based on a set of logical constraints which we designate *merging glue*. Alloy is a language for describing the *structural* information underlying a design model whereas labelled event structures are needed to make sure the semantics of the *behavioural* model and the composition are as expected.

The choice of Alloy as a target framework makes it straightforward to find a model (if available) for the composition of sequence diagrams. The approach converts each sequence diagram into a set of logical constraints to which it is simple to add additional constraints capturing the *merging glue*. Alloy solves these constraints to *find* a model that complies to both sequence diagrams and the glue.

3 Model Composition

For the integration of two or more scenarios we define syntactic composition of sequence diagrams and its underlying semantics.

Our mechanism for composition of sequence diagrams considers interleaving of diagrams and shared behaviour. In the first case, diagrams evolve completely autonomously whereas in the latter case diagrams have shared behaviour (shared objects and messages). We treat the cases separately and consider only the composition of two diagrams. The case for an arbitrary number of diagrams is easily generalised from here. In the sequel, let SD_1 and SD_2 be two sequence diagrams, with sets of instances and messages given by I_1, I_2, Mes_1 and Mes_2 respectively.

The *interleaving* of diagrams SD_1 and SD_2 with $Mes_1 \cap Mes_2 = \emptyset$ is written $SD_1 \parallel SD_2$ and is defined syntactically as $par(SD_1, SD_2)$. In other words, it consists of a diagram with a par fragment and two operands where each operand contains the behaviour described in SD_1 and SD_2 respectively.

Semantically, the model for $SD_1 \parallel SD_2$ is an event structure $M_{SD_1 \parallel SD_2} = (E, \mu)$ where $Ev = Ev_1 \cup Ev_2$, all relations are preserved, and $\mu(e)$ is defined for all e iff $\mu_i(e)$ is defined for some $i \in \{1, 2\}$ in which case $\mu(e) = \mu_i(e)$. For shared instances $o \in I_1 \cap I_2$ we further match the initial and maximal events in Ev_1 and Ev_2. We illustrate this with an example (see Fig. 3) showing shared objects but different messages.

The models associated to SD_1 and SD_2 are given in Fig. 4.

As described above, if we compose both models we can merge initial and maximal events for shared objects which in this case corresponds to events e_{a0} and e_{a0}', e_{b0} and e_{b0}', e_{a2} and e_{a2}', and e_{b2} and e_{b2}'. The final composition $SD_1 \parallel SD_2$ is shown in Fig. 5. This is the exact model obtained for a sequence diagram which consists of a parallel fragment with two operands where the first operand is taken from $SD1$ and the second operand is taken from SD_2.

The composition of diagrams SD_1 and SD_2 with *shared behaviour* is written $SD_1 \parallel_G SD_2$ where $G = Mes_1 \cap Mes_2$ indicates the shared behaviour.

If $G = Mes_1$, in other words, all the behaviour in SD_1 is shared, then we say that SD_1 is *syntactically contained* in SD_2, and the composition $SD_1 \parallel_G SD_2$ can be reduced to SD_2.

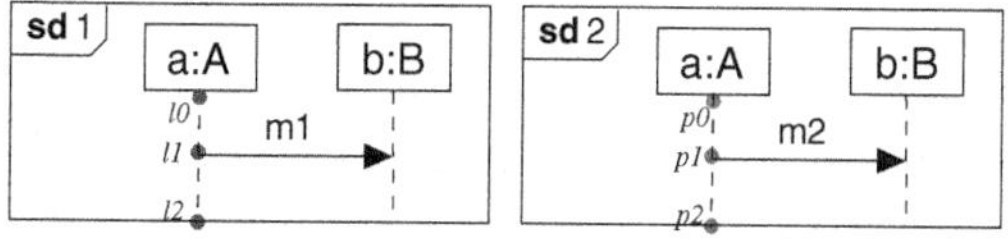

Fig. 3. Two simple sequence diagrams.

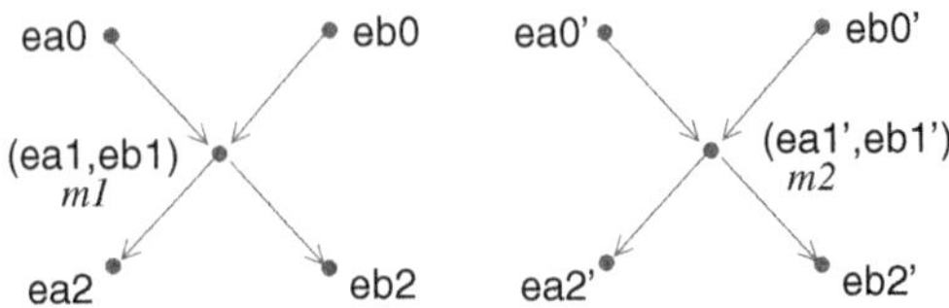

Fig. 4. Model for SD_1 (left) and SD_2 (right).

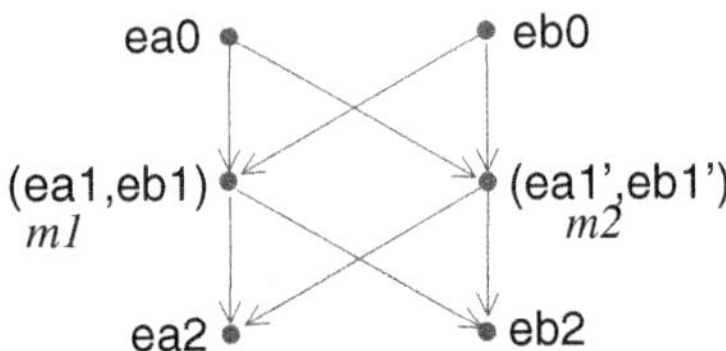

Fig. 5. Model for $SD_1 \parallel SD_2$.

We now consider the case that $G = \{m\}$. This case can be generalised to a finite number of messages, but we omit it here for simplicity.

Consider $SD_1 = seq(\varphi_0, m, \varphi_1)$ and $SD_2 = seq(\varphi_0', m, \varphi_1')$ where *seq* denotes a sequential fragment, φ_0, φ_1, φ_0' and φ_1' are interactions which on their own would define a valid sequence diagram and may be empty. The composition $SD_1 \parallel_G SD_2$ is defined syntactically by $seq(par(\varphi_0, \varphi_0'), m, par(\varphi_1, \varphi_1'))$.

Note that the *seq* fragment describes the default (sequential) behaviour of a sequence diagram and can be omitted in a diagram, but is useful here to describe composition in general. For example, SD_1 from Fig. 3 can be seen as $seq(\varphi_0, m_1, \varphi_1)$ with φ_0 and φ_1 both empty.

Consider a more complex case where $SD_1 = f(seq(\varphi_0, m, \varphi_1), \varphi_2)$ and $SD_2 = seq(\varphi_0', m, \varphi_1')$ where f denotes an arbitrary fragment (e.g., par, alt, etc.). The composition $SD_1 \parallel_G SD_2$ is defined syntactically by:

$$f(seq(par(\varphi_0, \varphi_0'), m, par(\varphi_1, \varphi_1')), \varphi_2)$$

In other words, if the shared behaviour is contained in an arbitrary fragment, then this fragment is preserved in the composed behaviour.

Consider the sequence diagrams SD_1 and SD_2 given in Fig. 6 which share message m_2.

The sequence diagrams can be seen as $SD_1 = alt(\varphi_0, seq(\emptyset, m2, \varphi_1))$ and $SD_2 = seq(\emptyset, m2, \varphi_1'))$, with φ_0 corresponding to a simple interaction with m_1, and similarly for φ_1 and message m_3, and φ_1' and message m_4. The composition $SD_1 \parallel_G SD_2$ as outlined above is given by $alt(\varphi_0, seq(\emptyset, m_2, par(\varphi_1, \varphi_1')))$. The composed diagram is our first sequence diagram from Fig. 1.

Given the syntactic composition of two sequence diagrams we derive the model (a labelled event structure) as described before.

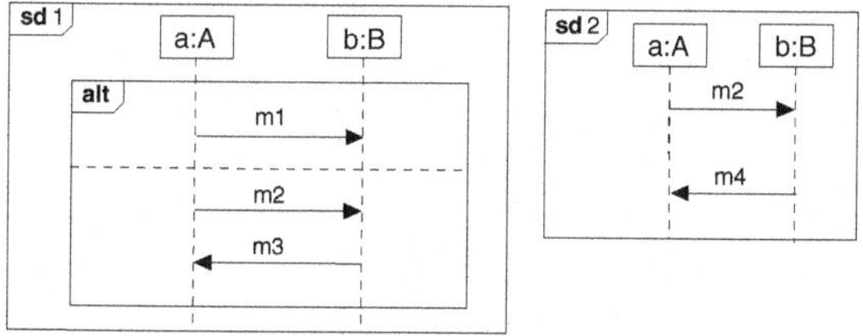

Fig. 6. Two sequence diagrams with shared message m_2.

4 Model Transformation to Alloy

We implement our composition method with the help of MDA techniques [7]. Due to space restrictions, in this paper we only discuss some of the transformation rules from sequence diagrams to Alloy. These rules can be implemented via any MDA transformation engine. Our approach is such that if an Alloy model can be solved, it generates all possible solutions each of which corresponds to a run of the original sequence diagram and in accordance to the formal semantics defined in the previous sections. The following transformation rules illustrate the transformation for `sd1` from Fig. 6.

4.1 Lifeline and Message

Each lifeline in a sequence diagram, which corresponds to an object with a name and of a given class (type), is transformed into Alloy code as follows.

```
1 abstract sig Lifeline {}
2 one sig A {}  //Lifeline Class
3 one sig a {} //Lifeline name
4 one sig sd1_L_1 extends Lifeline {name: a, type: A }
5 one sig sd1_L_2 extends Lifeline {name: b, type: B }
```

A `Lifeline` corresponds to an abstract signature refined further by concrete lifelines from a sequence diagram. The code above shows the transformation of `sd1` lifelines in Alloy. Lines 4 and 5 give concrete lifeline declarations `sd1_L_1` and `sd1_L_2`. The keyword `one` in the declaration indicates that there is exactly one instance of the signature. Furthermore, a lifeline signature has fields `name` to specify the object name and `type` to specify its class.

A message has two message ends, a send and a receive events, which cover a lifeline. A receive event cannot occur unless its corresponding send event has happened before. An event is either a send or a receive event.

```
7 abstract sig Event { cover :one Lifeline , next :set Event }
8 abstract sig Message { send :one Event , receive :one Event }
9 //a message send event always occurs before the associated receive event
10 fact MessageEventsOrder {all m: Message |
11     m.receive in m.send.next }
12 // all events correspond to send or receive events of one message
```

```
13 fact {all e: Event | one m: Message |
14     e = m.send or e = m.receive }
```

The rule above creates the domains Event and Message. In both cases these are abstract signatures with two fields. The `Event` signature has a field `cover` corresponding to a relationship with the lifeline it belongs to, and a field `next` denoting a relationship with a set of events. This relationship corresponds to the immediate causality relation from our labelled event structures. The `Message` signature has two fields `send` and `receive` both corresponding to one event. The facts on lines 10–14 describe two constraints over the elements in the domain as mentioned before and are straightforward.

A message also has a name which is introduced when creating a concrete message.

```
15 lone sig sd1_m1 extends Message { name : m1}
16 lone sig sd1_m2 extends Message { name : m2}
17 lone sig sd1_m3 extends Message { name : m3}
```

In diagram `sd1` of Fig. 6 we have three messages `m1,m2` and `m3`. The lines above show the declaration of these messages. The messages are declared as `lone` (a multiplicity keyword in Alloy meaning 0 or 1). This has to do with the fact that messages within an alternative fragment are not guaranteed to occur. We will explain this in more detail in the transformation rule for the alternative fragment.

```
18 lone sig sd1_e1 extends Event {}
19 lone sig sd1_e2 extends Event {}
20 lone sig sd1_e3 extends Event {}
21 lone sig sd1_e4 extends Event {}
22 lone sig sd1_e5 extends Event {}
23 lone sig sd1_e6 extends Event {}
24
25  // assigning events to messages
26 fact { sd1_m1.send = sd1_e1 and sd1_m1.receive = sd1_e2 and
27 sd1_m2.send = sd1_e3 and sd1_m2.receive = sd1_e4 and
28 sd1_m3.send = sd1_e5 and sd1_m3.receive = sd1_e6 }
29
30  // assigning events to lifelines
31 fact EventToLifeline {
32 sd1_e1. cover =sd1_L_1 and sd1_e2. cover =sd1_L_2
33 ...
34 sd1_e5. cover =sd1_L_1 and sd1_g6. cover =sd1_L_2 }
```

Six events are declared in lines 18–23 above. Events are always associated to the sending or receiving of messages. How these events are associated to the messages declared in lines 15–17 is given in the fact of lines 26–28, and which lifeline they cover is given in the fact of lines 31–34. All events are declared as lone as the corresponding messages fall within the scope of an alternative fragment and may therefore not occur.

In the case of sequential messages without interaction fragments, or messages within the same operand (e.g., `m2` and `m3`), this implies a total order among the events of the lifeline of an object. This is specified in Alloy by another logical constraint called `GeneralOrder` shown below for the events underlying messages `m2` and `m3`.

```
fact GeneralOrder {
  sd1_e6 in sd1_e3.^next and sd1_e5 in sd1_e4.^next
  }
```

The fact above specifies the expected ordering between events `e3` (`m2.send`) and `e6` (`m3.receive`), and between `e4` (`m2.receive`) and `e5` (`m3.send`). No statement is made about the relation between these events and those underlying `m1` because they belong to a different operand and are hence not related by causality.

4.2 Alternative Combined Fragment

For the alternative interaction fragment (aka combined fragment in UML's metamodel [4]), the transformation generates a set of abstract signatures as follows.

```
39 abstract sig Combinedfragment {
40             operand:set Operand}
41 abstract sig Operand{cover:set Event+Combinedfragment}
42
43 fact {all e: Event | lone op: Operand |
44  e in op. cover }
45
46 fact {all cf: Combinedfragment |
47  lone op: Operand | cf in op. cover }
48
49 fact {all op: Operand |
50  one cf: Combinedfragment | op in cf. operand }
51
52 // alt: exactly one operand will be executed
53 fact Alt-Execution {all CF: Combinedfragment |
54  ( CF.TYPE = CF_TYPE_ALT) => # CF.operand = 1}
```

These abstract signatures represent the main elements of combined fragments and how interactions are defined at the metamodel level in UML [4]. The abstract signature for `CombinedFragment` consists of one or more operands whereby operands contain events (i.e., cover the send and receive events of the messages defined inside it) and/or combined fragments nested within the operand. In addition, three facts impose further constraints on the elements of these domains. Fact on line 43 states that every event `e` belongs to at most one operand, and fact on line 46 states that every combined fragment `cf` belongs to at most one interaction operand (indicating fragment nesting). Fact in line 49 states that all interaction operands are operands of only one combined fragment. Finally, the `fact` in line 53 defines that at most one operand is executed. This implies that a different set of events may occur for each possible run of the code preserving the semantics of alternative combined fragments.

```
one sig CF_TYPE_ALT {}//Combinedfragment Type
one sig sd1_CF extends Combinedfragment{TYPE = CF_TYPE_ALT}
lone sig sd1_Operand_1 extends Operand{}
```

```
59 lone sig sd1_Operand_2 extends Operand{}
60
61 // Covering: Combined Fragment->Operands
62 fact{
63   sd1_Operand_1 in CF.operand
64   sd1_Operand_2 in CF.operand}
65 // Connect events to Operands
66 fact EventToOp{
67 sd1_e1 in sd1_Operand_1.cover and sd1_e2 in sd1_Operand_1.cover and
68 sd1_e3 in sd1_Operand_2.cover and sd1_e4 in sd1_Operand_2.cover and
69 sd1_e5 in sd1_Operand_2.cover and sd1_e6 in sd1_Operand_2.cover}
```

In line 56, the signature `CF_TYPE_ALT` declares the type of the combined fragment, in this case an `ALT`. Following this, in lines 57–59, three signatures define the combined fragment and the number of operands used, in this case `Operand_1` and `Operand_2`. The operands (lines 58–59) are declared as `lone` which allows the previous fact in line 53 to execute only one operand. Moreover, the facts in line 62 and 66 establish a connection between the combined fragment and its operands, and between the operands and their events, respectively.

4.3 Parallel Combined Fragment

In Alloy the representation of a parallel combined fragment (not present in Fig. 6) is similar to that of an alternative combined fragment, but without fact `Alt-Execution`. The following is an example.

```
1 one sig CF_TYPE_PAR {}//Combinedfragment Type
2 one sig sd1_CF extends Combinedfragment{
3    TYPE = CF_TYPE_PAR}
4 one sig Operand_1 extends Operand{}
5 one sig Operand_2 extends Operand{}
6 // Covering: Combined Fragment->Operands
7 fact{
8   Operand_1 in CF.operand
9   Operand_2 in CF.operand}
10   // Connect events to Operands
11 fact EventToOp{
12 sd1_e1 in sd1_Operand_1.cover and sd1_e2 in sd1_Operand_1.cover and
13 .........
14 sd1_e5 in sd1_Operand_2.cover and sd1_e6 in sd1_Operand_2.cover}
15
16 fact{all CF: Combinedfragment, OP1:  CF.operand,  OP2: CF.operand,
17    E1: OP1.cover, E2: OP2.cover, E3: OP1.cover | no  E4: OP2.cover | OP1 != OP2
18    and E2 in E1.next and E3 in E4.next  }
```

All operands of a parallel fragment are declared as `one` since they are necessarily executed. The Alloy model that contains a parallel combined fragment must show a parallel execution of `Operand_1` and `Operand_2`, i.e., the events covered by each operand are not related and can thus occur in an arbitrary order. This is given in the fact of line 16, and is in accordance to the labelled event structure semantics given earlier. It implies a relation of concurrency between events in different operands whilst the events within an operand remain ordered in the usual way. Therefore, this fact guarantees the preservation of the correct and intended order of events in a parallel fragment.

5 Composition via Alloy

In order to compose Alloy models that have been obtained by transformation from sequence diagrams, two fundamental conditions must be satisfied:

- *Matching* elements must indicate correspondence between equivalent elements of the source. The purpose of matching is to uncover how two models correspond to each other.
- *Merging* of equivalent elements identified earlier producing a composed version of the models.

In Alloy, these conditions can be encoded by adding facts that must be satisfied to match and merge equivalent elements. For example, consider two Alloy models A1 and A2 each with two lifelines, where these lifelines have the same name and type. In order to compose the lifelines with the same name from each one of the models we have to specify the following fact.

```
fact lifelineEquality {
all L1: A1_Lifeline_1 , L2: A2_lifeline_1 |
(L1.type=L2.type && L1.name=L2.name) =># L2 =0}
```

The Alloy code above shows that if the matching condition is satisfied, then lifelines will be merged into one given by L1 and L2 will be hidden. The same is true of messages. For example, if the two Alloy models A1 and A2 have two messages with the same name and involving the same objects (lifelines) then Alloy will compose these messages into one.

The idea of the procedure of merging entered models in Alloy is as follows. First we generate a new Alloy model A3 representing the result of merging the original models. Second, we copy all the elements of A1 to A3. Third, we copy all elements of A2 except the duplication elements such as abstract signatures that are shared in the two models. Fourth, for any pair of equal elements, one of the signatures keyword has to be changed from one to lone to be able to merge it and then add the merging facts mentioned above. Finally, in terms of merging messages, the merged message events (send and receive) are replaced with their equivalent message events to apply the behaviour environment of both models into this message.

To validate our approach, we implemented the example of Fig. 6 in Alloy. After solving the merged model, we obtained three Alloy solutions (also referred to as instances). These instances show exactly the expected behaviour underlying Fig. 1 with possible traces of execution: only $m1$ occurs, or $m2 \cdot (m3\ co\ m4)$ occur. Figure 7 shows two Alloy instances, one for each of the possible executions of the second operand of the alternative fragment. These instances show in particular that m_2 is always before $m3$ and $m4$, and $m3$ and $m4$ are in parallel. The complete Alloy code for the example used as well as the composed model is available from our research webpage[1].

[1] http://www.cs.bham.ac.uk/~bxb/research/matching-merging/alloy-example.

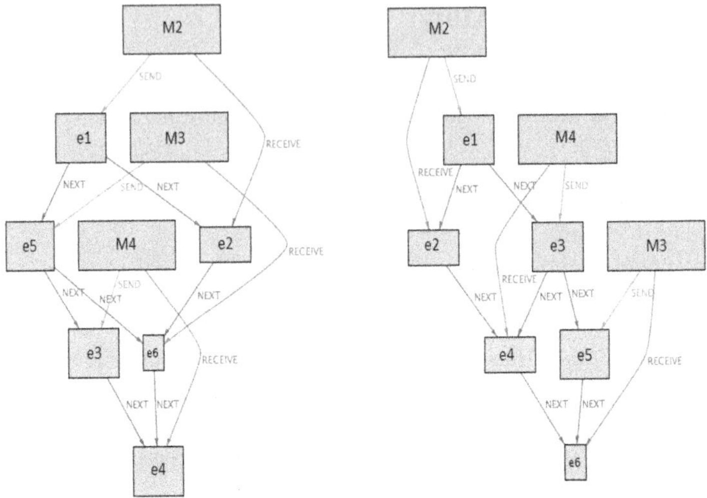

Fig. 7. Alloy instance obtained from merging sd1 and sd2 of Fig. 6.

6 The *SD2Alloy* Tool

Our approach relies on Model Driven Development (MDD) techniques that aim to enhance the role of modelling in software development [12]. It allows the developer to model the required functionality and the overall architecture of the system instead of calling on developers to spell out every detail of the system's implementation using a programming language. Hence, MDD results in reduced development cycles and lower cost of software production.

To ensure that the methods developed can be adopted by the software industry, it is crucial to follow standards set by the Model Driven Architecture (MDA) framework [7]. MDA is a framework for software development proposed by the Object Management Group (OMG). It provides a set of guidelines for the structuring of models and their specifications. It also defines a standard for applica-

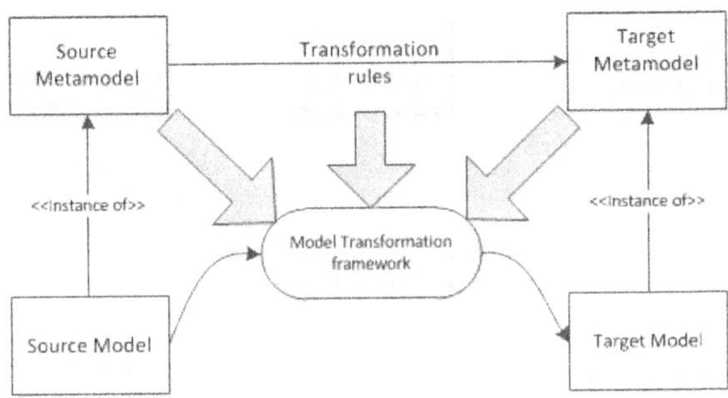

Fig. 8. An overview of MDA.

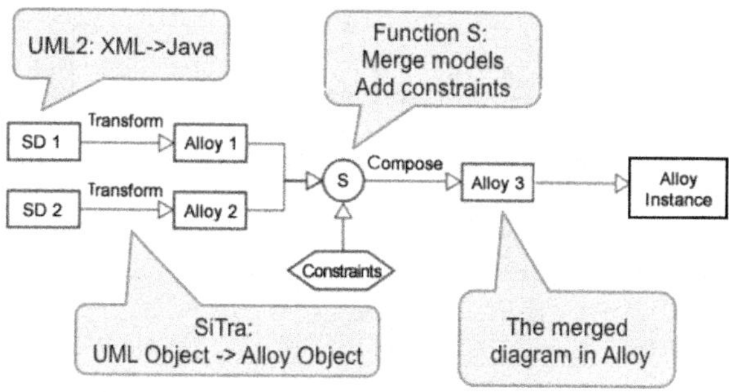

Fig. 9. The SD2Alloy architecture.

tion design and implementation. Central to MDA is the notion of metamodels [13]. A metamodel defines all elements that are available for a designer to use when modelling with a language. In MDA, a model transformation is defined by mapping the meta-elements, i.e., the constructs of the source metamodel (e.g., sequence diagrams) are mapped onto constructs in the target metamodel (e.g., Alloy) as Fig. 8 shows. Subsequently, every model arising from the source metamodel can be transformed automatically to an instance of the destination metamodel with the help of a model transformation framework such as SiTra [14].

We now give a brief description of our composition tool *SD2Alloy* which was built in accordance to MDA. The transformation rules have been implemented as an Eclipse plugin. Figure 9 depicts the *SD2Alloy* architecture. The tool includes a modified open source tool called Papyrus [16], which allows the user to generate any number of sequence diagrams, and exports these diagrams as XMI files so they can be parsed. *SD2Alloy* parses the XMI files generated by Papyrus into Java objects using the UML2 library. SiTra is used to transform the UML sequence diagrams and create the Alloy Java object that produces the Alloy code.

In Fig. 9, two sequence diagrams SD1 and SD2 are transformed individually to Alloy generating Alloy 1 and Alloy 2 respectively. Moreover, this tool allows the user to specify composition constraints required in Alloy to merge the entered models, shown as S and denoting the syntactic matching of model elements. The composition model obtained is shown as Alloy 3 which corresponds to the union of all constraints associated to the individual models Alloy 1, Alloy 2 and the glue contraints in S. If there are no conflicts in Alloy 3 then the Alloy Analyzer produces an Alloy instance (in fact as many as there are possible traces of execution in Alloy 3). If no solution can be produced, Alloy highlights the constraints that are causing a conflict. More details on the tool can be found in [15].

Figures 10 and 11 show two snapshots of the interface of *SD2Alloy*. In both cases, to the left we have a list of the current sequence diagrams used (here sd1.di and sd2.di where di is the extension name given by Papyrus) as well as the syntactic matching declarations of model elements from the different diagrams (here sd1-sd2Equality.eq). Different levels of detail can be shown on different panes in the tool with the editor in the middle showing the current diagram or

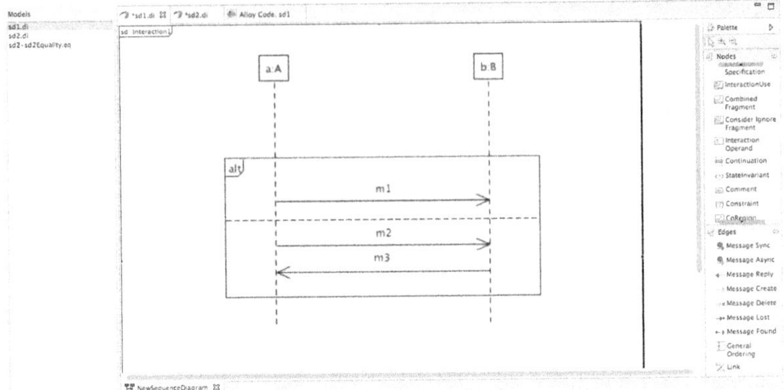

Fig. 10. A snapshot of the SD2Alloy interface.

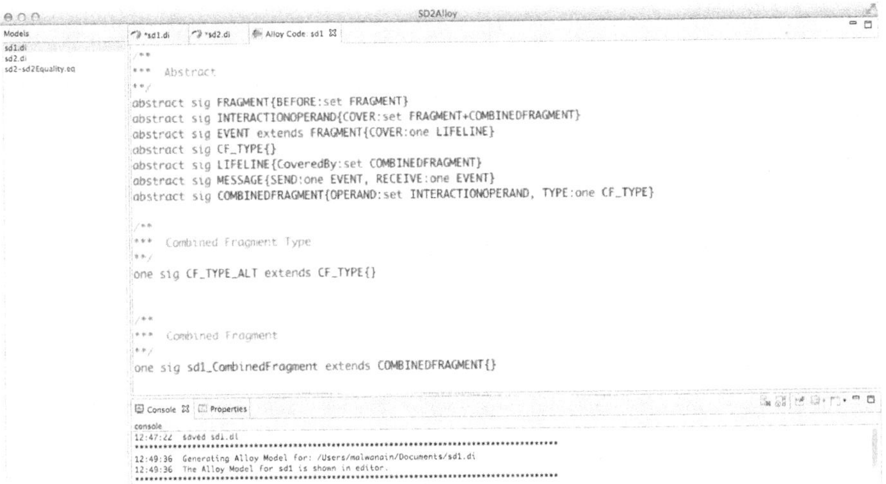

Fig. 11. Showing Alloy code in SD2Alloy.

code that is being edited. For example, in Fig. 10 we show a diagram and in Fig. 11 we look at the generated Alloy code for the same diagram. Properties of elements being edited can also be seen and changed on a separate pane at the bottom right of the tool.

7 Related Work

Over the last decade, a number of software tools and algorithms have been designed and implemented to compose behavioural models. Liang et al. [17], have presented a method of integrating sequence diagrams based on the formalisation of sequence diagrams as typed graphs. Rubin et al. [2], illustrate the use of the Alloy Analyzer to compose class diagrams based on syntactic properties of metamodels and the primary model. This approach uses UML2Alloy [18] to transform UML class diagrams into Alloy and the Alloy Analyzer to compose these classes. However, their method only composes static models and the compositional code produced is generated manually.

In addition, Widl et al. [3] present an approach for composing concurrently evolved sequence diagrams in accordance to the behaviour given in state machine models. They describe the problem of merging sequence diagrams formally using SAT solvers. However, similarly to [17], the approach does not merge complex sequence diagrams.

When looking at the integration of several model views or diagrams, [19] presents a method of mapping a design consisting of class diagrams, OCL constraints and sequence diagrams into a mathematical model for detecting and analysing inconsistencies. Finally, [20] propose a further approach to composition of sequence diagrams by composing sequence diagram operators directly. This approach is very different from ours and can be seen as a high-level composition strategy at the UML level.

8 Conclusions

In this paper, we have defined a new compositional semantics of sequence diagrams based on the true-concurrent model of labelled event structures, and presented an automated technique based on Alloy to generate a composed model in accordance to the true-concurrent semantics.

The underlying developed tool takes as input one or more sequence diagrams, and automatically constructs Alloy solutions for the composition. Each of the solutions corresponds to a run that can be derived from the underlying labelled event structure of the composed sequence diagram. Our approach has been evaluated through a series of examples and larger case studies.

References

1. La Rosa, M., Dumas, M., Uba, R., Dijkman, R.: Merging business process models. In: Meersman, R., Dillon, T.S., Herrero, P. (eds.) OTM 2010. LNCS, vol. 6426, pp. 96–113. Springer, Heidelberg (2010)
2. Rubin, J., Chechik, M., Easterbrook, S.: Declarative approach for model composition. In: MiSE 2008, pp. 7–14. ACM (2008)
3. Widl, M., Biere, A., Brosch, P., Egly, U., Heule, M., Kappel, G., Seidl, M., Tompits, H.: Guided merging of sequence diagrams. In: Czarnecki, K., Hedin, G. (eds.) SLE 2012. LNCS, vol. 7745, pp. 164–183. Springer, Heidelberg (2013)
4. OMG: UML: Superstructure. Version 2.4.1. OMG (2011). http://www.omg.org, Document id: formal/2011-08-06. Accessed 1 June 2012
5. Winskel, G., Nielsen, M.: Models for concurrency. In: Abramsky, S., Gabbay, D., Maibaum, T. (eds.) Handbook of Logic in Computer Science. Semantic Modelling, vol. 4, pp. 1–148. Oxford Science Publications (1995)

6. Küster-Filipe, J.: Modelling concurrent interactions. Theor. Comput. Sci. **351**, 203–220 (2006)
7. Kleppe, A., Warmer, J., Bast, W.: MDA Explained: The Model Driven Architecture: Practice and Promise. Addison-Wesley, Boston (2003)
8. Harel, D., Marelly, R.: Come, Let's Play: Scenario-Based Programming Using LSCs and the Play-Engine. Springer, Heidelberg (2003)
9. Micskei, Z., Waeselynck, H.: The many meanings of UML 2 sequence diagrams: a survey. Softw. Syst. Model. **10**, 489–514 (2011)
10. Jackson, D.: Software Abstractions: Logic, Language and Analysis. MIT Press, Cambridge (2006)
11. Berre, D.L., Parrain, A.: The SAT4j library, release 2.2 - system description. J. Satisfiability, Boolean Model. Comput. **7**, 59–64 (2010)
12. Stahl, T., Völter, M.: Model-Driven Software Development. Wiley, Chichester (2006)
13. Gonzalez-Perez, C., Henderson-Sellers, B.: Metamodelling for Software Engineering. Wiley, Chichester (2008)
14. Akehurst, D.H., Bordbar, B., Evans, M.J., Howells, W.G.J., McDonald-Maier, K.D.: SiTra: simple transformations in java. In: Wang, J., Whittle, J., Harel, D., Reggio, G. (eds.) MoDELS 2006. LNCS, vol. 4199, pp. 351–364. Springer, Heidelberg (2006)
15. Chen, Y.: Automated synthesis of sequence diagrams. Master's thesis, University of Birmingham (2013)
16. Lanusse, A., Tanguy, Y., Espinoza, H., et al.: Papyrus UML: an open source toolset for MDA. In: ECMDA-FA 2009, pp. 1–4 (2009)
17. Liang, H., Diskin, Z., Dingel, J., Posse, E.: A general approach for scenario integration. In: Czarnecki, K., Ober, I., Bruel, J.-M., Uhl, A., Völter, M. (eds.) MODELS 2008. LNCS, vol. 5301, pp. 204–218. Springer, Heidelberg (2008)
18. Bordbar, B., Anastasakis, K.: Uml2alloy: a tool for lightweight modelling of discrete event systems. In: IADIS International Conference in Applied Computing, vol. 1, pp. 209–216 (2005)
19. Bowles, J., Bordbar, B.: A formal model for integrating multiple views. In: ACSD 2007, pp. 71–79. IEEE (2007)
20. Araújo, J., Whittle, J., Kim, D.: Modeling and composing scenario-based requirements with aspects. In: RE 2004, pp. 58–67. IEEE (2004)

Use Case and User Interface Patterns for Data Oriented Applications

António Miguel Rosado da Cruz(✉)

Escola Superior de Tecnologia e Gestão, Instituto Politécnico de Viana do Castelo, Av. do Atlântico, s/n, Viana do Castelo, Portugal
miguel.cruz@estg.ipvc.pt

Abstract. Use case driven software development starts, in general, with abstract problem domain descriptions of how the users see themselves using the system being developed, and involves a series of iterative refinement steps that incrementally add detail to the use case model, bringing those descriptions to the solution domain. Use cases involve interactions between human actors and the system state. These interactions are held within interaction spaces, which are modeled through a user interface model. Business applications are in general data-driven, comprising a set of typical functions that the users can make on the system. When a use case driven approach is used to develop data-oriented applications those typical functions pop-up as use case patterns, and their interactions occur within a set of user interface patterns. This paper presents a set of use case patterns and the corresponding user interface patterns typically found in data-oriented business applications. For that, a user interface metamodel and corresponding concrete user interface modeling language are also proposed.

Keywords: Use case model · Use case patterns · Interaction modeling · User interface model · User interface patterns · Model-driven development

1 Introduction

Use cases are present in most software projects, and evolve iteratively since the first analysis activities until the activities of design and coding. Use case driven software development encourages software engineers to follow an approach that is guided by the system functionality. This approach, typically starts with high-level problem domain descriptions of how the users see themselves using the system being developed, and involves a series of iterative refinement steps that incrementally detail the use case model, bringing those descriptions to the solution domain [1]. These refinement steps comprise the simultaneous development of a domain model, which models the domain entities and the structural relations between them [2], and the model of the system state on which the system functionality will act upon. Such a process produces increasingly detailed use case models and domain entity models that must be kept consistent with each other [3].

According to the UML specification [4], a use case, being a *BehavioredClassifier*, specifies some offered behaviors, which involve interactions between its actors and a subject comprising a collection of classifiers. This collection of classifiers that form the

S. Hammoudi et al. (Eds.): MODELSWARD 2014, CCIS 506, pp. 117–133, 2015.
DOI: 10.1007/978-3-319-25156-1_8

subject of a use case may be the system state or a partial view of the system state containing the domain entities affected by the use case behaviors (its functionality). Use case behaviors may be semi-formally specified, in UML, through various means, including state machines, activities, interactions, pre-conditions, post-conditions and natural language text [4].

As the use case model becomes more detailed, with use cases including or being extended by other, more concrete, use cases, its use case specifications become more obvious, and each use case behaviors may be informally inferred from a short description or from the use case name itself. These use case behaviors act on one or more system domain entity instances (its subject or collaborative entity classes) [4], so the use case model needs to be closely related to the system domain model. This proximity is in the sense that the use case behaviors refer to entities from the domain model [5].

Indeed, at platform independent level, use case (UC) and domain models are two sub-models (views) of one and the same system model. The former models a vision of the system functionality, and the latter models a vision of its structural features [2]. Other relevant model views are the system user interface (UI) view, modeled by a user interface model (UIM), and a behavioral view, which is, in this approach, divided between class methods and invariant constraints in the domain model and through use case behaviors, which may be specified as mentioned above [5].

When confining ourselves to data-oriented applications, which constitute the vast majority of business applications, the use case model tends to present a set of use case patterns that comprise typical functions that the users can make on the system [6]. Similarly, the spaces (user interface) where those use case patterns interactions take place form, at a platform independent level, a set of user interface patterns. This paper's main contribution is the presentation, in Sect. 5, of the user interface patterns related to the use case patterns previously presented in [6], and summarized in Sect. 3. Another major contribution is the proposition of a UI metamodel, aligned with UML, and the corresponding UI modeling concrete notation, in Sect. 4.

The next section addresses some background issues concerning abstract user interface models and the UML use case metamodel. Section 3 presents the mentioned set of use case patterns typically found in business (data-oriented) applications. In Sect. 4, a UI metamodel and the concrete notation for constructing UI models is proposed, and in Sect. 5, the set of abstract user interface patterns corresponding to the use case patterns previously defined, is presented. Section 6 illustrates the relation between use case and UI patterns through a demonstration case. Section 7 overviews related work and, finally, Sect. 8 concludes the paper.

2 Background

This section addresses some background issues, namely user interface models and the Canonical Abstract Prototypes (CAP) notation for modeling abstract user interface models, in the next subsection, and the UML use case metamodel, in Subsect. 2.2.

CAP will be used, in Subsect. 4.2, as a basis for proposing a concrete notation for abstract UI models that conform to the metamodel proposed in Sect. 4.

2.1 Abstract User Interface Models

User Interface model-based development techniques build a more or less declarative User Interface Model (UIM), which is typically composed of various sub-models, or model views. This UIM captures the relevant aspects of the UI and is typically developed using a model-based user interface development environment (MB-UIDE) [7]. Different MB-UIDEs use different kinds of models specified with different kinds of modeling languages.

Typically, a model-based UI development process begins with the construction of a task model [7, 8]. Afterwards, an abstract interaction model (or abstract UI model) is built and at the end of the process a concrete interaction model (or concrete UI model) is constructed.

User Interface Models provide a description of the UI at different levels of abstraction. Platform dependent (concrete) user interface models make use of widgets and functionality that may be specific to one given platform. Platform independent declarative (abstract) user interface models provide an abstract description of the UI, which can be reused and can be refined to more concrete (platform dependent) models.

UIMs can, then, be found at different levels of abstraction during the UI design process. A UIM provides an infrastructure for allowing automated tasks in the UI design and implementation processes.

Canonical Abstract Prototypes is an approach and notation, proposed by Constantine [9], for capturing the presentation aspects of interactive systems. Canonical Abstract Prototypes capture only the abstract presentation aspects of a user interface, by making use of abstract interaction objects (AIO), which are UI elements that don't have a unique concrete representation.

CAP is based on 3 extensible generic universal symbols [9]:

1. Material (or generic container): represents information, data or other objects shown to the user during a task.
2. Tool (or generic action/operation): represents UI objects that can be used to manipulate, control or transform materials.
3. Hybrid (or active material): represents UI components with characteristics both from materials and tools like, for instance, editable fields or lists of selectable items.

Figure 1 shows the main symbols of the canonical abstract notation, which allow the development of abstract user interface models (AUIM) like the one shown in Fig. 2. The figure shows a prototype of a selectable list and the output of detailed information about the selected list item. The symbol ⋙ represents repetition and, in the example, it means that the aligned elements in the Film Clips selectable collection are repeated in every line.

2.2 Use Cases in the UML Metamodel

Use cases can be used both for modeling the external requirements of a subject and the functionality offered by a subject. In both cases the subject can be the system domain model or a subset of it. Moreover, use cases can also be used to specify the requirements the subject (the system) poses on its environment, by defining how the actors should interact with the subject [4].

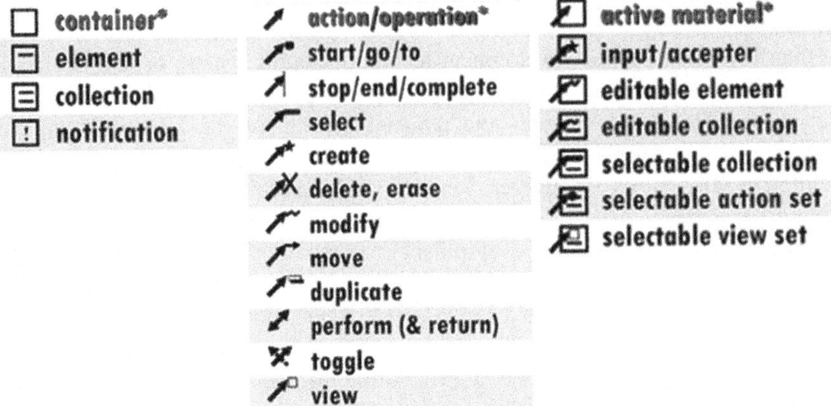

Fig. 1. Canonical abstract prototypes symbols (adapted from [9]).

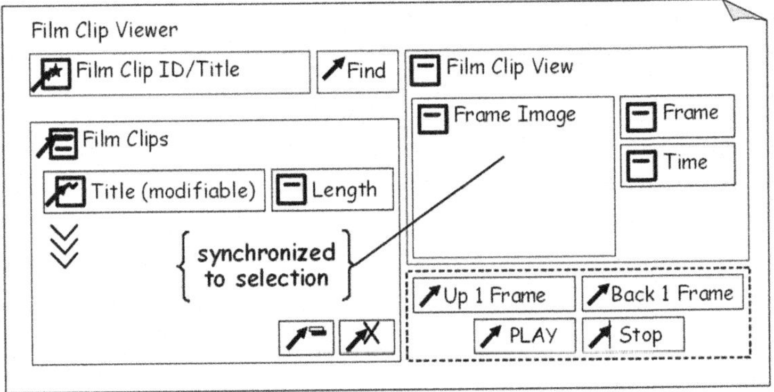

Fig. 2. Example of a CAP for a Film Clip Viewer (taken from [9]).

The UML metamodel for use cases (see Fig. 3) supplies two use case relations, namely Extend and Include, which allow the modeler to organize a use case behaviors into further refined behaviors that are included in a bigger, more complex, use case, and optional or conditional behaviors that may extend the bigger use case by the actors' option or when certain pre-conditions hold.

Besides those two relations, as a (*Behaviored*) Classifier, a use case may also specialize another use case through an Inheritance relation. A use case that inherits from another use case, inherits all its features (included use cases, associated Domain Model Classifiers and Features, etc.).

Use cases comprise behaviors that can be instantiated within an interaction. Those behaviors consist of a specification of events that may occur dynamically over time [4]. On a behavior invocation, the actual sequence of events that occur, and are consistent with the behavior specification, is called an execution trace [4]. An execution is, then, an instance of a Behavior.

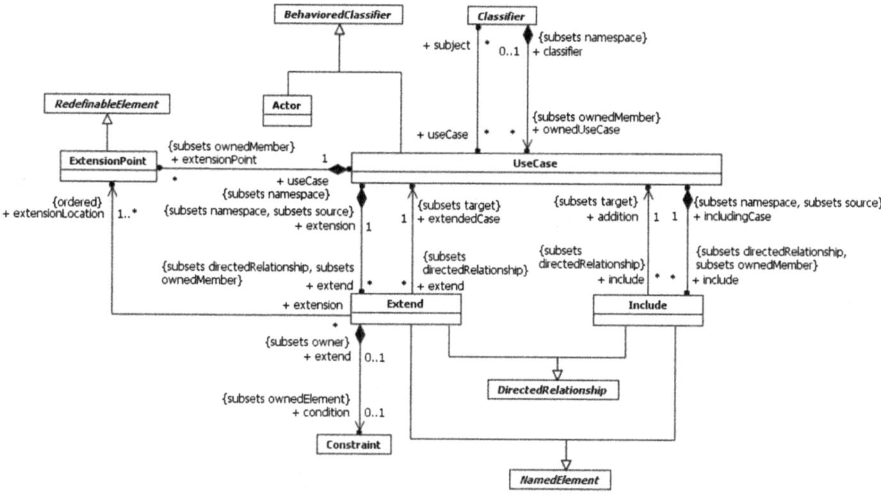

Fig. 3. Use cases portion of the UML metamodel (taken from [4]).

A system use case model acts upon the system domain model, whose instance forms the system state.

Use cases define behaviors that may modify the system state. Those behaviors occur within interactions, which form the space where actors interact with the system, in the scope of a use case.

A use case behavior can be seen as an orchestrator of its owned subject's behavioral features. In a model-driven setting, a use case behavior can be defined, for instance, through Alf, OMG's proposal for Action Semantics concrete notation [10].

The simpler types of use case behavior consist of calling CRUD (create/retrieve/update/delete) operations over domain entities (the use case subject), user-defined operations enclosed in methods within the use case subject, and navigational operations over domain entities that are available within each use case.

The use case model also identifies the actors (user roles) that have access to each use case (system functionality), thus providing authorization information about the system.

When focusing on data-oriented applications, a set of use case patterns, and associated behavior and domain model entities (subjects), can be identified, as addressed in the next section.

3 Use Case Patterns for Data-Oriented Applications

Data oriented applications have as main functionality the management of stored entities' information. Operations in such applications typically include listing the (possibly filtered) instances of an entity, editing entity properties, defining or modifying entities' relationships, etc., and may be grouped in the following use case patterns [3, 6]:

- Manage an entity instance;
- Manage dependent related entity instances;
- Manage independent related entity instances;
- Manage dependent related entity collections;
- Manage independent related entity collections.

This section presents these typical functionality patterns, modeled as use case diagrams, taking the form of use case patterns that can be used in constructing a system's use case model.

Two categories of use cases can be distinguished in the patterns presented herein [3, 11]:

- Independent use cases: can be initiated directly, and so can be linked directly to actors, which initiate them. Independent use cases cannot extend and cannot be included in any other use case.
- Dependent use cases: can only be initiated from within other use cases, called source use cases, because they depend on the context set by these. Dependent use cases extend or are included by the source ones, according to their optional or mandatory nature, respectively.

Some use cases may exhibit characteristics from either of these categories, depending on the use case where the actor-system interaction begins.

3.1 Manage an Entity Instance

Managing an entity instance typically involves listing all or some of the existing instances, and selecting one of those instances for editing (retrieving its information for visualizing, updating or deleting it), or creating a new instance.

"Manage an entity instance" is, thus, a use case pattern comprising three use cases where use cases for creating an entity instance (Create E1; see Fig. 4(a)) and editing an existing instance (Retrieve, Update, Delete E1) are dependent of, and extend, the use case for listing existing instances (List E1).

List E1 may also be extended with a use case for defining filtering criteria. And, of course, Create E1 might also be directly accessed by actors.

As specified in [3, 11], each use case references an entity (its subject) through a tagged value, for consistency between models. All use cases of this pattern refer to the same entity in the domain model (E1).

3.2 Manage Dependent Related Entity Instance

A dependent related entity instance is an instance of an entity E2 that has a "one to one" or a "zero-or-one to one" association with E1 (refer to Fig. 4(b)).

Managing the instance of E2 associated to a given instance of E1 typically involves creating a new related instance (Create Related E2, in Fig. 4(b)), or editing the existing related instance (Retrieve, Update, Delete Related E2).

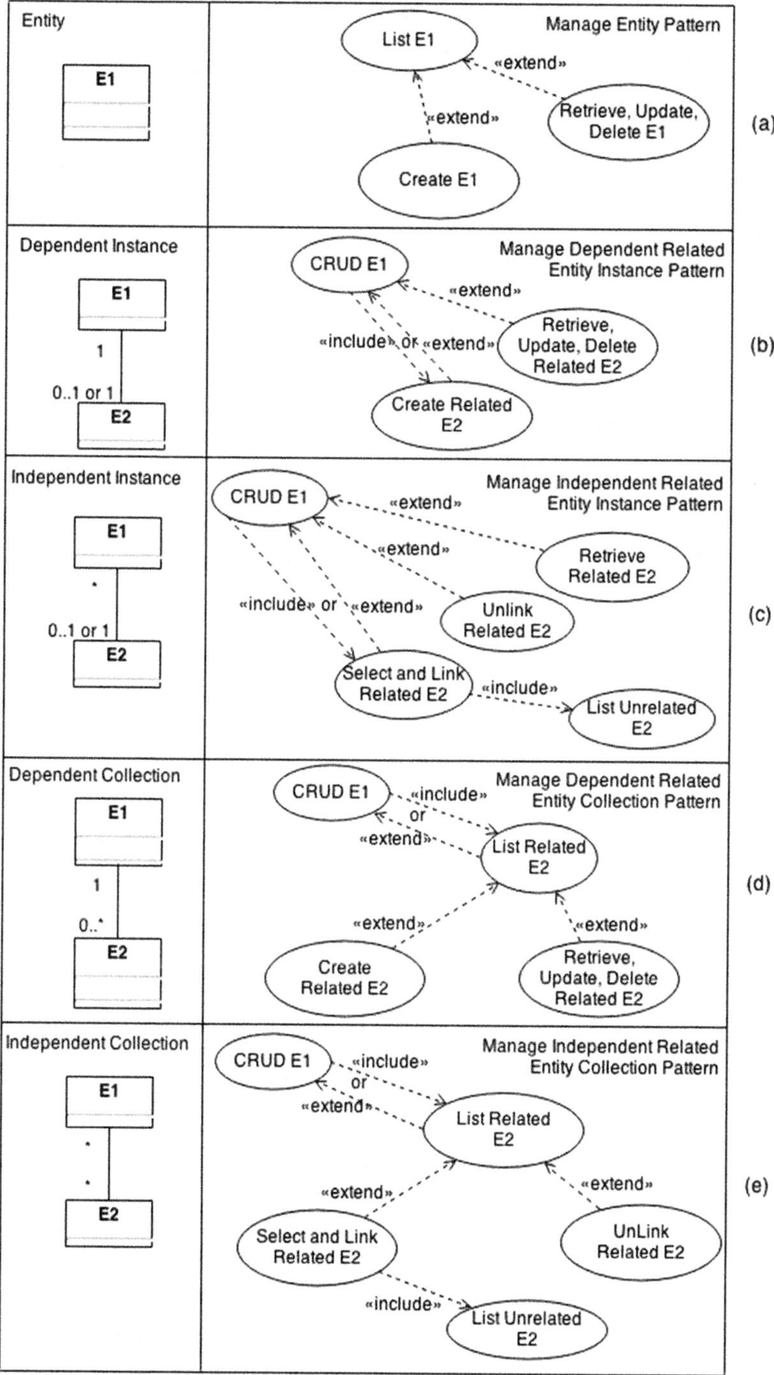

Fig. 4. Use case patterns and the corresponding appropriate patterns in the domain model.

These two use cases are available from within the use case that allows creating or editing the instance of E1 (CRUD E1, in Fig. 4(b)).

"Manage dependent related entity instance" is, therefore, a use case pattern comprising the three use cases referred to above, where CRUD E1 references instance E1, in the case of a "zero-or-one to one" association between E2 and E1, and it needs to reference E1 and E2, in the case of a "one to one" association between the two instances.

The other two use cases need to reference, as subject, both instance E1 and E2, because, creating or updating E2 always demands a related E1.

3.3 Manage Independent Related Entity Instance

An independent related entity instance is an instance of an entity E2 that has a "one to many" or a "zero-or-one to many" association with E1.

Managing the instance of E2 associated to a given instance of E1 typically involves linking (Select and Link Related E2, in Fig. 4(c)) or unlinking (Unlink Related E2) an existing instance of E2, or simply retrieving its information (Retrieve Related E2). These three use cases are available from within the use case that allows creating or editing the instance of E1 (CRUD E1, in Fig. 4(c)).

Use case "Select and Link Related E2" includes a use case for listing existing instances of E2 not related to the instance of E1 being managed (List Unrelated E2).

As a result, "Manage independent related entity instance" is a use case pattern comprising the five use cases referred to above, where CRUD E1 references an instance of E1, in the case of a "zero-or-one to many" association between E2 and E1, and it needs to reference E1 and E2, in the case of a "one to many" association between the two instances.

The other use cases need to reference instances of both E1 and E2, because, creating or updating E2 may imply a related instance of E1.

3.4 Manage Dependent Related Entity Collection

Dependent related entities are the instances of an entity E2 that have a mandatory "to one" association to E1. Managing the collection of instances of E2 associated to a given instance of E1 typically involves listing all or some of the existing related instances, and selecting one of those instances for editing (retrieving its information for visualizing, updating or deleting it), or creating a new related instance.

"Manage dependent related entity collection" is, hence, a use case pattern comprising four use cases where use cases for creating a new related instance (Create Related E2, in Fig. 4(d)) and editing existing related instances (Retrieve, Update, Delete Related E2) extend the use case for listing existing related instances (List Related E2), which in turn extends or is included in a use case where E1 is managed (CRUD E1).

3.5 Manage Independent Related Entity Collection

Independent related entities are the instances of an entity E2 that have an optional shared "to one" or "to many" association with E1. Managing the collection of instances of E2 associated to a given instance of E1 typically involves listing all or some of the existing related instances, and selecting one of those instances retrieving its information or unlinking it, or selecting an existing unrelated instance of E2 and link it to E1.

"Manage independent related entity collection" is, so, a use case pattern comprising five use cases where use cases for selecting and linking a related instance (Select and Link Related E2, in Fig. 4(e)) and unlinking existing related instances (Unlink Related E2) extend the use case for listing existing related instances (List Related E2), which in turn extends or is included in a use case where E1 is managed (CRUD E1). Also, use case "Select and Link Related E2" includes a use case for listing existing instances of E2 not related to the instance of E1 being managed (List Unrelated E2).

4 UI Metamodel and Modeling Notation

Use cases comprise behaviors that occur within interactions between a user playing the role of an actor (user role) and the system. An Interaction occurs within an interaction space. As seen in Sect. 2, interaction spaces may be specified through a User Interface Model, which, just as the use case and domain models we have been addressing, shall be defined in a platform independent manner.

As we are focusing on data-oriented applications, and these typically exhibit form-based user interfaces, the following subsections present a metamodel for developing form-based abstract user interface models (AUIM) at a platform independent level, and the concrete notation for modeling UIs according to the defined metamodel.

4.1 A Metamodel for User Interface Modeling

For enabling the construction of an AUIM, a metamodel for form-based UI modeling is proposed in this subsection. The proposed metamodel (see Fig. 5), extends UML by importing its packages, and is an evolution of the metamodel presented in [5, 11], which has been refined and simplified.

An interaction space (*InteractionSpace* in the figure) is an abstract UI space where interaction between a human actor (user role) and the system takes place, in the context of a use case. An *InteractionSpace* is composed of *InteractionBlocks*, which may contain a set of *DataAIO* elements. Both interaction spaces and interaction blocks may contain *ActionAIO* objects, which may navigate to another interaction space, trigger operations on the user interface (e.g.: *CancelOp*), or execute domain operations, which are behaviors associated to the use cases whose interactions take place within that interaction space, or methods of the domain entities belonging to the subject of those use cases (e.g.: CRUD operations).

An *InteractionBlock* is associated to one entity class (entity), from the domain model, and may be optionally associated to another class (master_entity) associated with the former, enabling master-detail information in an interaction space, provided

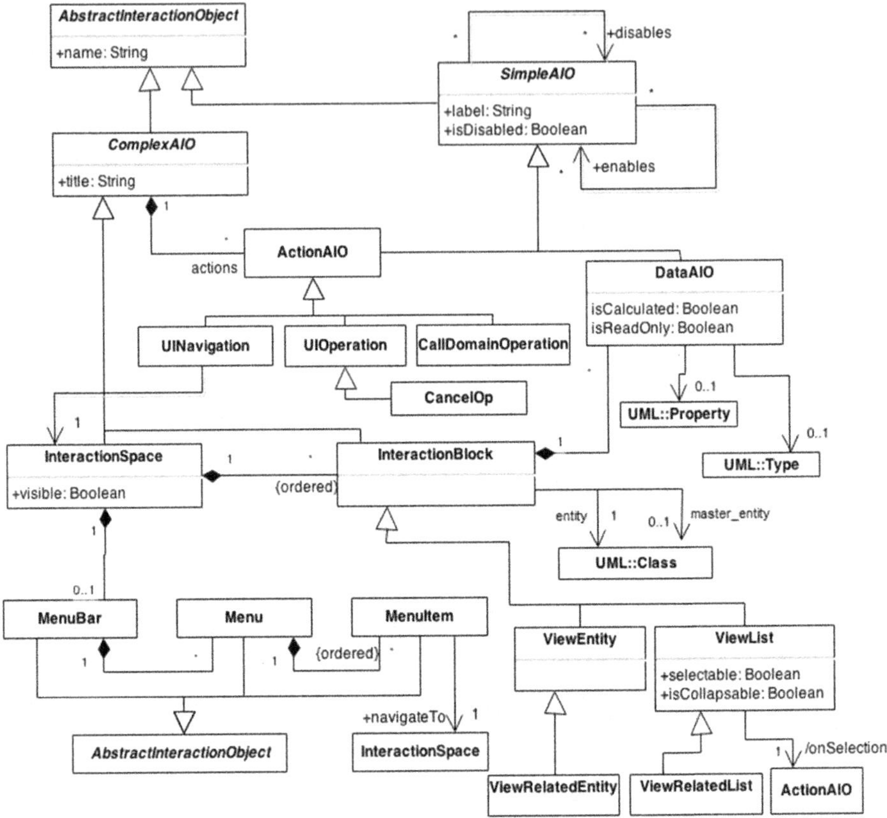

Fig. 5. User interface metamodel.

that in the same interaction space another interaction block is associated to the latter entity as its mandatory entity.

An *InteractionSpace* may contain a menu bar, composed of menus that aggregate menu items, each one of these allowing the navigation to another interaction space.

An *InteractionBlock* has four specializations:

- *ViewEntity,* which represents a *form* associated to an entity in the domain model;
- *ViewList,* which represents a *list* associated to an entity in the domain model;
- *ViewRelatedEntity,* representing a *form* associated to two entities in the domain model that have a dependent instance ("one to one" or "one to zero-or-one") or independent instance ("many to one" or "many to zero-or-one") relation between them, the one side entity being the master_entity and the other side entity being the main entity;
- *ViewRelatedList,* that represents a *list* associated to two entities in the domain model that have a dependent collection ("one to many") relation between them, the one side entity being the master_entity and the other side entity being the main entity, or

an independent collection ("many to many"), being either one of them the master_entity and the other one, the main entity.

An *InteractionBlock* may contain *DataAIO*s, which may have a type and may be associated to properties in the domain model entities. A *SimpleAIO* (*DataAIO* or *ActionAIO*) may enable or disable other *SimpleAIO*s when interacted with.

4.2 UI Model Concrete Notation

In this subsection, a concrete notation for abstract UI models that conform to the previously presented metamodel, is proposed.

Note that the concrete presentation of the final UI is not the goal of an AUIM. This way, the concrete notation for the AUIM shall be simple and leverage the aspects we want to address within this kind of models, that include the user interface interaction spaces, their contents, the relation between UI elements, navigation between spaces or action elements and the behavior triggered by them.

Table 1 shows the proposed concrete symbols for the UI modeling concepts defined in the proposed UI metamodel. The language symbols are borrowed from CAP.

Table 1. Relation between concrete symbols from CAP and the UI modeling language concepts proposed in the metamodel.

CAP symbol	CAP meaning	Proposed Metaclass Identified by symbol	Constraints
	container	InteractionSpace	
	container	InteractionBlock	
	container	ViewEntity / ViewRelatedEntity	
	collection	ViewList / ViewRelatedList	
	Selectable collection	ViewList / ViewRelatedList	selectable = true
	input/accepter	DataAIO	
	editable element	DataAIO	isCalculated = true
	element	DataAIO	isReadOnly = true
	action/operation	ActionAIO	
	delete, erase	CancelOp (UIOperation)	
	start/go/to	UINavigation	
	perform (&return)	CallDomainOperation	

5 UI Patterns for Use Case Patterns' Interactions

Just as data-oriented systems typically include the use case patterns identified in Sect. 3, which can be used in constructing the use case model, also their UIM typically includes a set of UI patterns in which the use case patterns' interactions take place.

Figure 6 presents the previously identified use case patterns and the corresponding UI patterns. The presented UI patterns comprise a set of *InteractionBlocks*, which may be in the same or different *InteractionSpaces*.

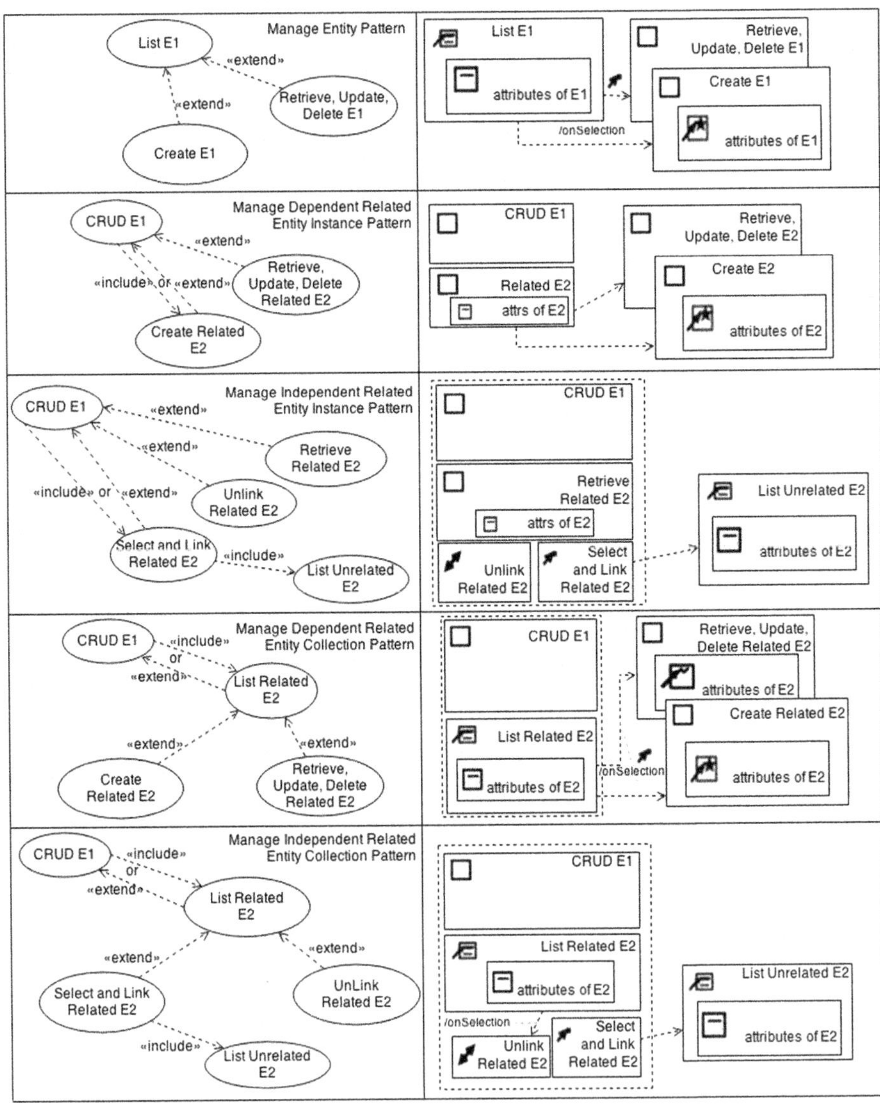

Fig. 6. Use case patterns for data-centered applications and the corresponding UI patterns.

The UI pattern for the "Manage Entity" use case pattern comprises a *ViewList* that lists instances of domain entity E1, from where a *ViewEntity* block for creating new instances of E1, or a *ViewEntity* block for retrieving, updating or deleting an existing instance of E1, may be accessed. Both of these *ViewEntity* blocks will contain *DataAIOs* related to the attributes of E1. *ViewList* for listing instances of E1 may contain *DataAIOs* related to all attributes of E1 or to attributes used for unique identification of instances by the users (e.g.: stereotyped as «ident», as proposed in [11]).

UI pattern corresponding to the "Manage Dependent Related Entity Instance" use case pattern comprises, besides the *ViewEntity* for performing CRUD operations on an instance of E1, a *ViewEntity* for displaying the identification attributes of the related instance of E2, which will contain *UINavigation ActionAIOs* for allowing navigating to *ViewEntity* blocks for creating a new related instance of E2 or for retrieving, updating or deleting the existing related instance of E2.

UI pattern corresponding to the "Manage Independent Related Entity Instance" use case pattern comprises, besides the *ViewEntity* for performing CRUD operations on an instance of E1, a *ViewEntity* for retrieving and displaying all or the identification attributes of the related independent instance of E2. A "Select and Link Related E2" *UINavigation ActionAIO* will allow navigating to a *ViewList* block for selecting and linking a new related instance of E2. An *ActionAIO* is also present for performing the domain operation of unlinking the existing related instance of E2.

Besides the *ViewEntity* for performing CRUD operations on an instance of E1, the UI pattern corresponding to the "Manage Dependent Related Entity Collection" use case pattern, comprises a *ViewList* for displaying all or the identification attributes of the related instances of E2. On selecting an instance of E2 from the list, a *UINavigation ActionAIO* will allow navigating to an interaction space containing a *ViewEntity* block for retrieving, updating or deleting an existing related instance of E2. Other *UINavigation ActionAIOs* will allow navigating to a *ViewEntity* block for creating a new related instance of E2.

UI pattern corresponding to the "Manage Independent Related Entity Collection" use case pattern comprises, besides the *ViewEntity* for performing CRUD operations on an instance of E1, a *ViewList* for displaying all or the identification attributes of the related independent instances of E2. A "Select and Link Related E2" *UINavigation ActionAIO* will allow navigating to a *ViewList* block for selecting and linking new related instances of E2. An *ActionAIO* is also present for performing the domain operation of unlinking an existing related instance of E2.

6 Demonstration Case

This section shows a demonstration case to illustrate some of the use case patterns, and the corresponding user interface patterns.

Figure 7 shows the partial domain and use case models for a car rental system. The use case model in the figure has three blocks marked, corresponding to three previously identified use case patterns: (A) "Manage Entity", (B) "Manage Dependent Related Entity Collection", and (C) "Manage Independent Related Entity Instance".

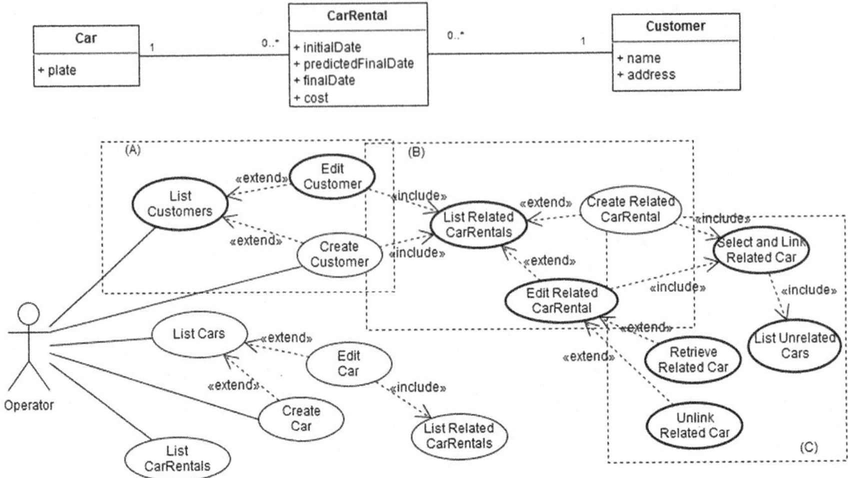

Fig. 7. Car rental partial domain and use case models.

The UI model excerpt corresponding to the bold use cases in the three blocks marked in the use case model is illustrated in Fig. 8. It starts with an interaction space "List Customers" with a selectable *ViewList* associated to Customer, which lists the instances of Customer. Selecting a customer from the list triggers the navigation to an interaction space with two interaction blocks: a *ViewEntity* with editable *DataAIOs*, associated to Customer, and a *ViewRelatedList* associated to CarRentals, with Customer as master entity. The selection of a car rental navigates to interaction space "Edit Related CarRental", that has a *ViewEntity* with read only *DataAIOs* displaying the

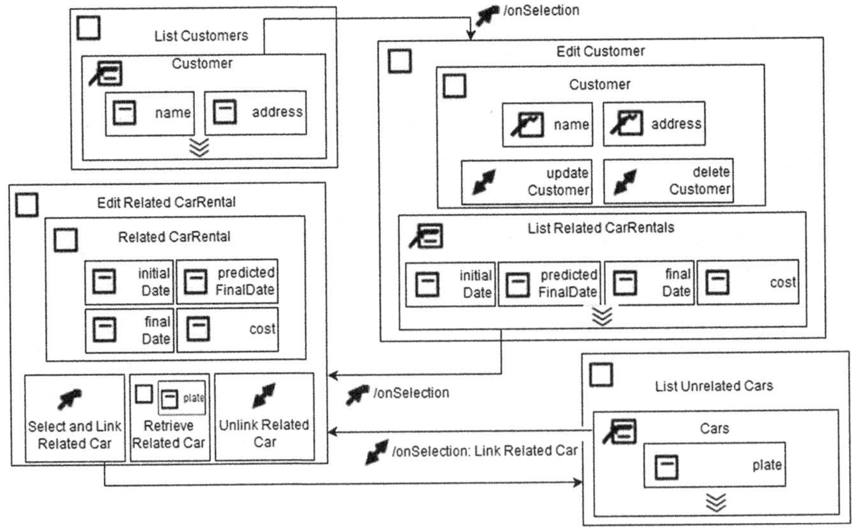

Fig. 8. Partial UI model for the car rental example.

selected car rental details. From there, the user may unlink the Car from the CarRental or navigate to another space with a *ViewList* listing the cars unrelated to the selected car rental, where the selection of a car triggers its linking to the previously selected CarRental.

7 Related Works

A few works that relate abstract UI elements with use cases have been proposed. Radeke *et al.* [12] propose an approach that interactively generates an abstract UI model, and then a concrete UI, by applying UI-patterns to elements of UI sub-models (e.g. task models). The approach is based on the manual selection of patterns, from a repository, that drives the UI model construction.

Costa *et al.* [13] combine CAP and task models to build abstract UI models, and from there obtain concrete Web Interfaces. The approach is based on the specification of a UI model comprising an abstract presentation model, a dialog model and a task model, together allowing the generation of a final concrete UI.

Martínez *et al.* [14] present a methodology for deriving UIs from early requirements existing in an organization's business process model. Their approach involves building a use case model and specifying each use case normal and alternative scenarios, which are then enriched with UI related information. The UI enriched scenario specifications are used in the generation of graphic components of the interface.

Elkoutbi *et al.* [15] propose formalizing use cases through a set of UML collaboration diagrams, each corresponding to a use case scenario. Each collaboration diagram message is manually labeled with UI constraints, from which it will then automatically produce message constraints with UI widget information. Elkoutbi's approach is then able to derive UI standalone prototypes for each interface object defined in the domain model.

Elkoutbi *et al.* and Martinez *et al.* approaches are able to produce a UI from the structural, use case and UI behavioral models, but demand the attachment of UI related information (input/output fields and/or widgets) to the use case detail specification, respectively collaboration diagrams and message sequence charts.

None of the surveyed approaches is restricted to data-oriented applications, but they all demand building a complete UIM. By restricting ourselves to data-oriented systems, our approach enables the generation of an UIM, from a system's use case model, easing the process of constructing the UIM. This is made by identifying patterns in use case models and generating the corresponding UI patterns in the UIM. Our approach also provides a concrete UI modeling language that enables modifying and completing the generated UIM, especially for the parts of the use case model that do not form an identifiable pattern and for which a UIM portion is not, consequently, generated.

8 Conclusions

This paper is based on the assertion that a system model has four views: structural view, where informational requirements are modeled through a domain model; functional view, where system functionality, and the user roles that may access it, are modeled through a use case model; user interface view, modeling the spaces where interaction within use cases take place, and a behavioral view, modeling the system behaviors or behavioral constraints.

Use cases, then, control which roles (actors) may access which system functionality, and hold the functionality that is executed in the context of an interaction, through execution traces, by instantiating available behaviors. Use cases may, then, be seen as providing services to the UI, which are based on the CRUD or user defined operations distributed as behavioral features in the system state (the domain model).

This view allowed us to propose the modeling of the abstract UI for use case interactions, based on a proposed UI metamodel and corresponding concrete notation. We also proposed a set of use case patterns and the corresponding UI patterns, which may be used when modeling data-oriented systems. These relations between use case and UI patterns enable the pattern based generation of the abstract UIM from the use case and domain models, as proposed in [5, 11], and for which a model-transformation prototype has been built [5]. In this setting, the proposed UIM concrete language allows the abstract UIM modification after its generation and before generating concrete UIMs for different target platforms [5].

Ongoing work, in the context of project Amalia (**A**gile **M**odel-driven **A**pp**LI**c**A**tion Development Method and Tools), aims at developing a modeling tool for the integrated modeling of the domain, use case and user interface model views of a system. The domain and use case models may be, however, developed using any UML tool, as the UML alone provides the needed mechanisms to associate domain entities and use cases, namely tagged values. In fact, a UML profile can be defined as a convenient and lightweight means, associated with a UML modeling tool, of building the domain and use case models. For developing the UIM, an appropriate modeling tool needs to be constructed, though. And that is one of the ongoing Amalia project's goals.

References

1. Jacobson, I., Booch, G., Rumbaugh, J.: The Unified Software Development Process. Addison Wesley, Reading (1998)
2. Frankel, D.S.: Model Driven Architecture - Applying MDA to Enterprise Computing. Wiley Publishing Inc., Indianapolis (2003)
3. Cruz, A.M.R., Faria, J.P.: Automatic generation of user interface models and prototypes from domain and use case models. In: Proceedings of the ICSoft 2009, Sofia, Bulgaria, vol. 1, pp. 169–176. INSTICC Press (2009)
4. OMG: OMG Unified Modeling Language (OMG UML), version 2.5 (2013). http://www.omg.org/spec/UML/2.5/Beta2/
5. Cruz, A.M.R.: Automatic generation of user interfaces from rigorous domain and use case models. Ph.D. dissertation, FEUP, University of Porto, Portugal (2010)
6. Cruz, A.M.R.: A pattern language for use case modeling. In: Proceedings of the 2nd International Conference on Model-Driven Engineering and Software Development (Modelsward 2014). INSTICC Press, Lisboa, Portugal, January 2014

7. Pinheiro da Silva, P.: User interface declarative models and development environments: a survey. In: Paternó, F. (ed.) DSV-IS 2000. LNCS, vol. 1946, pp. 207–226. Springer, Heidelberg (2001)
8. Dix, A., Finlay, J., Abowd, G., Beale, R.: Human-Computer Interaction, 2nd edn. Prentice Hall, Upper Saddle River (1998)
9. Constantine, L.L.: Canonical abstract prototypes for abstract visual and interaction design. In: Jorge, J.A., Jardim Nunes, N., Falcão e Cunha, J. (eds.) DSV-IS 2003. LNCS, vol. 2844, pp. 1–15. Springer, Heidelberg (2003)
10. OMG: Action language for foundational UML (Alf) - concrete syntax for a UML action language, version 1.0.1 (2013)
11. da Cruz, A.M.R., Faria, J.P.: A metamodel-based approach for automatic user interface generation. In: Petriu, D.C., Rouquette, N., Haugen, Ø. (eds.) MODELS 2010, Part I. LNCS, vol. 6394, pp. 256–270. Springer, Heidelberg (2010)
12. Radeke, F., Forbrig, P., Seffah, A., Sinnig, D.: PIM tool: support for pattern-driven and model-based UI development. In: Coninx, K., Luyten, K., Schneider, K.A. (eds.) TAMODIA 2006. LNCS, vol. 4385, pp. 82–96. Springer, Heidelberg (2007)
13. Costa, D., Nóbrega, L., Jardim Nunes, N.: An MDA approach for generating web interfaces with UML concurtasktrees and canonical abstract prototypes. In: Coninx, K., Luyten, K., Schneider, K.A. (eds.) TAMODIA 2006. LNCS, vol. 4385, pp. 137–152. Springer, Heidelberg (2007)
14. Martinez, A., Estrada, H., Sánchez, J., Pastor, O.: From early requirements to user interface prototyping: a methodological approach. In: International Conference on ASE 2002, pp 257–260 (2002)
15. Elkoutbi, M., Khriss, I., Keller, R.K.: Automated prototyping of user interfaces based on UML scenarios. J. Autom. Softw. Eng. **13**(1), 5–40 (2006)

Staged Translation of Graph Transformation Rules

Sabine Winetzhammer(✉) and Bernhard Westfechtel

Applied Computer Science I, University of Bayreuth,
Universitätsstraße 30, 95440 Bayreuth, Germany
{sabine.winetzhammer,bernhard.westfechtel}@uni-bayreuth.de
http://btn1x4.inf.uni-bayreuth.de/modgraph/homepage

Abstract. Graph transformation rules provide an opportunity to specify model transformations in a declarative way at a high level of abstraction. So far, compilers have translated graph transformation rules into conventional programming languages such as Java, C, or C#. In contrast, we follow a staged translation approach: We developed a compiler which translates graph transformation rules into a procedural language for behavioral modeling (Xcore). By reusing the Xcore compiler, the code may be compiled down to a conventional programming language in a second step. The generated Xcore code is significantly more concise and readable than programming language code. Furthermore, the code is portable since it is completely programming language independent.

Keywords: Graph Transformation Rules · Behavioral Modeling · Code Generation

1 Introduction

Model transformation languages have been developed for specifying transformations of models at a higher level of abstraction than in conventional programming languages. Among many features [5], model transformation languages may be classified according to their underlying paradigm: In *procedural languages*, the transformation is described by specifying the order in which elementary transformation steps are executed. In contrast, *rule-based languages* specify transformations with rules for matching and replacing patterns. Since the algorithms for pattern matching and replacement need not be provided by the user, rule-based languages are located at a higher level of abstraction.

A model may be considered as a *graph* whose nodes and edges correspond to the model's objects and links. *Graph transformation rules* [8] are ideally suited for specifying model transformations in a declarative way. Essentially, a graph transformation rule consists of a left-hand side — the graph pattern to be searched — and a right-hand side — the replacing pattern. Quite a number of graph transformation languages have been proposed, including PROGRES [17],

This paper is an extended and revised version of [24].

S. Hammoudi et al. (Eds.): MODELSWARD 2014, CCIS 506, pp. 134–152, 2015.
DOI: 10.1007/978-3-319-25156-1_9

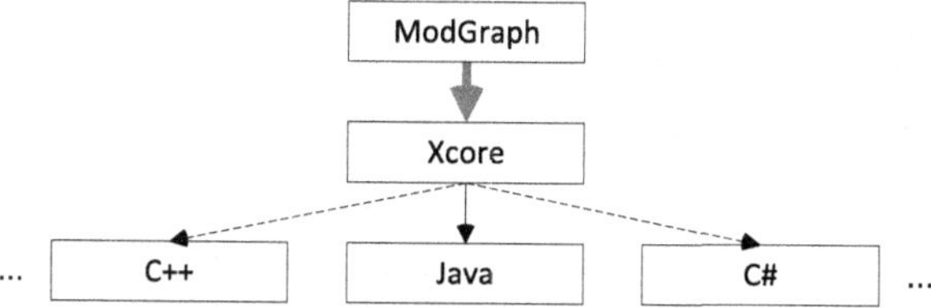

Fig. 1. Staged translation.

Fujaba [14], GReAT [1], GrGen.NET [11], Henshin [3], MDELab [10], VIATRA2 [21], eMOFLON [2], and ModGraph [4]. Users of these languages specify transformations with the help of high-level graph transformation rules. Users are not concerned with the algorithms for pattern matching and replacement, which are taken care of by the underlying execution engines.

To support the execution of graph transformation rules, both *interpreters* and *compilers* have been developed. An interpreter provides excellent support for debugging, which is slowed down by a compiler. On the other hand, compiled code is more efficient. So far, compilers have translated graph transformation rules into conventional programming languages such as Java, C, or C#. This approach results in rather complicated generated code which is difficult to understand.

In contrast, we built a *compiler* which translates *graph transformation rules* into a *procedural language* for *behavioral modeling* (Figure 1). The compiler accepts *ModGraph* rules and translates them into *Xcore* [6], a recently developed modeling language which is based on Ecore. Xcore is a textual language which covers both structural and behavioral modeling. Our compiler transforms ModGraph rules into procedural Xcore operations, specifically making use of Xcore's expression language. The Xcore environment in turn translates Xcore into Java (and prospectively into other target languages in the future). Within our work we follow our goal to provide *total model driven software engineering* as explained in [23] and [24]. Xcore interacts with ModGraph in order to provide high level control structures for rules. The translation to Xcore unifies the level of abstraction between rules and procedural code.

This *staged translation approach* (Figure 1) provides the following advantages over the traditional approach of compiling into a conventional programming language directly, which is followed by all competing tools:

Conciseness. The generated code is concise (but it still takes care of the details of pattern matching and replacement which should be shielded from the user).

Readability. The generated code is human readable, which facilitates e.g. code-level debugging.

Simplicity. The task of compiling is simplified significantly since Xcore provides more high-level language constructs than conventional programming languages such as Java.

Portability. With direct compilation into a programming language, one compiler is required for each target language. In our approach, the compiler does not depend on the programming language which is eventually used for execution.

Section 2 provides background information on ModGraph and Xcore. Section 3 introduces a running example. Section 4 describes the generation of Xcore code from graph transformation rules. Section 5 illustrates this approach with the help of the running example. Section 6 discusses our approach. Section 7 compares related work, and Sect. 8 concludes the paper.

2 Background

The *Eclipse Modeling Framework (EMF)* [19] has been designed with the intent to improve the software process by providing lightweight support for model-driven software engineering. For this reason, EMF provides a fairly minimalistic metamodel for structural modeling (*Ecore*, an implementation of Essential MOF (EMOF) [16]). Using the components of the EMF core, software engineers create Ecore models as instances of the Ecore metamodel. From an Ecore model, the EMF code generator creates code for classes, including methods for creating objects, assigning attribute values, as well as creating and deleting links. However, for user-defined operations, the EMF code generator may only create empty method bodies.

Xcore [6] adds behavioral modeling to EMF. Xcore provides a single language for both structural and behavioral modeling. To this end, Xcore introduces a textual syntax for Ecore models as well as procedural behavioral models. Xcore is driven by the vision that software engineers need no longer deal with code in a programming language such as Java (as current programmers do not inspect assembly or byte code). In Xcore, the sublanguage Xbase [7] is used to model behavior, i.e. the bodies of operations. Xbase is an expression language that was designed to be reused in different domain-specific languages. Xbase expressions provide both control structures and program expressions in a uniform way. Its program expressions may be used e.g. for navigation in models and checking constraints. Altogether, Xbase programs specify computations in a procedural way at a higher level of abstraction than Java.

ModGraph [4] is an EMF-based language for specifying graph transformation rules. With ModGraph, an operation defined in an Ecore or Xcore model may be realized as a *graph transformation rule* (or *rule* in short form). A graph pattern forms the core of a ModGraph rule. The graph pattern describes both the pattern to be searched and the replacing pattern in a single diagram. If no replacement is specified, the rule describes a test or a query rather than a transformation. In addition to the core, a rule may comprise optional components such as textual pre- and postconditions and graphical negative application conditions (NACs).

A *graph pattern* may be composed of several kinds of nodes and edges. Nodes are distinguished into a current object, named `this`, bound nodes, representing

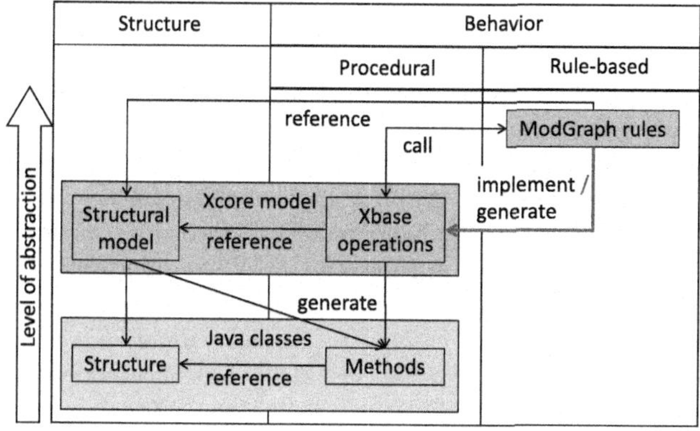

Fig. 2. Interplay between ModGraph and Xcore.

the non-primitive parameters of the operation, and unbound nodes, representing the objects to be searched in the model instance. Both bound and unbound nodes may be single- or multi-valued. Nodes provide a status which may be preserved (grey, no marker), created (green, ++), or deleted (red, −−). They can be marked as return parameter (<<out>>) or as optional (<<optional>>) nodes. Nodes to preserve or to delete may be constrained, nodes to create or to preserve may be modified, for example by setting an attribute value or calling an operation (operation calls allow ModGraph rules to interact directly with each other). All nodes may be connected by two kinds of edges: links and paths (instances of intrinsic and derived references, respectively). Analogously to nodes, links have a status. Paths are marked with a path expression, written in OCL [15] or Xbase. *Negative application conditions* describe patterns which must not occur when the main pattern has been matched. NACs are specified in a similar way as graph patterns; however, nodes and edges do not have a status and nodes may only be single-valued. *Pre- and postconditions* may be written in OCL or Xbase.

The *interplay* between *ModGraph* and *Xcore* is illustrated in Fig. 2. The user defines the structural model in Xcore's textual notation or migrates an existing Ecore model to Xcore. With respect to behavioral modeling, the user may choose between the procedural and the rule-based paradigm. Simple operations may be defined directly in Xcore using Xbase to implement its body. Complex operations may be specified in ModGraph, taking advantage of its expressiveness and its easily readable graphical notation. If a complex operation may not be coded as a single rule, the user may resort to Xbase control structures for controlling the application of multiple rules. In general, Xbase operations may call ModGraph rules and vice versa. For the purpose of execution, ModGraph rules are first compiled into Xcore operations. The second stage of compilation (currently targeting Java) is performed by the Xcore compiler. Please note that the user gets in touch only with Xcore and ModGraph (orange boxes); there is no need to inspect the generated Java code (yellow boxes).

3 Example

This section introduces a running example which illustrates modeling with ModGraph and Xcore. As running example, we study the *refactoring* of *structural models*. The example was drawn from our tool support for consistent refactoring of structural models and graph transformation rules which is described elsewhere [25]. Altogether, we implemented 19 refactoring transformations with a total of 35 graph transformation rules and 71 Xcore operations.

We consider two refactoring operations on an Ecore model: *changing a uni- to a bidirectional reference* and *collapsing the inheritance hierarchy* as defined by Fowler [9]. The graph transformation rules were selected (and adapted) to serve as demonstration examples for the generation of Xcore code.

An excerpt from the *Xcore specification* of the *structuralmodel for refactoring* is shown in Listing 1. A refactoring class references the elements of the Ecore model to be refactored (classes, operations, etc.), and provides the refactoring operations to be applied. Each refactoring operation is applied to model elements fixed by parameters. The operations are invoked through an interactive user interface; thus, the user decides which refactoring transformations are applied to which elements of the structural model to be refactored. For demonstration purposes, both strings and objects are used to identify model objects. In the first example, the use of string parameters implies the insertion of nested loops into the generated code. In the second example, objects are used instead of strings to focus on other issues of code generation. In the actual implementation, parameters are supplied consistently as objects rather than as strings.

Listing 1. Xcore Model for refactoring.

```
class Refactoring {
  refers EOperation[] referenceToEOperation
  refers EClass[] referenceToEClass
  refers EReference[] referenceToEReference
  refers EParameter[] referenceToEParameter
  refers EStructuralFeature[] referenceToEStructuralFeature

  op void changeUniToBidirectionalReference(
    String class1Name, String class2Name)
  op void collapseHierarchy(ClassType classType,
        EClass superClass, EClass subClass)
  op void removeSub(EClass superClass, EClass subClass)
  op void removeSuper(EClass superClass, EClass subClass)
}
```

The rule for *changing a uni- to bidirectional reference* is supplied with two string parameters which identify the source class and the target class of the unidirectional reference (Figure 3). The precondition (in OCL) on the top requires that both strings must not be empty. The graph pattern on the left is rooted at the current object (this) on which the refactoring operation is invoked. Starting at the current object, two classes need to be found (class1 and class2) whose names equal the supplied string parameters (see the checks in the Constraints compartment). Furthermore, there must be a reference (reference1) which is owned by class1 and is typed by class2. The negative application condition on the right ensures that the reference is unidirectional (there is no opposite reference (oppositeRef). If the

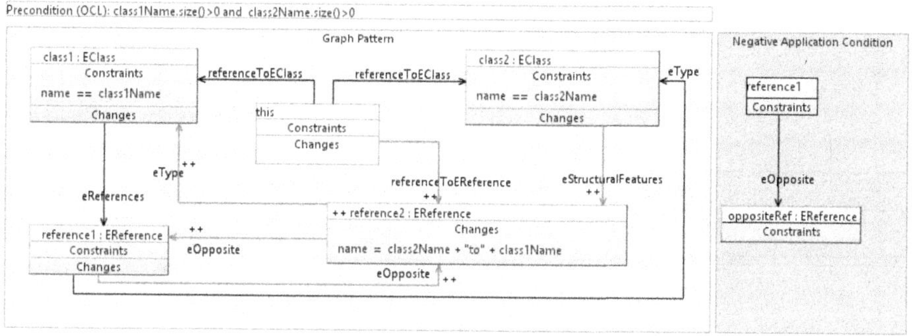

Fig. 3. ModGraph rule for changeUniToBidirectionalReference.

graph pattern can be matched and the NAC holds, as well, the transformation may be applied, resulting in a new reference (reference2) which is connected to its opposite reference (reference1) as well as to its source class, its target class, and the current object. The name of the new reference is composed from the names of the connected classes (Changes compartment).

Our second refactoring operation — *collapsing a class hierarchy* — demonstrates the interplay of procedural and rule-based operations. This refactoring is applied to two classes connected by inheritance. Collapsing a hierarchy means eliminating either the sub- or the superclass. Both alternatives may be modeled in separate ModGraph rules implementing the methods removeSub and removeSuper.

Listing 2. Xcore implementation of method collapseHierarchy.

```
op void collapseHierarchy(ClassType classType, EClass superClass,
        EClass subClass){
    if(classType == ClassType::SUPER_CLASS) try {
      removeSuper(superClass, subClass)
    } catch (GTFailure f) {/*do sth.*/}
    if(classType == ClassType::SUB_CLASS) try {
      removeSub(superClass, subClass)
    } catch (GTFailure f) {/*do sth.*/}
}
```

At the user interface, we would like to offer a single refactoring operation with a parameter controlling whether the sub- or the superclass is removed. Its Xcore implementation is shown in Listing 2. The method selection is realized by a condition, depending on the given value of enumeration classType. Exception handling, using try-catch blocks, is necessary because each method implemented by a graph transformation rule may raise an exception of type GTFailure.

The rule to *remove the subclass* is shown in Figure 4[1]. An Xcore precondition ensures the parameters not to be null[2]. In contrast to the rule for changing

[1] The rule was simplified by omitting various positive and negative application conditions which are immaterial in the context of this paper.

[2] This precondition is redundant and was included to demonstrate that Xcore expressions may be used alternatively to OCL expressions.

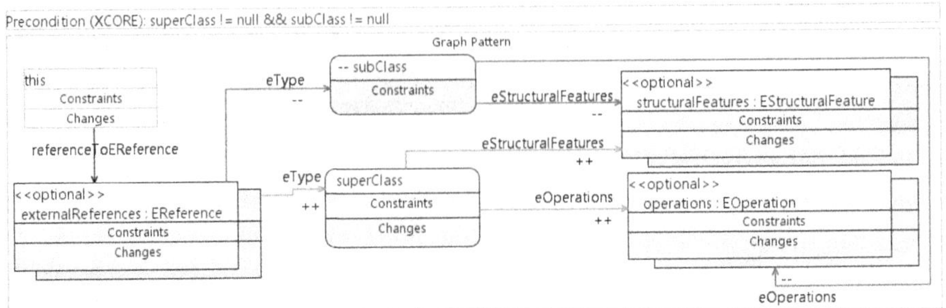

Fig. 4. ModGraph rule for removeSub.

a uni- to a bidirectional reference, the classes required as parameters are now supplied directly as objects (while they had to be searched via their names in the previous rule). In addition to the current object, the subclass, and the superclass, the rule includes only multi-objects (shaded rectangles) which are designated as optional (stereotypes inside the top compartments of the rectangles). The multi-objects are obtained by traversing instances of multi-valued references. Since the subclass object is deleted, all adjacent links are deleted, as well. All outgoing containment links to structural features and operations are transferred to the superclass. Furthermore, references which were typed with the subclass have to be retyped with the superclass.

4 Code Generation

According to our *staged translation approach*, graph transformation rules are compiled into Xcore operations. Each graph transformation rule is translated into a single Xcore operation. The generated code is injected into the overall Xcore model as described in [24]. The resulting extended Xcore model may then be compiled down to Java, using Xcore's code generator. Alternatively, the Xcore code may be interpreted directly, which may accelerate the debugging cycle considerably.

In the following, we provide a brief overview of our code generation approach at a conceptual level (leaving out implementation details). To this end, let us explain first the *execution steps* to be performed at run time:

1. *Check All Preconditions.* If some precondition fails, execution terminates with failure.
2. *Match Graph Pattern.* Graph pattern matching will be described below. If no (new) match can be found, execution terminates with failure.
3. *Check Negative Application Conditions.* If at least one of the patterns specified as NACs is present, backtrack to the previous step.
4. *Evaluate All Attribute Expressions.* Before any change is performed, all expressions are evaluated whose values are needed later for attribute assignments.

5. *Perform Deletions.* Delete objects and links with status −−.
6. *Perform Insertions.* Insert objects and links with status ++.
7. *Perform Assignments.* Assign the values of expressions evaluated in Step 4 to attributes, as specified in the Changes compartments.
8. *Call Operations.* Perform operation calls, as specified in the Changes compartments.
9. *Check Postconditions.* If any postcondition is violated, terminate with failure. Otherwise, terminate successfully.

Only Step 2 is required for each rule; the presence of all other steps depends on the presence of corresponding optional elements of the rule. If no changes are specified at all, the rule constitutes a test or a query; in the latter case, one or more nodes of the pattern are marked as output parameters.

The *order* of the *steps* is fixed such that graph transformation rules have a well-defined semantics:

- In general, insertions and deletions do not commute; consider, e.g., single-valued references. Therefore, an appropriate order needs to be fixed. In ModGraph, deletions are performed first because otherwise insertions could be undone by subsequent deletions.
- Attribute expressions are evaluated in the pre-state of the transformation, e.g., because they may refer to objects which are deleted by the transformation.
- Called operations provide for a simple way of rule chaining. Since they are executed as the last modification step, the called operations may rely on the fact that the rule has been executed completely. Furthermore, the execution of called rules may contribute to the satisfaction of postconditions, which are checked only in the very last step of rule execution.

Pattern matching constitutes the most complex step of executing a graph transformation rule. In the simplest case, a graph pattern defines a subgraph to be searched in the model graph. However, in ModGraph the notion of graph pattern is more general since ModGraph provides abstraction mechanisms such as multiplicities of nodes and paths. Therefore, a graph pattern defines a set of matching subgraphs which may vary with respect to the number of nodes and the paths by means of which these nodes are connected. In general, a *match* is defined by a relation between pattern nodes and model graph nodes which meets the following conditions:

1. Each single-valued pattern node is matched to a single model graph node, each multi-valued pattern node is matched to a set of model graph nodes.
2. Each mandatory pattern node must be matched to at least one model graph node.
3. The class of a matched node must conform to the class of its pattern node.
4. Each edge in the pattern graph must be present between the matched nodes in the model graph, as well. This condition applies to both links and paths.
5. Each matched node must satisfy all constraints defined on its pattern node.

ModGraph provides a *localized search* for matches. This means that matching starts from one or more anchor nodes. Both the current object and the bound objects (supplied as parameters) serve as anchor nodes. From the anchor nodes, all unbound nodes are determined by a navigational search, i.e., by traversing links or paths. Thus, all unbound nodes must be reachable from the anchor nodes. This eliminates the need for global searches.

For efficient pattern matching, it is crucial to search nodes in such an order that the number of match candidates to be considered is kept as small as possible. Therefore, ModGraph constructs a *spanning forest* from which the search order is derived. The spanning forest covers all nodes of the pattern and determines for each node a unique path from one of the anchor nodes. The spanning forest is constructed by a *heuristic greedy algorithm* as follows:

1. The forest is initialized with all anchor nodes, each of which acts as a root of a tree inside the forest.
2. Next, all mandatory unbound nodes are processed. The forest is extended step by step with unvisited nodes. Each iteration considers all unvisited nodes which may be reached from visited nodes by a link or a path. If possible, an unvisited node is selected which is connected to a visited node by a unique link (an instance of a single-valued reference). Paths are treated in the same way as multi-valued references[3].
3. Finally, all optional unbound nodes are processed in the same way as done in the previous step for mandatory unbound nodes. This ensures that the search path for a mandatory node never contains an optional node.

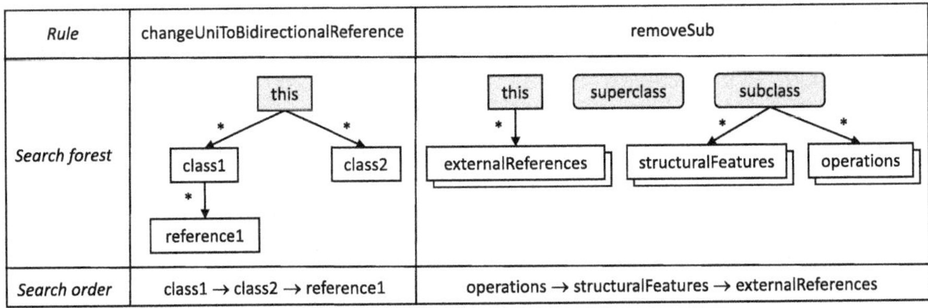

Fig. 5. Search forests and search order for the sample rules.

The *search order* for unbound nodes is derived from the search forest in an analogous way. Thus, all mandatory nodes are ordered before all optional nodes. Furthermore, a child node is appended to the search sequence only after its parent node. Finally, among the candidate nodes to be appended next to the search sequence, nodes are preferred which are reachable over unique links.

[3] This is a pessimistic assumption which could be improved only by analyzing the path expression.

The Xcore code is generated by a template-based *model-to-text transformation*. The templates are written in Xpand, a template language provided by the Eclipse Modeling Project[4]. The generated code is structured according to the execution steps explained above. Pattern matching is implemented by *nested loops*: For each node for which multiple match candidates need to be considered, a loop is created in the generated code. The loops are nested according to the search order derived from the spanning forest.

5 Example Revisited

In this section, we revisited the example introduced in Sect. 3 and present the Xcore code which is generated from the sample graph transformation rules for refactoring.

For the graph transformation rule for changing a uni- to a bidirectional reference (Fig. 3), the ModGraph compiler creates the search forest which is displayed on the left-hand side of Fig. 5. In search forests, anchor nodes are shown in grey. Arrows are annotated with multiplicities (either 1 for a single-valued reference or * for multi-valued references or paths). From the search forest, ModGraph derives a search order which complies with the rules explained in Sect. 4.

The Xcore code generated for this rule is shown in Listing 3. In line 1 a Genmodel annotation is used to mark the operation as generated by ModGraph. Line 2 checks the OCL precondition (shown at the top of Fig. 3), using the EMF OCL Pivot evaluator via an annotation. Lines 3 and 4 show the Xcore generated operation head. For each unbound object in the rule's graph pattern, the generator declares variables as shown in lines 5–7. Lines 8–20 implement the matching of the graph pattern. Nested `for` loops are built up according to the search order defined in Fig. 5. These loops use the Xbase λ-expression language to filter the collections they iterate by the constraints given to the objects in the rule, e.g., `name == class1Name`. The innermost loop contains a condition that checks the NAC. If matching succeeds, the variables defined above the loops are set. Unfortunately Xcore does not support `break` commands. Therefore, the variables are eventually set with the last match found[5]. Line 20 checks if matching has succeeded; otherwise, an exception is raised.

Line 21 shows the calculation of the name for the new reference depending on the pre-state of the model. The reference itself is created in line 22 and its name is set to the calculated one in line 23. Lines 24–28 put the new reference into its context by executing the following expressions: The new reference's opposite is set to the existing one and vice versa. `class2` is set as a container for the new reference by adding the latter to its structural features. A link is added from the refactoring object to the new reference, and the reference's type is set to `class1`.

[4] http://eclipse.org/modeling/

[5] Since we expect that `break` commands will be added soon to Xcore, we refrain from rewriting the generated code with more awkward `while` loops returning the first match.

Listing 3. Generated Xcore implementation of changeUniToBidirectionalReference.

```
@GenModel(documentation="Generated by ModGraph. ")
@OCL(pre_pre1="class1Name.size()>0 and class2Name.size()>0 ")
op void changeUniToBidirectionalReference(
        String class1Name , String class2Name) {
    var EClass class1 = null
    var EClass class2 = null
    var EReference reference1 = null
    for (_class1 : referenceToEClass.filter(e|e.name == class1Name)) {
      for (_class2 : referenceToEClass.filter(e|e.name == class2Name)){
        for (_reference1 : class1.EReferences.
                filter(e|e.EType.equals(_class2))) {
        if (! ( reference1.EOpposite != null )) {
          class1 = _class1
          class2 = _class2
          reference1 = _reference1
          }
        }
      }
    }
    if(class1 == null) throw new GTFailure
    val reference2NameValue = class2Name + "to" + class1Name
    var reference2 = EcoreFactory::eINSTANCE.createEReference()
    reference2.name = reference2NameValue
    reference2.EOpposite = reference1
    reference1.EOpposite = reference2
    class2.EStructuralFeatures.add(reference2)
    referenceToEReference.add(reference2)
    reference2.EType = class1
}
```

Listing 4 shows the generated Xcore code for the ModGraph rule removeSub; the respective search forest and the search order are illustrated on the right-hand side of Fig. 5. Lines 1 and 2 include an annotation containing the documentation which was attached to the ModGraph rule. The head of the method follows in line 3. Line 4 checks the Xcore precondition. Lines 5–7 declare variables for storing matches of multi-objects. In lines 8–11, values for these variables are

Listing 4. Generated Xcore implementation of removeSub.

```
1  @GenModel(documentation="Generated by ModGraph: Removes the
2     subclass. Part of the collapse hierarchy refactoring. ")
3  op void removeSub(EClass superClass , EClass subClass) {
4    if(! ( superClass != null && subClass != null )) throw new GTFailure
5    var EList<EStructuralFeature> structuralFeatures = null
6    var EList<EOperation> operations = null
7    var EList<EReference> externalReferences = null
8    val _operations = subClass.EOperations
9    val _structuralFeatures = subClass.EStructuralFeatures
10   val _externalReferences = referenceToEReference
11     .filter(e|e.EType.equals(subClass)).asEList
12   structuralFeatures = _structuralFeatures
13   operations = _operations
14   externalReferences = _externalReferences
15   org::eclipse::emf::ecore::util::EcoreUtil::remove(subClass)
16   superClass.EStructuralFeatures.addAll(structuralFeatures)
17   superClass.EOperations.addAll(operations)
18   externalReferences.forEach(e|e.EType = superClass)
19   }
20
21 op void removeSuper(EClass superClass , EClass subClass) {
22   /*analogously to removeSub*/
23   }
```

retrieved which are assigned in lines 12–14. Line 15 removes the subclass. Since all adjacent links are deleted automatically anyway, there is no need to generate additional code for the deleted links specified in the graph pattern. Lines 16 and 17 assign the structural features and operations to the superclass, respectively, and line 18 retypes the references.

6 Discussion

6.1 Staged Translation

Staged translation is a well-known engineering approach for decomposing translations into manageable, modular parts. It has been applied for long in many different contexts, including (but not limited to) model transformations [20]. For example, Java makes use of staged translation by compiling Java programs into portable byte code which is translated into machine code in a second step. Furthermore, staged translation reduces the effort of writing converters between different data formats: The introduction of an intermediate neutral data format reduces the number of data converters from $O(n^2)$ to $O(n)$.

In ModGraph, we applied staged translation to make the generated code portable (i.e., programming language independent). Furthermore, by compiling graph transformation rules to Xcore, we may reuse the Xcore interpreter for debugging. Finally, the task of code generation is simplified significantly, compared to the direct generation of Java code.

To demonstrate the advantages of our staged translation approach, we consider the three implementations to delete a subclass in an Ecore model in order to collapse the hierarchy: the ModGraph rule (Fig. 4), the generated Xcore implementation (Listing 4), and the Xcore generated Java code (Listing 5).

Comparing the ModGraph rule to the Xcore implementation, we observe that a rule is still more intuitive than the generated code: its clearly structured format with the graphical, color-coded, nodes and edges visualize the pattern to be matched and the actions to be performed. The Xcore code is a clearly structured, target language independent text which we consider to be still concise and simple enough to be human readable. Its high level of abstraction increases the readability especially when the functional expressions provided by Xbase come into play.

The generated Xcore code shown in Listing 4 could be written more concisely if written by hand. In fact, lines 5–14 could be expressed by only three lines of hand-written code. In contrast, the code generator creates declarations of variables which are assigned values only when a complete match has been found. During the matching, intermediate variables are used to store partial matches. In this way, it can be checked conveniently whether matching has succeeded (if it has not, the variables for complete matches will still be null). This code generation approach supports the most general case, in which matching has to be performed in (potentially nested) loops (see Listing 3 for the refactoring rule converting a unidirectional to a bidirectional reference).

Listing 5. Xcore generated Java code for method removeSub.

```
/**
 * <!-- begin-user-doc --> <!-- end-user-doc -->
 * @generated
 */
 public void removeSub(final EClass superClass, final EClass subClass){
    try {
      boolean _and = false;
      boolean _notEquals = (!Objects.equal(superClass, null));
      if (!_notEquals) {
        _and = false;
      } else {
        boolean _notEquals_1 = (!Objects.equal(subClass, null));
        _and = (_notEquals && _notEquals_1);
      }
      boolean _not = (!_and);
      if (_not) {
        GTFailure _gTFailure = new GTFailure();
        throw _gTFailure;
      }
      EList<EStructuralFeature> structuralFeatures = null;
      EList<EOperation> operations = null;
      EList<EReference> externalReferences = null;
      final EList<EOperation> _operations = subClass.getEOperations();
      final EList<EStructuralFeature> _structuralFeatures =
                subClass.getEStructuralFeatures();
      Refactoring _this = this;
      EList<EReference> _referenceToEReference =
                _this.getReferenceToEReference();
      final Function1<EReference,Boolean> _function =
                new Function1<EReference,Boolean>()
      {
          public Boolean apply(final EReference e){
            EClassifier _eType = e.getEType();
            boolean _equals = _eType.equals(subClass);
            return Boolean.valueOf(_equals);
          }
        };
      Iterable<EReference> _filter = IterableExtensions.<EReference>filter(
          _referenceToEReference, _function);
      final EList<EReference> _externalReferences =
          ECollections.<EReference>asEList(
          ((EReference[])Conversions.unwrapArray(_filter, EReference.class)));
      structuralFeatures = _structuralFeatures;
      operations = _operations;
      externalReferences = _externalReferences;
      EcoreUtil.remove(subClass);
      EList<EStructuralFeature> _eStructuralFeatures =
                                superClass.getEStructuralFeatures();
      _eStructuralFeatures.addAll(structuralFeatures);
      EList<EOperation> _eOperations = superClass.getEOperations();
      _eOperations.addAll(operations);
      final Procedure1<EReference> _function_1 = new Procedure1<EReference>()
      {
          public void apply(final EReference e) {
            e.setEType(superClass);
          }
        };
      IterableExtensions.<EReference>forEach(externalReferences, _function_1);
    } catch (Throwable _e){
      throw Exceptions.sneakyThrow(_e);
      }
 }
```

This example demonstrates that hand-written code may be shorter than generated code. This is not surprising and quite common. Nevertheless, the generated code is still concise and readable. Thus, debugging may be performed quite conveniently on the generated code.

The result of compiling the Xcore code of Listing 4 to Java code is shown in Listing 5. Comparing them, we note a significant difference in length: The generated Java code is much longer than the Xcore code. In general, we may expect Xcore code to be more concise than Java code. However, the actual factor obtained by dividing the code lengths depends heavily on the way code is generated. We have already discussed above that hand-written Xcore code usually is shorter than the code produced by the ModGraph compiler. However, this argument holds for the Java code generated by Xcore, as well (to a greater extent!): The generated code makes massive use of variables for storing intermediate results.

The decisive argument for decomposing the translation is Xcore's higher level abstraction, e.g., with respect to its expression language (λ expressions). Compare, e.g., the precondition initially written as one line Xcore expression in the rule in Fig. 4 and the Xcore implementation in Listing 4, line 4. The Java implementation uses lines 7–19 to ensure this condition. A closer look at the Xcore generated Java code reveals that internal functions need to be called or even implemented. The filter function shown in Listing 4, lines 10–11 to filter the references typed over the subclass is mapped to lines 38–42 in Listing 5. An additional Java filter function is called to map the procedural expression to Java. The `foreach` expression shown in Listing 4, line 18, even forces a reimplementation to be mapped to Java, see lines 52–58.

6.2 Higher Order Transformations

The ModGraph2Xcore compiler performs a *higher order transformation*: It transforms a rule-based transformation specification written in ModGraph into a procedural transformation specification written in Xcore. In general terms, a higher order transformation transforms a source transformation into a target transformation.

However, the definition given in [20] is less general: It demands that both the source transformation and the target transformation are represented as models, and the higher order transformation is realized as a *model-to-model transformation.* [20] employs the language ATL [13] for this purpose; many other languages are available, as well [12].

Since we had already developed a compiler from ModGraph to Java [22], we could have bootstrapped the ModGraph2Xcore compiler. However, we refrained from an implementation as a model-to-model transformation (in whatever language) and instead decided to implement a template-based *model-to-text transformation.* We consider this approach superior in conciseness and readability: Building up the target model in terms of its abstract syntax requires much longer transformation definitions which are more difficult to read.

6.3 Hybrid Behavioral Modeling

The integration of ModGraph and Xcore provides for *hybrid behavioral modeling*, combining rule-based modeling in ModGraph and procedural modeling in Xcore in an opportunistic way. This approach is not new, and it has been applied in all languages and tools to be compared in Section 7 (Related Work). Evaluating the hybrid modeling approach goes beyond the focus of this paper, which is devoted to the ModGraph2Xcore compiler. Nevertheless, we discuss this topic briefly, mainly referencing other publications.

Opportunistic combination of rule-based and procedural modeling means that graph transformation rules are employed only when they pay off; otherwise, transformations are encoded as procedures. In earlier work, we evaluated this approach by examining several medium-sized to large projects written in different languages [26]. The evaluation was performed both qualitatively and quantitatively (by analyzing data such as the number of rules and procedures, the number of nodes and edges per rule, etc.). Based on our analysis, we concluded that typically large fractions of the behavior may be implemented best as procedures, but graph transformation rules do provide an added value if complex transformations are to be performed requiring structural consistency checks.

The development of ModGraph builds upon these observations: we intend to focus ourselves exactly on the added value of graph transformations, and reuse everything else (the data model provided by Ecore and the procedural abstractions provided by Xcore). In the refactoring project which we used as a running example in this paper, we wrote graph transformation rules only when they provided an added value, and resorted to Xcore code otherwise. For a more comprehensive presentation of this project, the reader is referred to [26]. Altogether, we implemented 19 refactoring transformations; see [25] for a complete list. The transformations provided to the end user were realized with a total of 35 graph transformation rules and 71 Xcore operations.

The rules which we selected for this paper roughly have average complexity; thus, they are (more or less) representative. Concerning the generated Xcore operations, it might be argued that we were "too successful" in generating concise and readable code: Why should we write the rules if the generated operations are fairly simple (and hand-written operations would be even simpler and shorter)? However, this argument is too simplistic: Still, rules are specified declaratively, while Xcore operations have to deal with all the algorithmic details of pattern matching and transformation. If the rules are more complex than the sample rules given in this paper, encoding the pattern matching and the transformation by hand may be considerably more complex and error-prone. Furthermore, the rule provides a graphical documentation of the transformation which is much easier to understand than the corresponding procedural code.

7 Related Work

This paper is related to our *own previous work* as follows: Originally [4], ModGraph was strongly based on *Java* in several respects. First, Java was used as

Table 1. Graph transformation languages and tools.

language/tool	interpreter	compiler	target language(s) (if compiled)
eMOFLON [2]	x	x	Java
Fujaba [14]	x	x	Java
GReAT [1]	x	-	-
GrGen.NET [11]	-	x	C#
Henshin [3]	x	-	-
MDELab [10]	x	-	-
ModGraph	(x)	x	*Xcore* or Java
PROGRES [17]	x	x	C or Java
VIATRA2 [21]	-	x	Java

the control flow language. Thus, the ModGraph user has to encode both simple operations and the composition of graph transformation rules as Java methods. This results in a hybrid approach, mixing high level rules with low level methods written in a conventional programming language. Subsequently, we integrated ModGraph with Xcore to support *total model-driven software engineering* [23]: the ModGraph user may provide a complete behavioral model and need not leave the level of modeling any more.

Second, the ModGraph compiler generated Java code directly [22]. For various reasons which have been explained repeatedly in this paper, we developed the ModGraph2Xcore compiler. It differs from the ModGraph2Java compiler not only in generating Xcore rather than Java code. Furthermore, the generated code is structured differently: The ModGraph2Java compiler does not generate the code for a graph transformation rule into a single method; rather, the code is distributed over several methods to keep the generated methods small. The selection of Xcore as target language obviates the need for such a procedural decomposition. Thus, the ModGraph2Xcore compiler generates a single, yet concise method.

Table 1 provides a short comparison of *related tools / languages*. Here we consider only tools related to EMF and based on the theory of graph transformation.[6] Some tools provide a direct interpreter. Quite a number of tools compile graph transformation rules into widely used programming languages such as C, C#, or Java. Only ModGraph provides *model-level code generation* (into Xcore code). None of the competing tools supports a *staged translation approach* as illustrated in Fig. 1.

[6] Please note, that PROGRES is not EMF related, but needs to be mentioned as godfather of practically oriented graph transformation tools.

8 Conclusions

We presented a new approach of compiling high level graph transformation rules into a procedural language for behavioral modeling (Xcore). Summing up, the integration of Xcore and ModGraph offers the following general benefits:

- Complex transformations which are awkward to program in Xcore may be specified with ModGraph's high-level graph transformation rules.
- Graph transformation rules may be composed with control structures provided by Xcore.
- Simple operations may be encoded exclusively in Xcore.
- Complete application code may be generated by relying on the code generators of EMF, Xcore, and ModGraph.
- Re-targeting the ModGraph code generator to Xcore gains *platform independence* for ModGraph: Generating code for a specific programming language may be delegated completely to Xcore.

Using this approach, the modeler may resort to graph transformation rules for complex operations, while simple operations may be directly implemented in Xcore using Xbase. The code produced by the ModGraph2Xcore compiler may be compiled as well as interpreted. It is much more concise, readable, and simple than programming language code due to the fact that we do not leave the modeling level. Furthermore, the Xcore code is portable since it is programming language independent. The approach presented here is unique with respect to these properties: All competing tools for generating code from graph transformation rules create code in a conventional programming language (see Section 7).

We applied the ModGraph/Xcore environment in a recent project addressing the consistent refactoring of Ecore models and graph transformation rules [26]. The experiences we gained so far are promising. In future work, we intend to employ ModGraph/Xcore for other applications such as e.g. model merging [18].

Acknowledgements. The constructive comments of the unknown reviewers are gratefully acknowledged.

References

1. Agrawal, A., Karsai, G., Neema, S., Shi, F., Vizhanyo, A.: The design of a language for model transformations. Software and Systems Modeling **5**, 261–288 (2006)
2. Anjorin, A., Lauder, M., Patzina, S., Schürr, A.: eMoflon: Leveraging EMF and Professional CASE Tools. In: INFORMATIK 2011. Lecture Notes in Informatics, vol. 192, p. 281. Gesellschaft für Informatik, Gesellschaft für Informatik, Bonn (October 2011), extended abstract
3. Arendt, Thorsten, Biermann, Enrico, Jurack, Stefan, Krause, Christian, Taentzer, Gabriele: Henshin: Advanced Concepts and Tools for In-Place EMF Model Transformations. In: Petriu, Dorina C., Rouquette, Nicolas, Haugen, Øystein (eds.) MODELS 2010, Part I. LNCS, vol. 6394, pp. 121–135. Springer, Heidelberg (2010)

4. Buchmann, T., Westfechtel, B., Winetzhammer, S.: ModGraph – A Transformation Engine for EMF Model Transformations. In: Proceedings of the 6th International Conference on Software and Data Technologies (ICSOFT 2011). pp. 212–219. Sevilla, Spain (2011)
5. Czarnecki, K., Helsen, S.: Feature-based survey of model transformation approaches. IBM Systems Journal **45**(3), 621–646 (2006)
6. Eclipse Foundation: Xcore (2013), http://wiki.eclipse.org/Xcore
7. Efftinge, S., Eysholdt, M., Köhnlein, J., Zarnekow, S., Hasselbring, W., von Massow, R., Hanus, M.: Xbase: Implementing domain-specific languages for Java. In: Proceedings of the 11th International Conference on Generative Programming and Component Engineering (GPCE 2012). pp. 112–121. ACM, Dresden, Germany (2012)
8. Ehrig, H., Engels, G., Kreowski, H.J., Rozenberg, G. (eds.): Handbook on Graph Grammars and Computing by Graph Transformation: Applications, Languages, and Tools, vol. 2. World Scientific, Singapore (1999)
9. Fowler, M.: Refactoring: Improving the Design of Existing Code. Addison-Wesley, Boston, MA, USA (1999)
10. Giese, H., Hildebrandt, S., Seibel, A.: Improved flexibility and scalability by interpreting story diagrams. In: Boronat, A., Heckel, R. (eds.) Proceedings of the 8th International Workshop on Graph Transformation and Visual Modeling Techniques (GT-VMT 2009). Electronic Communications of the EASST, vol. 18. York, UK (Mar 2009), 12 p
11. Jakumeit, E., Buchwald, S., Kroll, M.: GrGen.NET – the expressive, convenient and fast graph rewrite system. International Journal on Software Tools for Technology Transfer **12**, 263–271 (2010)
12. Jakumeit, E., Buchwald, S., Wagelaar, D., Dan, L., Hegedüs, A., Herrmannsdörfer, M., Horn, T., Kalnina, E., Krause, C., Lano, K., Lepper, M., Rensink, A., Rose, L., Wätzold, S., Mazanek, S.: A survey and comparison of transformation tools based on the transformation tool contest. Science of Computer Programming **85A**, 41–99 (2014)
13. Jouault, F., Allilaire, F., Bézivin, J., Kurtev, I.: ATL: A model transformation tool. Science of Computer Programming **72**(1–2), 31–39 (2008)
14. Norbisrath, U., Zündorf, A., Jubeh, R.: Story Driven Modeling. CreateSpace Independent Publishing Platform (2013), iSBN-10: 1483949257
15. Object Management Group: Object Constraint Language Version 2.3.1. Needham, MA, formal/2012-01-01 edn. (Jan 2012)
16. OMG: Meta Object Facility (MOF) 2.0 Query/View/Transformation, v1.1. OMG (Jan 2011)
17. Schürr, A., Winter, A., Zündorf, A.: The PROGRES approach: Language and environment. In: Ehrig et al. [8], pp. 487–550
18. Schwägerl, F., Uhrig, S., Westfechtel, B.: Model-based tool support for consistent three-way merging of EMF models. In: Proceedings of the Workshop on ACadeMics Tooling with Eclipse (ACME 2013). pp. 2:1–2:10. ACM, Montpellier, France (2013)
19. Steinberg, D., Budinsky, F., Paternostro, M., Merks, E.: EMF Eclipse Modeling Framework, 2nd edn. The Eclipse Series, Addison Wesley, Boston, MA (2009)
20. Tisi, Massimo, Jouault, Frédéric, Fraternali, Piero, Ceri, Stefano, Bézivin, Jean: On the Use of Higher-Order Model Transformations. In: Paige, Richard F., Hartman, Alan, Rensink, Arend (eds.) ECMDA-FA 2009. LNCS, vol. 5562, pp. 18–33. Springer, Heidelberg (2009)
21. Varró, D., Balogh, A.: The model transformation language of the VIATRA2 framework. Science of Computer Programming **68**(3), 214–234 (2007)

22. Winetzhammer, S.: ModGraph – generating executable EMF models. In: Margaria, T., Padberg, J., Taentzer, G., Krause, C., Westfechtel, B. (eds.) Proceedings of the 7th International Workshop on Graph Based Tools. Electronic Communications of the EASST, vol. 54. Bremen, Germany (September 2012), 13 p
23. Winetzhammer, S., Westfechtel, B.: ModGraph meets Xcore: Combining rule-based and procedural behavioral modeling for EMF. In: Tichy, M., Ribeiro, L., Margaria, T., Padberg, J., Taentzer, G. (eds.) Proceedings of the 12th International Workshop on Graph Transformation and Visual Modeling Techniques (GTVMT 2013). Electronic Communications of the EASST, vol. 58. Rome, Italy (March 2013), 13 p
24. Winetzhammer, S., Westfechtel, B.: Compiling graph transformation rules into a procedural language for behavioral modeling. In: Pires, L.F., Hammoudi, S., Filipe, J., das Neves, R.C. (eds.) Proceedings of the 2nd International Conference on Model-Driven Engineering and Software Development (MODELSWARD 2014). pp. 415–424. SCITEPRESS Science and Technology Publications, Portugal, Lisbon, Portugal (2014)
25. Winetzhammer, S., Westfechtel, B.: Propagating model refactorings to graph transformation rules. In: ICSOFT-PT 2014 - Proceedings of the 9th International Conference on Software Paradigm Trends. pp. 17–28. Vienna, Austria (Aug 2014)
26. Winetzhammer, S., Westfechtel, B.: Model refactorings for and with graph transformation rules. In: Holzinger, A., Cardoso, J., Libourel, T., Maciaszek, L., van Sinderen, M. (eds.) Software Technologies. Communications in Computer and Information Science, Springer, Heidelberg (2015), invited paper, selected from ICSOFT-PT 2014, 18 p

Towards Bidirectional Higher-Order Transformation for Model-Driven Co-evolution

Bernhard Hoisl[1,2](✉), Zhenjiang Hu[3], and Soichiro Hidaka[3]

[1] Institute for Information Systems and New Media, Vienna University of Economics and Business (WU Vienna), Vienna, Austria
bernhard.hoisl@wu.ac.at

[2] Secure Business Austria Research (SBA Research), Vienna, Austria

[3] National Institute of Informatics (NII), Tokyo, Japan
{hu,hidaka}@nii.ac.jp

Abstract. In model-driven development (MDD), numerous metamodels, models, and model transformations need to be taken into account. These MDD-based artifacts—although highly interdependent—are autonomously maintained. Changes in one artifact (e.g., in a model) are not automatically reflected in other dependent artifacts (e.g., in a model transformation). The barrier for a tight integration of MDD-based artifacts stems from two limitations of current approaches. On the one hand, model transformations are unidirectional and changes can be propagated in one direction only. On the other hand, changes can only be propagated into output artifacts of transformations, not into transformation definitions themselves. In order to overcome these co-evolution problems, our approach is based on establishing bidirectional transformations (BX) between modeling artifacts and on applying higher-order transformations (HOTs) on first-class model representations of transformation specifications. In this paper, we present a generic approach and provide initial prototypes for an integrated tool support which integrates BX into well-established Eclipse-based MDD frameworks, thereby neither being restricted to a specific modeling nor model transformation language.

Keywords: Model-driven development · Model co-evolution · Bidirectional transformation · Higher-order transformation

1 Introduction

In model-driven development (MDD; see, e.g., [2,3]), numerous models and transformations on different abstraction levels need to be taken into account. The high number of models involved originate from a layered modeling architecture (i.e. metamodels, MMs) as well as from refinements (i.e. transformations) from generic to implementation-centric model representations [4]. On the one hand,

This is an extended version of the paper published as Hoisl et al. [1].

S. Hammoudi et al. (Eds.): MODELSWARD 2014, CCIS 506, pp. 153–167, 2015.
DOI: 10.1007/978-3-319-25156-1_10

the need for model transformations is inherent to the abstraction mechanism in MDD to represent platform-specific concepts (e.g., statements in a programming language) as platform-independent models [5]. On the other hand, model transformation necessities stem also from, for instance, changes in MMs (e.g., changes from the original MM to a new MM are implemented by model-to-model transformations, M2M) or the support for multiple platforms (e.g., platform-specific textual representations, such as, source code or configuration and deployment documents, are provided by different model-to-text transformations, M2T).

MDD-based artifacts are frequently subject to change and evolve over time [6]. In most cases, the evolution of (meta)models and model transformations is a manual process [7]. Individually maintain and manually evolve MDD specifications is a tedious and error-prone task [8,9]. For instance, consider an evolution of a MM and accompanying constraints. First, all instance models need to be migrated in order to conform to the new MM definition. Furthermore, all model transformations need to be adapted (e.g., due to model type changes). Moreover, tests need to be rewritten to check that the generated source code fulfills the specified constraints.

The artifacts which make up a MDD process (models, M2M/M2T transformations, model and transformation constraints etc.)—although highly interdependent—are autonomously maintained. Changes in one artifact (e.g., in a model) are not automatically reflected in other dependent artifacts (e.g., in a M2T transformation). The barrier for a tight integration of MDD-based artifacts stems from two limitations of current approaches: (1) Model transformations are unidirectional and changes can be propagated in one direction only (e.g., a model change is reflected in generated code); (2) changes can only be propagated into output artifacts of transformations (e.g., models), not into transformation definitions themselves.

In order to overcome these co-evolution problems, our approach, on the one hand, is based on (1) establishing bidirectional transformations (BX) between modeling artifacts (see, e.g., [8]). *BX* is a mechanism for maintaining the consistency of two (or more) related sources of information. A BX between two sources of information A and B (e.g., two different models) comprises a pair of unidirectional transformations: one from A to B (*forward transformation*) and another from B to A (*backward transformation*) [10].

On the other hand, we apply (2) higher-order transformations (HOTs) on first-class model representations of transformation specifications [11]. A *HOT* "is a model transformation such that its input and/or output models are themselves transformation models. [...] This demands the representation of the transformation as a model conforming to a transformation MM" [11].

In this way, we are able to propagate changes in two directions (1): From a source model to a target model and vice versa. These changes can be propagated into models on the same or on different abstraction levels. Furthermore, we ensure not only the co-evolution of models, but (2) model transformations, as well. We represent transformation definitions as models and are able to propagate changes into horizontal and vertical model transformations (i.e. transformations between models on the same and on different abstraction levels).

Our contributions are as follows:

- *A Method for MDD-based Co-evolution:* Our approach of bidirectional higher-order transformation (B-HOT) for the co-evolution of model artifacts builds on former work [12–15]. This paper presents first enhancement steps which will allow for coupling, synchronization, and tracing of all model artifacts involved in a MDD process.
- *Integrated Tool Support:* We provide initial prototypes for an integrated MDD-based tool support for B-HOTs via the Eclipse IDE. Our implementations build on well-established MDD tools (e.g., Eclipse EMF [16], ATL [17], Epsilon [18])[1].
- *Conformance between BX and MDD:* To facilitate reproduction and transferability, we present an approach independent of any transformation language and we prepare for generalizations according to OMG specifications, for example, MOF [19], QVT [20], MOFM2T [21]. Besides integrated BX and MDD tooling, we also want to contribute to establish a common terminology to bridge the gap between the BX and MDD communities [10,22].

The remainder of this paper is structured as follows. Section 2 reviews traditional model-driven architectures and explains why current approaches cannot sufficiently cope with the co-evolution of multiple MDD-based artifacts. Section 3 describes our approach to overcome the shortcomings of current methods. Requirements of our approach are discussed in Sect. 4. Our initial MDD-based developments are briefly explained in Sect. 5. Section 6 concludes the paper by discussing implications and mentioning limitations of our approach as well as pointing to ongoing and future work.

2 Current Approaches

A traditional model-driven architecture (MDA), as proposed by the OMG [23,24] and as supported by a variety of tools, is sketched in Fig. 1. MMs provide the reference frame to which instance models must conform to, for example, a UML class model conforms to its MM defined in the UML specification [25]. M2M transformations are applied over one or more input models with the purpose of generating one or more output models conforming to the same or different MMs. A typical M2M transformation example is the generation of platform-specific models (PSMs) from platform-independent models (PIMs). As models are a means for abstraction, they mostly do not capture enough implementation details to be directly executable. Hence, M2T transformations generate textual artifacts (e.g., source code, configuration documents) which can be deployed on a specific platform.

When a MDD-based artifact evolves, changes must be reflected in all dependent (meta)models, transformations, and platform artifacts. The complexity of

[1] All software artifacts are publicly available at http://www.biglab.org and http://nm.wu.ac.at/modsec.

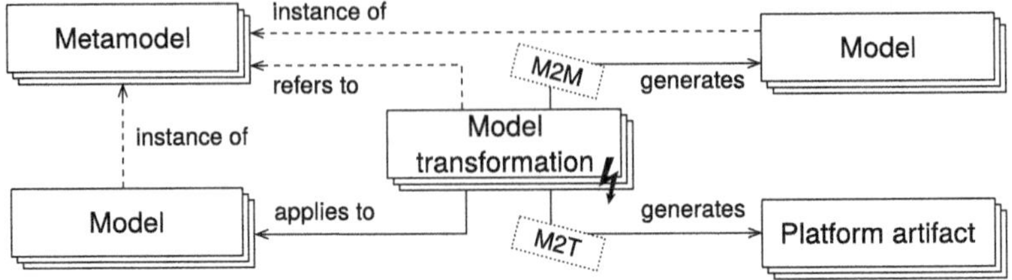

Fig. 1. Traditional model-driven architecture.

change operations increases with the number of different MMs and models (e.g., due to different modeling languages), M2M transformations (e.g., due to intermediary model representations), and M2T transformations (e.g., due to multiple supported platforms) involved. Current approaches cannot sufficiently cope with the co-evolution of multiple MDD-based artifacts because of restrictions to express and propagate changes which manifest in (1) unidirectional model transformations and (2) disregarding transformation definitions as first-class models (see Fig. 1). An example for evolution mismatches is the inability to reflect changes in generated platform artifacts back to their corresponding instance models. For example, in Eclipse EMF, changes to the generated Java source code may be lost when executing the unidirectional M2T transformation once again. Furthermore, by default, the generation templates (i.e. Java Emitter Templates, JETs) cannot be easily adapted, excluding the possibility to reflect changes in the code generator logic (i.e. transformation definitions are not treated as first-class artifacts).

Yu et al. [26] provide a platform-specific (i.e. Java-bound) solution for the co-evolution problem stated above. In the approach, BX is used to synchronize models with generated and user-modified code. Prerequisites are that the platform-specific language encodes a textual duplicate of the PIM (i.e. `@model` annotations) and that a MM representation exists for the platform-specific language (i.e. a Java Ecore MM).

To establish BX, triple graph grammars [27] are commonly employed in MDD for keeping related models consistent (see, e.g., [28]). Triple graph transformations relate a source and a target graph (i.e. a model) by some correspondence graph. In this way, source and target graphs are coupled which provides a basic structure for their co-evolution.

Wachsmuth [29] considers MM/model co-evolution as a step-wise adaptation of MMs (via transformation relations) and instance-preservation of models. Instead of describing the co-evolution of models as a transformation between two MMs, Wimmer et al. [30] employ in-place transformations. Herrmannsdoerfer et al. [31] present a framework to model the co-evolution of MMs/models via the composition of coupled transactions to adapt the MM and specify the corresponding model migrations.

Furthermore, state-based MM/model co-evolution approaches, for instance, adopt HOTs which take a difference model obtained by comparing two MMs and generate a model transformation able to produce the co-evolution of involved models [9].

Although all of these co-evolution methods cope with model transformation restrictions, a combined and uniform solution is missing, so far. Either the approaches provide only one-way co-evolution possibilities (i.e. unidirectional) or only for a subset of MDD artifacts (e.g., only MM/model co-evolution). Therefore, in the next section, we propose a generic approach for co-evolving MDD-related artifacts.

3 Model Co-evolution via B-HOT

With our approach (Fig. 2 provides an overview) we want to overcome shortcomings of current methods and offer a generic solution for co-evolving MDD artifacts. The upper part of Fig. 2 reflects a traditional MDA. Model co-evolution is achieved by integrating (1) BX capabilities (lower part of Fig. 2) and (2) support for HOTs into the MDA.

As an example, consider a model transformation from an object-oriented representation (e.g., a class diagram) to a relational database model. For instance, both MMs are defined in a MOF-based language (see upper part of Fig. 2). Hence, their instance models (e.g., using Ecore as technological projection) conform to the (E)MOF MM. A transformation (e.g., specified via ATL or ETL) is

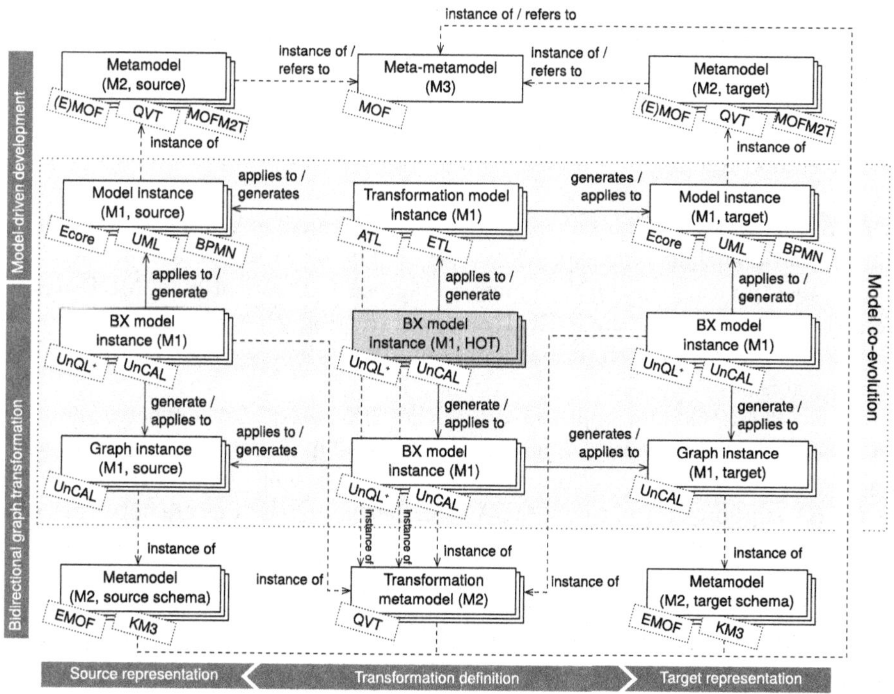

Fig. 2. Overview of our model co-evolution approach.

applied to class models and generates database models. This forward transformation proves useful in one case only: Changes in evolving class models should be reflected in database models, as well. Updates in database models cannot be propagated back to their source class models. A coupling of both representations limits the target model to be read-only (otherwise changes get lost when re-executing the transformation).

In our approach, we integrate BX capabilities by reusing native MDD concepts. *Every* transformation is represented as a first-class model conforming to a transformation MM. B-HOTs (see Fig. 2) provide for the mapping of unidirectional MDD-based transformation models (e.g. defined via ATL or ETL) into a bidirectional graph transformation model (and vice versa). Reconsidering the BX of the class-to-database model transformation example, in a next step, both source and target models (i.e. class and database models) are mapped to a graph structure (defined via UnCAL [32], a graph algebra). Source and target graph schemas are represented as MOF-based MMs. In order to establish bidirectionality between the class-to-database transformation, the unidirectional transformation model need to be mapped to a bidirectional transformation model. This is done via a B-HOT (defined via UnQL$^+$ [13], a SQL-like graph query/transformation language) which provides the forward and backward transformations between two transformation specifications (in our example, transformation models specified in ATL/ETL and UnQL$^+$). The result of the B-HOT is a BX specification (again defined via UnQL$^+$) which provides both, a forward transformation from class to database graphs as well as a corresponding backward transformation. Thus, changes in the database graph can be propagated back to the class graph. As the transformation of models to graphs is also bidirectional, updated class and database graphs can be represented in their initial model-based forms. Therefore, a BX of source and target models (class and database models in our example) is established. The backward database-to-class transformation is distinct to the BX and no corresponding MDD-based transformation equivalent exists (i.e. no backward transformation defined via, e.g., ATL or ETL). Therefore, as a last step, the backward transformation (in UnQL$^+$) must be represented in its original MDD-based form (in ATL, ETL) via the B-HOT mapping (see Fig. 2).

We discuss co-evolution properties of our approach according to the following four categories.

Model Relations: Our approach establishes BX-based relations between models, graphs, and model and graph representations. The mapping relation between traditional MDD-based transformations and BX representations (B-HOT) allows to add BX support in traditional MDAs. Furthermore, relations are not restricted to one source and one target artifact only, but can be used for the transformation of multiple dependent models/graphs, as well (see also compositional BX down below). The coupling of models via BX allows, on the one hand, to establish synchronization definitions and, on the other hand, to collect transformation traces. As many modeling artifacts make up a MDD process, keeping models consistent is of special importance. Moreover, trace information are a relevant source for documentation and debugging purposes.

Model Co-evolution Scenarios: Our approach supports any M2M relation and any number of MM-layers. Horizontal co-evolution examples are, for instance, the synchronization of different MMs or different instance models. Vertical co-evolution examples are, for instance, keeping instance models and corresponding MMs or PIMs and PSMs consistent. Consider, for example, a PIM representing a MM of an object-oriented system and a Java-based MM as its PSM equivalent. Both MMs are synchronized via a B-HOT keeping them consistent. In this case, changes in the PIM can be propagated into the PSM (and vice versa). If the Java-based MM needs to be modified (e.g., due to the release of a new Java version), these changes—when affecting the object-oriented system representation, as well—can be propagated back into the PIM via the B-HOT. Moreover, transformation models permit to propagate changes also in horizontal and vertical M2M and M2T transformation definitions, for instance, for the co-evolution of MMs and transformation models or different transformation models. Referring to the example of synchronizing a general object-oriented MM and a Java-based MM, consider that their instance models are transformed into a textual object-oriented representation and Java source code, respectively. Changes in the Java-based MM (again, e.g., because of a new Java version) must also be reflected in its M2T transformation (e.g., type changes). Via a B-HOT between the PIM and PSM M2T transformations, changes in one of the M2T transformations can be propagated into the other M2T transformation keeping them consistent.

Language-independent Integration: Our approach is not dependent on a specific model transformation language, i.e. it does not matter if the model transformation is defined via ATL, ETL, or any other language. This is because we do not integrate bidirectionality into a model transformation language directly. The B-HOT definition serves as a language-specific binding between the concepts of the unidirectional MDD-based transformation and the bidirectional graph transformation. These bindings must be specified only once for each MDD-based transformation language (e.g., ATL, ETL) and facilitate reuse of our approach.

BX Properties: We develop B-HOTs via a functional bidirectional graph transformation language named UnQL$^+$ [13]. UnQL$^+$ is an extension of UnQL [32], a graph querying language based on structural recursion (which can be expressed in first-order logic extended with transitive closure) [33]. The BX ensures the *well-behavedness* of forward and backward transformations (i.e. that they are consistent with each other) and satisfy the round-trip property [10]. As the BX does not restrict forward transformations to be information preserving, a backward transformation requires not only the modified target graph/model, but also the original source graph/model. Large BX can be developed in a *compositional* way of reusing existing information (e.g., via intermediate models). Compositional BX can be employed, on the one hand, for a pair of consecutive transformations, where the output of transformation A is the input of transformation B; for example, the output of the source model-to-graph transformation is fed into the forward source-to-target graph transformation (see Fig. 2). On the other hand, compositional BX can be used for a pair of transformations that share an identical input model, for instance, transformations from one PIM to multiple PSMs [12].

4 B-HOT Requirements

This paper provides a first step to make co-evolution in MDD via B-HOTs possible. Initial work regarding the methodology and accompanying tool support has been performed, but is far from being finalized. In this section, we list challenging requirements for the implementation of our approach. We present completed work and discuss prerequisites for future developments.

Transformation MMs: Our B-HOT approach relies on transformation (meta)models. MDD-based M2M transformation MMs exist, for instance, for ATL [11] and for a subset of the Epsilon-language family [34]. Regarding M2T transformations, Hoisl et al. [15] extended the Epsilon model representations of Wei [34]. The BX framework [13] does not need MM representations for the UnQL$^+$ and UnCAL languages. Syntax definitions in Backus-Naur Form (BNF) exist for both languages and need to be mapped to EMOF-compliant (e.g. Ecore-based) MM representations (ongoing work; see also Sects. 5 and 6).

MM-specific Bindings: For a B-HOT, language-specific bindings need to be established between uni- and bidirectional transformation MMs. Initial work provides a unidirectional transformation from a subset of the ATL language to UnQL$^+$ (excluding imperative code and OCL expressions of ATL). This transformation does not take the model representation of ATL into account [14][2]. Thus, language-specific bindings for, for instance, ATL and/or ETL to UnQL$^+$ and/or UnCAL via B-HOT is future work. Furthermore, a first prototype exists for the BX of model-to-graph representations (Ecore-based models to UnCAL and vice versa), but needs improvements (future work).

Round-tripping of Transformation Definitions: Our B-HOT approach demands transformation models as input. In contrast, most model transformation engines cannot execute model representations of transformation definitions. Therefore, the round-tripping of executable (i.e. text-based) transformation specifications and their model representations must be provided. For M2M transformations, "an ATL transformation is itself a model, conforming to the ATL MM" [11]. Furthermore, Wei [34] developed initial round-tripping support for an Epsilon subset which was extended for M2T transformations (i.e. EGL) by Hoisl et al. [15]. Currently, the automatically derived backward transformation of a BX can neither be expressed as UnQL$^+$ or UnCAL textual statements nor via corresponding model representations (future work).

Generic Mappings: Prototype developments define transformations in a specific language as implementation vehicle (e.g., ATL, ETL). To support uptake and transferability of our approach we need to establish mappings to OMG specifications (see also Fig. 2). Hoisl et al. [15] provide mappings between EGL-based M2T transformation concepts used for the prototype and the MOFM2T specification. As future work, uni-/bidirectional M2M transformation concepts (e.g., ATL, ETL, UnQL$^+$) will be mapped to the QVT specification.

[2] This separate work of integrating ATL and BX is performed in collaboration with the AtlanMod team, uses the same BX framework (*GRoundTram*), but in contrast focuses on unidirectional transformations from ATL to UnQL$^+$ with a concrete semantic alignment between these two technical spaces.

Development Support: Initial support for the requirements-driven testing of (meta)models and model transformations via scenarios is provided by Sobernig et al. [35] and is extended/evaluated by Hoisl et al. [36,37]. Furthermore, validation for source and target models as well as for BX is presented by Hidaka et al. [13]. We have started implementing an IDE (e.g., a text editor) to support the development of UnQL$^+$ BX (see Sect. 5) and UnCAL-based graphs (future work). For this task, we have chosen Eclipse Xtext as candidate framework because it combines the grammar specification for a textual syntax with an Ecore-based model representation and provides for an Eclipse-based IDE.

Combine BX and MDD: Model (i.e. graph) transformations are important to both BX and MDD [10,22]. Our approach allows to integrate BX into MDD, thereby reusing native methods and tools for both. We want to support the creation of a shared terminology [10] via the generalization and mapping of language-specific uni-/bidirectional transformation concepts to OMG specifications. After our developments have matured, as future work, we need to provide for a larger case study to show that our approach works in practice.

5 Prototypical MDD-Based Support for UnQL$^+$

This section introduces our initial MDD-based developments for the UnQL$^+$ BX language: an Ecore-based UnQL$^+$ MM (see Fig. 3), an Xtext grammar specification for the UnQL$^+$ textual syntax (see Listing 1), and editors to support the development of UnQL$^+$ BX in both textual and model-based syntax notations (see the example text- and model-based transformation definitions in Listing 2 and Fig. 4, respectively)[3] These developments are based on Eclipse EMF and matured versions will fulfill the following B-HOT requirements (see Sect. 4): The mapping of BNF-compliant/Xtext-based UnQL$^+$ grammar definitions to EMOF-compliant/Ecore-based MM representations. This allows the *specification of an UnQL$^+$ BX MM* with two corresponding and interchangeable concrete syntax variants (textual and model-based). As the Xtext grammar describes how an Ecore model is derived from a textual notation, *round-tripping of UnQL$^+$ BX definitions* is partially fulfilled (i.e. transformations specified textually are automatically mapped to their model representations). Furthermore, the implemented software artifacts (e.g., text/model editors) *support the development of UnQL$^+$ BX.*

Figure 3 shows an excerpt of the Ecore-based UnQL$^+$ MM. For this, the BNF grammar of UnQL$^+$ was mapped to a model representation consisting of (abstract) classes and class attributes as well as containment references and inheritance relationships between these classes. From Fig. 3 it can be seen that four different `Statement` types can be contained in an `UnQLplus` expression: `Selection`, `Replacement`, `Deletion`, and `Extension`. All of these statements operate on graphs (`Template`); for example, to select a graph based on certain conditions.

[3] All software artifacts can be obtained from the URLs mentioned in the footnote of Sect. 1.

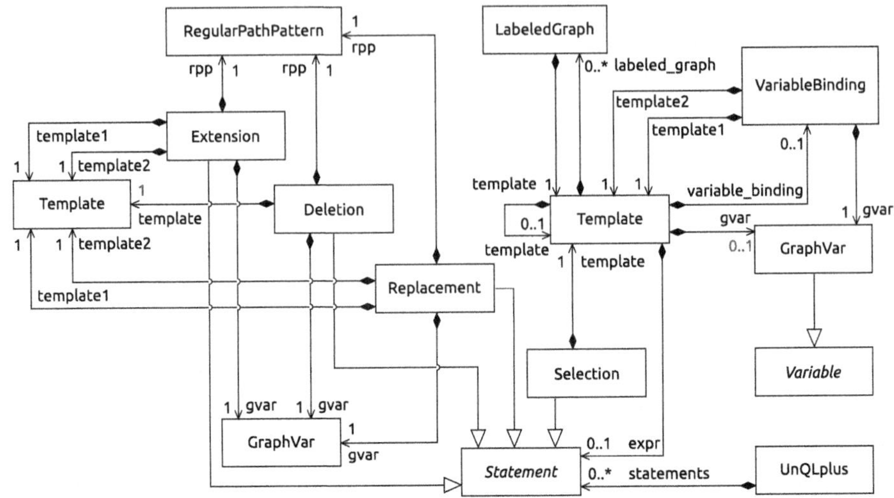

Fig. 3. Ecore-based UnQL$^+$ MM (excerpt).

Listing 1 shows an excerpt of the Xtext grammar for the UnQL$^+$ textual syntax. The grammar definition of UnQL$^+$ was translated from BNF to Xtext and aligned to match the Ecore model concepts. The entry rule on lines 7–8 in Listing 1 defines that an `UnQLplus` expression contains `Statements`. The `Statement` rule (lines 10–12) delegates in line 11 to the four alternative statement rules (defined later) and specifies the syntax of an optional condition (line 12). As examples, the syntax of two statements is specified in the `Selection` rule (lines 14–15) and in the `Replacement` rule (lines 17–18). Furthermore, the definition of graphs is shown in lines 22–23 (`Template` rule) and lines 25–33 (`TemplateExpression` rule), respectively (delegated rules are omitted).

```
1 grammar org.biglab.groundtram.bx.UnQLplus
2   hidden(WS, SL_COMMENT, ML_COMMENT)
3
4 import "http://unqlplus/0.1"
5 import "http://www.eclipse.org/emf/2002/Ecore" as ecore
6
7 UnQLplus:
8   statements+=Statement*;
9
10 Statement:
11   (Selection | Replacement | Deletion | Extension)
12   ('where' condition+=Condition (',' condition+=Condition)*)?;
13
14 Selection:
15   'select' template=Template;
16
17 Replacement:
18   'replace' rpp=RegularPathPattern '->' gvar=GraphVar 'by' template1=
        Template 'in' template2=Template;
19
20 ...
```

```

Template:
  TemplateExpression (=>'U' template=Template)?;

TemplateExpression returns Template:
  {Template} '{' labeled_graph+=LabeledGraph? (',' labeled_graph+=
       LabeledGraph)* '}' |
  '(' expr=Statement ')' |
  fname=FunctionTemplate |
  conditional=Conditional |
  variable_binding=VariableBinding |
  structural_recursion=StructuralRecursion |
  mutual_structural_recursion=MutualStructuralRecursion |
  gvar=GraphVar;

VariableBinding:
  'let' gvar=GraphVar '=' template1=Template 'in' template2=Template;

...
```

Listing 1. Xtext grammar definition for the UnQL$^+$ textual syntax (excerpt).

With the Ecore MM and the Xtext grammar defined in Fig. 3 and Listing 1, it is possible to provide editor support for textual as well as model-based UnQL$^+$ BX. Listing 2 shows an example class-to-database UnQL$^+$ BX replacing attributes by columns (excerpt taken from Hidaka et al. [13]). The BX in Listing 2 makes use of `Selection` (e.g., starting from line 1 and line 3) and `Replacement` statements (starting from line 7). The UnQL$^+$ BX was created using our Eclipse-based textual editor providing features, such as, syntax coloring, auto completion, error detection, and so forth. In this way, it is ensured that developed UnQL$^+$ BX conform to the Xtext grammar defined in Listing 1. A benefit of using the editor to write UnQL$^+$ BX is the early detection and immediate correction of syntactical errors.

```
 1 select {tables : $table} where
 2   $persistentClass in
 3     (select $class where
 4       {Association.(src|dest).Class : $class} in $db,
 5       {is_persistent : {Boolean : true}} in $class),
 6   $table in
 7     (replace attrs -> $g
 8       by (select {Column : $a} where
 9           {attrs.Attribute : $a} in $persistentClass)
10       in $persistentClass)
```

Listing 2. Example class-to-database UnQL$^+$ BX (excerpt).

Figure 4 shows an excerpt of a tree-based view on a model representation of the same class-to-database UnQL$^+$ BX example introduced in Listing 2. Via the Ecore MM and the corresponding Xtext grammar, a model representation can be derived from textual UnQL$^+$ BX definitions. This instance model conforms to the Ecore-based UnQL$^+$ MM in the same way as a textual UnQL$^+$ BX definition conforms to the Xtext grammar. The representation of transformation models (e.g., expressing UnQL$^+$ BX as models as exemplified in Fig. 4) is one of the main requirements to realize our B-HOT approach.

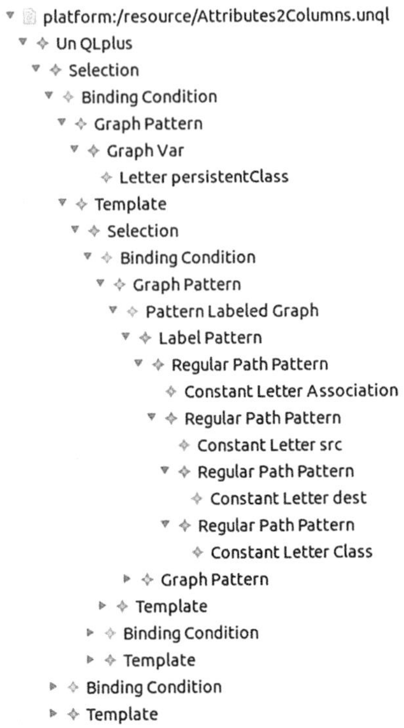

```
▾ platform:/resource/Attributes2Columns.unql
  ▾ Un QLplus
    ▾ Selection
      ▾ Binding Condition
        ▾ Graph Pattern
          ▾ Graph Var
              Letter persistentClass
        ▾ Template
          ▾ Selection
            ▾ Binding Condition
              ▾ Graph Pattern
                ▾ Pattern Labeled Graph
                  ▾ Label Pattern
                    ▾ Regular Path Pattern
                        Constant Letter Association
                      ▾ Regular Path Pattern
                          Constant Letter src
                        ▾ Regular Path Pattern
                            Constant Letter dest
                        ▾ Regular Path Pattern
                            Constant Letter Class
                  ▸ Graph Pattern
              ▸ Template
            ▸ Binding Condition
            ▸ Template
      ▸ Binding Condition
      ▸ Template
```

Fig. 4. Tree-based view on example class-to-database UnQL$^+$ BX model (excerpt).

6 Concluding Discussion

In this paper, we presented an approach for model co-evolution by combining BX and HOT for MDD. The developed method (B-HOT) intends to overcome current limitations for model co-evolution as transformations are represented as models and model transformations are bidirectionalized. In our approach, models are coupled via BX providing the benefit that synchronization of models is ensured via forward/backward transformations. Another advantage is that changes can be propagated into model transformations keeping them consistent with their evolving dependent artifacts (MMs, model instances). Our approach of integrating BX into MDD is generic and can be applied to any model transformation language via binding specifications.

With our work and according to the feature-based classification of BX approaches presented in [38], we combine graph-based and MDD-based artifact representations involved in BX. In particular, the employed demonstrator BX framework (GRoundTram) is based on graphs, while metamodels in Eclipse approximate the MOF specification (implemented via Ecore models). Therefore, the technical space of GRoundTram needs to cope with MDD-based artifact representations, as well. In GRoundTram (for further BX approaches and their characteristic features see [38]), the correspondence relation between source and target artifacts is defined via user-provided unidirectional transformation specifications. In this case, the backward transformation is not explicitly stated (see also Sect. 4) and is automatically derived by the bidirectional engine (inversion). Thus, the results of the computed backward transformation needs to be conceptualized in the technical space of GRoundTram (i.e. represented in UnQL$^+$ or UnCAL). The proposed B-HOT approach presented in this paper demands to switch from an implicit to an explicit representation of the backward transformation.

Please note that BX approaches (see, e.g., [38]) differ in terms of feature characteristics and implementation methods, for example, according to the technical space (e.g., text-, graph-, MDD-based), the directionality of the consistency definition (e.g., unidirectional, bidirectional transformation specifications), the representation of changes (e.g., state-, operation-based), or the definition of the backward transformation (e.g., explicit, implicit) [38]. Although we focus in this paper specifically on one BX approach (i.e. GRoundTram), other BX methods which conceptually conform to the requirements discussed in the former paragraph as well as in Sect. 4 are candidates for consideration, as well.

A drawback of our proposal is that the efforts of creating initial modeling and transformation artifacts can be high. Transformation MMs may have to be defined for the intended target language. Currently, no bindings for transformation languages exist. Although these have to be defined only once for each language, this is a barrier for uptake. Transformation engines might not execute transformation models directly making model/text round-tripping functions necessary (but again these can be reused per language). Adequate tool support must be provided to facilitate the development of models and transformations.

Currently, we are developing an EMOF-based MM for the UnQL$^+$ BX language (in Ecore). In parallel, we transfer the BNF-based grammar definition to Xtext. This will ensure the consistent mapping of transformations written in UnQL$^+$ to their modeling equivalents. An editor to support the definition of UnQL$^+$ statements will be provided, as well. Initial developments (see also Sect. 5) are available at the URLs mentioned in the footnote of Sect. 1 and are continuously updated. UnQL$^+$ concepts will be mapped to the QVT-Relations language in the near future.

Acknowledgements. This work has partly been funded by the Austrian Research Promotion Agency (FFG) of the Austrian Federal Ministry for Transport, Innovation and Technology (BMVIT) through the Competence Centers for Excellent Technologies (COMET K1) initiative and the FIT-IT program.

References

1. Hoisl, B., Hu, Z., Hidaka, S.: Towards co-evolution in model-driven development via bidirectional higher-order transformation. In: Proceedings of the 2nd International Conference on Model-Driven Engineering and Software Development, pp. 466–471. SciTePress (2014)

2. Mellor, S., Clark, A., Futagami, T.: Model-driven development - guest editor's introduction. IEEE Softw. **20**, 14–18 (2003)
3. Stahl, T., Völter, M.: Model-Driven Software Development: Technology, Engineering, Management. Wiley, New York (2006)
4. Sendall, S., Kozaczynski, W.: Model transformation: the heart and soul of model-driven software development. IEEE Softw. **20**, 42–45 (2003)
5. Schmidt, D.C.: Guest editor's introduction: model-driven engineering. Computer **39**, 25–31 (2006)
6. Di Ruscio, D., Iovino, L., Pierantonio, A.: Coupled evolution in model-driven engineering. IEEE Softw. **29**, 78–84 (2012)
7. Meyers, B., Vangheluwe, H.: A framework for evolution of modelling languages. Sci. Comput. Program. **76**, 1223–1246 (2011)
8. Stevens, P.: Bidirectional model transformations in QVT: semantic issues and open questions. Softw. Syst. Model. **9**, 7–20 (2010)
9. Di Ruscio, D., Iovino, L., Pierantonio, A.: What is needed for managing co-evolution in MDE? In: Proceedings of the 2nd International Workshop on Model Comparison in Practice, pp. 30–38. ACM (2011)
10. Czarnecki, K., Foster, J.N., Hu, Z., Lämmel, R., Schürr, A., Terwilliger, J.F.: Bidirectional transformations: a cross-discipline perspective. In: Paige, R.F. (ed.) ICMT 2009. LNCS, vol. 5563, pp. 260–283. Springer, Heidelberg (2009)
11. Tisi, M., Jouault, F., Fraternali, P., Ceri, S., Bézivin, J.: On the use of higher-order model transformations. In: Paige, R.F., Hartman, A., Rensink, A. (eds.) ECMDA-FA 2009. LNCS, vol. 5562, pp. 18–33. Springer, Heidelberg (2009)
12. Hidaka, S., Hu, Z., Kato, H., Nakano, K.: Towards a compositional approach to model transformation for software development. In: Proceedings of the 24th Symposium on Applied Computing, pp. 468–475. ACM (2009)
13. Hidaka, S., Hu, Z., Inaba, K., Kato, H., Nakano, K.: GRoundTram: an integrated framework for developing well-behaved bidirectional model transformations. In: Proceedings of the 26th International Conference on Automated Software Engineering, pp. 480–483. IEEE (2011)
14. Sasano, I., Hu, Z., Hidaka, S., Inaba, K., Kato, H., Nakano, K.: Toward bidirectionalization of ATL with GRoundTram. In: Cabot, J., Visser, E. (eds.) ICMT 2011. LNCS, vol. 6707, pp. 138–151. Springer, Heidelberg (2011)
15. Hoisl, B., Sobernig, S., Strembeck, M.: Higher-order rewriting of model-to-text templates for integrating domain-specific modeling languages. In: Proceedings of the 1st International Conference on Model-Driven Engineering and Software Development, pp. 49–61. SciTePress (2013)
16. Steinberg, D., Budinsky, F., Paternostro, M., Merks, E.: EMF: Eclipse Modeling Framework, 2nd edn. Addison-Wesley, Reading (2008)
17. Jouault, F., Kurtev, I.: Transforming models with ATL. In: Bruel, J.-M. (ed.) MoDELS 2005. LNCS, vol. 3844, pp. 128–138. Springer, Heidelberg (2006)
18. Kolovos, D., Rose, L., García-Domínguez, A., Paige, R.: The Epsilon book (2015). http://www.eclipse.org/epsilon/doc/book/
19. Object Management Group: OMG meta object facility (MOF) core specification (2015). http://www.omg.org/spec/MOF, version 2.5, formal/2015-06-05
20. Object Management Group: Meta object facility (MOF) 2.0 query/view/transformation specification (2015). http://www.omg.org/spec/QVT, version 1.2, formal/2015-02-01
21. Object Management Group: MOF model to text transformation language (2008). http://www.omg.org/spec/MOFM2T, version 1.0, formal/2008-01-16

22. Hu, Z., Schurr, A., Stevens, P., Terwilliger, J.F.: Dagstuhl seminar on bidirectional transformations (BX). SIGMOD Rec. **40**, 35–39 (2011)
23. Bézivin, J., Gerbé, O.: Towards a precise definition of the OMG/MDA framework. In: Proceedings of the 16th International Conference on Automated Software Engineering, pp. 273–280. IEEE (2001)
24. Object Management Group: MDA guide (2003). http://www.omg.org/cgi-bin/doc?omg/03-06-01, version 1.0.1, omg/2003-06-01
25. OMG unified modeling language (OMG UML), superstructure (2015). http://www.omg.org/spec/UML, version 2.5, formal/2015-03-01
26. Yu, Y., Lin, Y., Hu, Z., Hidaka, S., Kato, H., Montrieux, L.: Maintaining invariant traceability through bidirectional transformations. In: Proceedings of the 34th International Conference on Software Engineering, pp. 540–550. IEEE (2012)
27. Schürr, A.: Specification of graph translators with triple graph grammars. In: Mayr, E.W., Schmidt, G., Tinhofer, G. (eds.) WG 1994. LNCS, vol. 903, pp. 151–163. Springer, Heidelberg (1995)
28. Giese, H., Wagner, R.: From model transformation to incremental bidirectional model synchronization. Softw. Syst. Model. **8**, 21–43 (2009)
29. Wachsmuth, G.: Metamodel adaptation and model co-adaptation. In: Ernst, E. (ed.) ECOOP 2007. LNCS, vol. 4609, pp. 600–624. Springer, Heidelberg (2007)
30. Wimmer, M., Kusel, A., Schönböck, J., Retschitzegger, W., Schwinger, W., Kappel, G.: On using inplace transformations for model co-evolution. In: Proceedings of the 2nd International Workshop on Model Transformation with ATL, INRIA & Ecole des Mines de Nantes (2010)
31. Herrmannsdoerfer, M., Benz, S., Juergens, E.: COPE - automating coupled evolution of metamodels and models. In: Drossopoulou, S. (ed.) ECOOP 2009. LNCS, vol. 5653, pp. 52–76. Springer, Heidelberg (2009)
32. Buneman, P., Fernandez, M., Suciu, D.: UnQL: a query language and algebra for semistructured data based on structural recursion. VLDB J. **9**, 76–110 (2000)
33. Hidaka, S., Hu, Z., Inaba, K., Kato, H., Nakano, K.: GRoundTram: an integrated framework for developing well-behaved bidirectional model transformations. Prog. Inf. **10**, 131–148 (2013)
34. Wei, W.: EpsilonLabs: Epsilon static analysis (2012). http://code.google.com/p/epsilonlabs/wiki/EpsilonStaticAnalysis
35. Sobernig, S., Hoisl, B., Strembeck, M.: Requirements-driven testing of domain-specific core language models using scenarios. In: Proceedings of the 13th International Conference on Quality Software, pp. 163–172. IEEE (2013)
36. Hoisl, B., Sobernig, S., Strembeck, M.: Natural-language scenario descriptions for testing core language models of domain-specific languages. In: Proceedings of the 2nd International Conference on Model-Driven Engineering and Software Development, pp. 356–367. SciTePress (2014)
37. Hoisl, B., Sobernig, S., Strembeck, M.: Comparing three notations for defining scenario-based model tests: a controlled experiment. In: Proceedings of the 9th International Conference on the Quality of Information and Communications Technology, pp. 95–104. IEEE (2014)
38. Hidaka, S., Tisi, M., Cabot, J., Hu, Z.: Feature-based classification of bidirectional transformation approaches. Softw. Syst. Model. (2015)

Methodologies, Processes and Platforms

Reducing Complexity of Process Tailoring Transformations Generation

Luis Silvestre(✉), María Cecilia Bastarrica, and Sergio F. Ochoa

Computer Science Department, University of Chile,
Beauchef 851, 8370459 Santiago, Chile
{lsilvest,cecilia,sochoa}@dcc.uchile.cl
http://www.dcc.uchile.cl

Abstract. Tailoring software processes to particular contexts applying model transformations has proved to be appropriate and technically feasible. However, the use of this approach can become awkward for most process engineers, because it requires knowledge about the process and its tailoring needs, and also about building model transformations. In a previous work we have proposed a tool based on model-driven engineering (MDE) for automatically generating software process model tailoring transformations. This paper presents an improved user interface of the tool and proposes a process for guiding its application for tailoring processes. We illustrate its use by applying it for tailoring the process of Rhiscom, a Chilean small software company. The tool and the process balance the formally required by MDE with the usability needed by the process engineers.

Keywords: Software process · Tailoring transformations

1 Introduction

Software process tailoring allows process engineers to adapt the organizational software process to the needs of particular projects. Although there is a variety of approaches for implementing tailoring processes, during the last years several researchers have identified in MDE a promising opportunity to address it [3,6,7]. MDE-based tailoring takes as input the organizational process model including its variability, and the project context model, and generates the project adapted process model through a model transformation. For each variable process element in the process model, there will be a rule in the tailoring transformation that determines if it is to be included or not (for optional elements) or which element should be included in the adapted process (for alternative elements), according to the values of the project context model attributes.

MDE-based approaches in general allow software modeling at different abstraction levels and addressing different application domains [12]. However, it requires mastering new concepts and formalisms relating model definition and writing model transformations in specific languages [13]. Particularly, generating

S. Hammoudi et al. (Eds.): MODELSWARD 2014, CCIS 506, pp. 171–182, 2015.
DOI: 10.1007/978-3-319-25156-1_11

appropriate tailoring transformations requires two different kinds of knowledge. On the one hand, process engineers, who are in charge of this activity, should know precisely how the context attribute values impact the process variation. And on the other hand, they should be able to write the model transformation, mastering the syntax and semantics of the transformation language. Most process engineers usually have the first kind of knowledge (i.e., how the process should be tailored), but they are usually not experienced in the use of transformation languages and MDE concepts. Moreover, software engineers that know how to build models and transformations are almost never in charge of processes and tailoring.

Costa-Silva et al. [5] present a qualitative study where they compare eight of the most relevant approaches for developing model transformations. The comparison considers aspects about the approaches foundations, features and applicability. The study shows that these proposals have rigorous foundations (from a theoretical perspective), they include most of the features required in the transformations, but they are difficult to use by developers. These results highlight the need for developing new solutions that simplify rule definition, while still providing all the expressive power required for software process model tailoring. This type of tailoring is only an example of the application scenarios that are not well supported by the current way of developing model transformations.

In order to address this challenge, in a previous work [20] we have presented a model-based tool that uses a generative approach to define tailoring transformations. This tool allows process engineers to interactively define rules using a graphical user interface, taking advantage of the formality provided by MDE, but hiding its inherent complexity. Thus, the process engineer defines transformation rules to tailor the organizational software process, only by instantiating on a graphical user interface the project context attributes that impact variable process elements. In this paper we describe an improved tool user interface and we provide a process that different stakeholders should follow for using the tool.

The rest of the paper is structured as follows. Next section presents and discusses some related work. Section 3 presents the foundations and the general structure used for the MDE software process tailoring tool. Section 4 presents the tool-based tailoring process and its application to a real world case using the improved user interface. Finally, conclusions and future work are presented in Sect. 5.

2 Related Work

Building appropriate model transformation requires expertise for choosing the right kind of transformation, and also for mastering the transformation language syntax and semantics. Therefore writing these transformations is usually difficult and requires knowledge that is not usually available in process engineers. These knowledge-gap barriers are partly addressed by transformation-by-example techniques [11]. Particularly, MOLA [10] and GREaT [1] allow specifying transformation rules through visual mapping patterns. They specify rules and mappings using class diagrams, but considering an environment inspired in activity diagrams. Both works also allow establishing relationships between metamodel attributes and elements. A limitation of MOLA and GREaT is that they need the user to directly interact with metamodels and class diagrams, which still represents a strong restriction for process engineers in terms of usability.

Varró and Balogh, through the VIATRA framework [25], provide a text-based rule editor. Although this proposal is supported by Eclipse, it does not provide an easy-to-use environment that can be used by process engineers for defining tailoring rules.

There are also some recent proposals, such as MTBE (Model Transformations By Example) [24,26] and MTBD (Model Transformation By Demonstration) [22], that use strategies and patterns with a visual support to simplify the implementation of model transformations. These strategies generate part of the code required for the model transformations, however, the process engineer still needs to understand and complete such a code. Therefore, using these approaches also represents a challenge for process engineers.

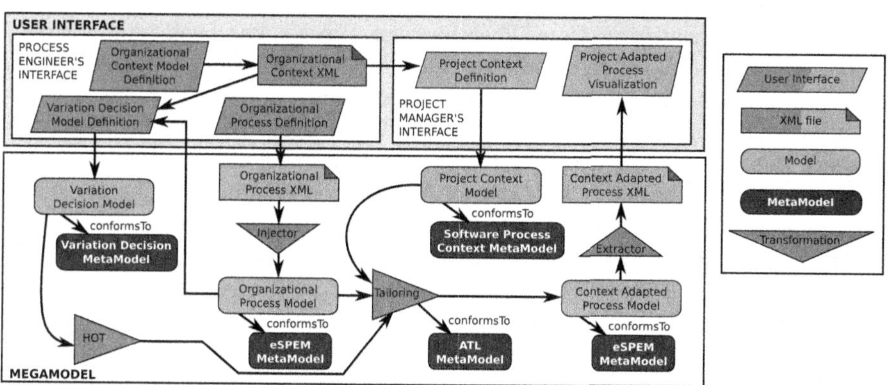

Fig. 1. MDE-based software process tailoring (Colour figure online).

Hurtado et al. [7] proposes a tailoring approach that generates an adapted process model from a general process model, which is adapted according to a project context model. The tailoring transformation is written in ATL [17] and it demonstrates the feasibility of this approach for tailoring software processes; however, it does not help overcame the stated problem due the rules still need to be written using ATL.

This knowledge-gap has lately been addressed by new proposals such as Domain-specific transformation languages [18]. For instance, Irazabal et al. [8] have proposed a DSTL implementation using MOFScript [15] (transformation language Model-to-Text) for the domain of data bases. Canovas et al. [9] have development Gra2Mol using Java (general purpose language) for generating grammar-to-model transformations.

3 MDE-based Software Process Tailoring

Figure 1 shows the general architecture of the MDE-based process tailoring approach organized as a megamodel [2]. This approach requires two input models: an *organizational software process model* that conforms to the eSPEM (experimental SPEM) metamodel that is a subset of SPEM (Software Process Engineering Metamodel) [14], and a *project context model* that is an instance of the *Organizational Context Model.* This approach uses a model-to-model transformation (the yellow triangle in the middle of Fig. 1) to generate a *project adapted software process model* as output. The resulting process model also conforms to eSPEM but includes no variability.

The *organizational software process model* is defined using the Eclipse Process Framework Composer (EPFC)[1], including its variabilities [21]. This tool has been well received by software companies' process engineers because it is free and provides an intuitive user interface. The process, as specified in EPFC, conforms to the UMA (Unified Method Architecture) metamodel in its internal representation, and the tool exports an xml file that cannot be directly used as input for the tailoring transformation. Therefore, an injector has been built for converting the process representation between format,s obtaining an *organizational software process model* in xmi format and conforming to eSPEM as needed.

The *organizational context model* indicates the project attributes that may influence the process tailoring along with their potential values. A *project context model* is an instance of this organizational context model. The organizational context model is defined using Eclipse Modeling Framework (EMF) and conforming to the SPCM (Software Process Context Metamodel) metamodel [7].

The *Variation Decision Model* (VDM), which conforms to a *Variation Decision MetaModel* (VDMM) [20], is a mapping that defines the tailoring rules using domain concepts. Each mapping has two subcomponents: Condition and Conclusion. Conditions may be simple (conditions [attribute and its value] with logical connectors), or complex (conditions are formed by combining simple conditions [attributes and its values] with logical connectors). Conclusions indicate if the process indicate a boolean value (true or false) for optional process elements, or a particular process element identification for alternative process elements.

Provided that model transformations can be also considered as models conforming to their language metamodel [4], a Higher-Order Transformation (HOT) is a transformation in itself, but it either takes a transformation model as input or generates a transformation model as output [23]. We use a HOT to generate the tailoring transformation, thus avoiding writing it directly. Our HOT takes the VDM previously built as input, and its output is the desired process tailoring transformation. There are two approaches for building HOTs: model-to-model (M2M) and model-to-text (M2T) transformations. We choose M2T and therefore the output is the ATL source code of the tailoring transformation. We have decided to use a general purpose language, such as Java, to build the HOT, at least for the first version, because it is a mature language that is easily mas-

[1] https://eclipse.org/epf/downloads/tool/tool_downloads.php.

tered by developers [19]. A final version of the HOT will be implemented in a transformation-specific language, probably ATL for symmetry of the solution.

The *tailoring* transformation in this proposal is written in ATL. For each variable element identified as part of the organizational process, there is a rule included in the transformation. For optional process elements, the rule decides, according to the values in the project context model attributes, if it should be included or not in the adapted process. For process elements defined with alternatives, the rule decides which of them will be included in the adapted process. Even though this strategy seems quite clear, translating it into ATL rules is a challenging task.

4 Applying the MDE-Based Tool

In this section we first describe who, what and when the tool should be used for process tailoring, i.e., its associated process. Afterwards, we illustrate the application of the tool and process for tailoring the software process of Rhiscom, a small Chilean software company.

4.1 The Process

The stakeholders for tool application process are: the process engineer, the project manager and the tool itself. Next, we will briefly describe each of them.

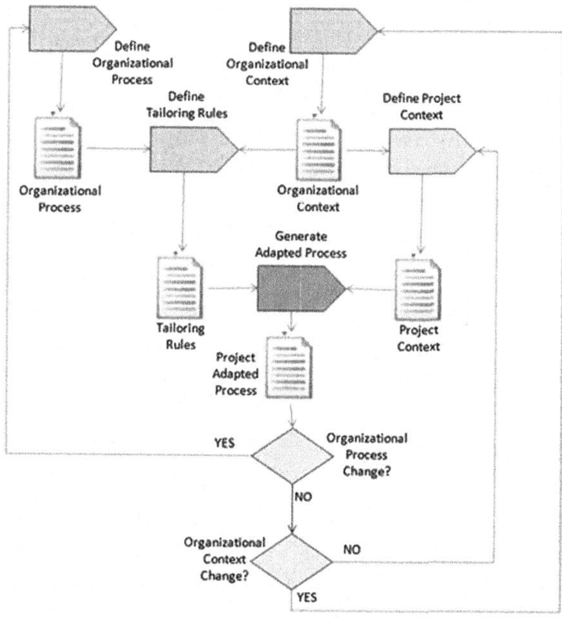

Fig. 2. Process supported by the proposed tool.

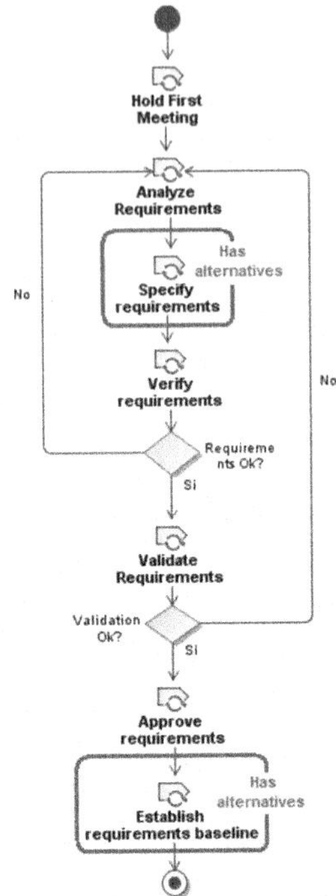

Fig. 3. Rhiscom's requirements activity.

Process Engineer. According to Fig. 2, the process engineer is in charge of the tasks *Define Organizational Process*, *Define Organizational Context*, and *Define Tailoring Rules* (orange in the figure). The definition of the process, together with its variability, is addressed using EPF Composer. Figure 3 shows a part of Rhiscom's process highlighting its variability. We have also developed a web-based tool to support the process engineer to *Define Organizational Context* [16]. The only task the process engineer should do applying the proposed tool is to *Define Tailoring Rules.*

Project Manager. The most appealing feature of the proposed tool is that the project manager should only *Define Project Context*, i.e., the characteristics of the project at hand. However, as shown in Fig. 2, he/she can only do this once the *Organizational Context* has been defined. Afterwards, once the *Project Adapted Process* is available, he/she can apply it for developing the concrete project.

The Proposed Tool. The tool plays an active role in the process. Once the *Organizational Process* and the *Project Context* have been defined, the tool is in charge of generating the *Project Adapted Process.* However, and according to the description in Sect. 3, the internal structure of the tool is much more complex than just a task.

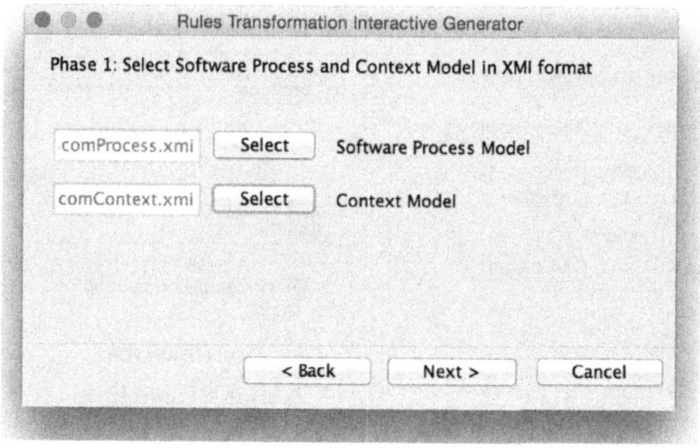

Fig. 4. User interface for input models selection.

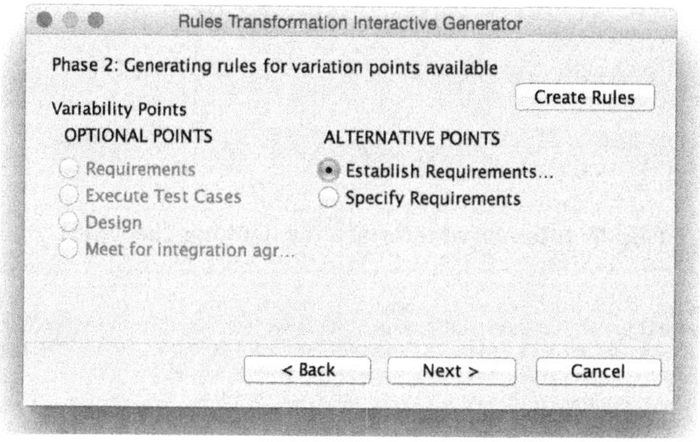

Fig. 5. Selection of process variation points.

4.2 Application Case

Rhiscom is a Chilean software company that develops integrated software and hardware solutions for points-of-sale. It is a 15 year old company and it has defined its development process around five years ago. Since two years ago, they have been addressing the issue of systematically tailoring its process, provided that is was being tailored anyway but with no agreed criterion. In this section we illustrate how the proposed tool supports this activity for tailoring Rhiscom's process.

The process engineer uses a visual interface to indicate the models that will be used in the definition of tailoring rules (Fig. 4). After that, she/he can define tailoring rules for each process variation point. This activity involves two steps: the interactive definition of a decision model (using the visual user interface) and the automatic generation of the tailoring transformation, based on the previously built decision model.

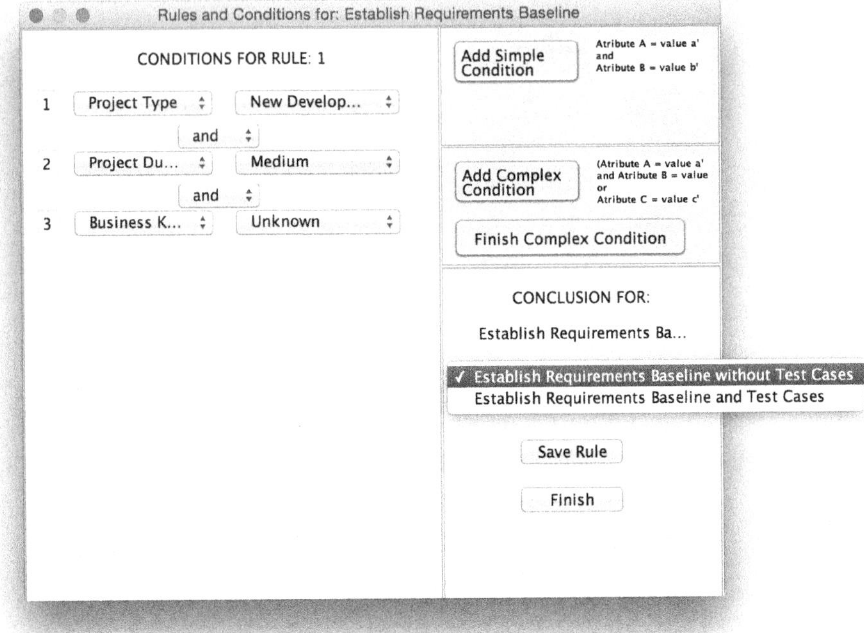

Fig. 6. Interactive interface for defining the VDM.

```
helper def:ruleAlt1(tu:MM!TaskUse): MM!TaskDefinition=if(thisModule.getValue('Project Type')
        = 'New Development' and thisModule.getValue('Project Duration') = 'Medium'
        and thisModule.getValue('Business Knowledge') = 'Unknown')
    then thisModule.getTaskDefinition('Establish Requirements Baseline and Test Cases')
else thisModule.getTaskDefinition(tu.name)
endif;
```

Fig. 7. Tailoring transformation. "Establish Requirements Baseline" has alternatives so a decision is made with respect to which one is included.

During the first step, the process engineer uses the tool to indicate which variation point he/she will define (see Fig. 5) and then interactively define the relationships between the context attribute values and the process variable element. Repeating this for all variable elements will yield a *Variation Decision Model* (VDM). This VDM is a mapping, i.e., a high-level representation of the transformation rules. The VDM is then used as input for a Higher Order Transformation (HOT) to automatically generate the tailoring transformation that will be used to adapt the organizational software process model.

Interactive Definition of the Variation Decision Model. Once the process engineer has specified the models that will be used as input, she/he can start with the interactive definition of the *Variation Decision Model*. Figure 5 shows five optional variation points for Rhiscom's process: *Requirements*, *Execute Test Cases*, *Meet for integration agreement*, and *Design*, and also two alternative

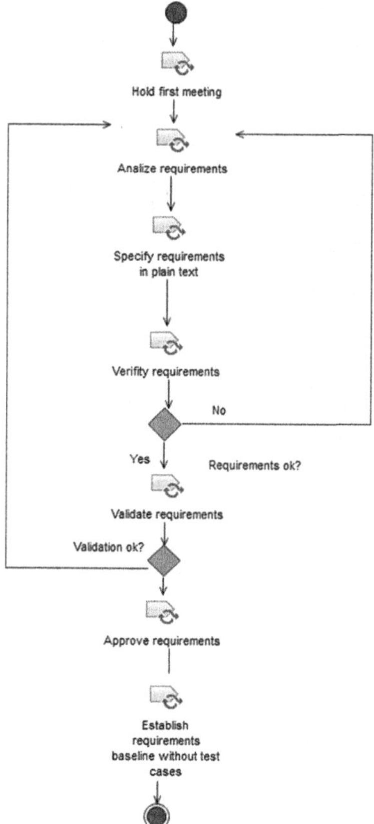

Fig. 8. Rhiscom's process after applying the tailoring transformation.

variation points: *Establish Requirements Baseline* and *Specify Requirements*. If the user selects a variation point (e.g., *Establish Requirements Baseline*) and clicks on the "Create Rules" button, she/he can define the rules that will be used to tailor the organizational process in such a point, depending on the values of the context attributes of a specific project.

Figure 6 shows the interactive interface that allows the process engineer to define the decision model. Each decision has a *condition* and a *conclusion*. The condition is a predicate that could be simple or complex. Simple predicates are typically a conjunction of context attributes and particular values. Complex conditions also consider the use of disjunctions. In the upper right part of the figure we can see the conditions defined so far.

In this example, the engineer defines that the *Establish Requirements Baseline* activity should be replaced by "Establish Requirements Baseline without Test Cases" when the "Project Tye" is New Development, "Project Duration" is Medium and "Business Knowledge" is Unknown. This decision is part of the adaptations defined by Rhiscom for its organizational process. The actual ATL rule, that is generated according to this interactive definition, is shown in Fig. 7.

Resulting Process. Figure 8 shows the resulting process after applying the tailoring transformation interactively generated. As can be seen, the "*Establish Requirements Baseline*" task has been replaced by "*Establish Requirements Baseline without Test Cases*" as indicated by the process engineer.

5 Conclusions and Future Work

We have presented model-based tool for interactively defining and automatically generating process tailoring transformations, as well as shown its practical application in a real world example. The tool combines MDE and generative programming aspects, together with a web-based user interface. The resulting tool is powerful enough to generate the tailoring transformation for a real world company's process and yet usable for process engineers.

The main purpose of building an interactive tool was aiding the process engineer to tailor her/his process. We provided a running example that shows how to apply MDE concepts without directly interacting with the code or requiring knowledge about transformation languages. Transformations in general could be quite complex. However, we have shown that building process tailoring transformations requires only a few types of rules that may be automatically generated from a VDM. Although we have been able to generate transformations automatically, this kind of tool is only applicable for the software process domain, but this experience can be the starting point to be extended to other domains.

Complex rules can be generated using simple conditions, logical operators and complex conditions (with logical connectors). In this sense, if there are rules with different conclusions on the same variability point, it still does not solve it; this can be addressed by adding constraint definitions. Future work is necessary to extend the VDM to support constraints definition between software process elements and complex rules.

We are currently conducting industrial experiments in order to collect empirical evidence to help us validate the tool expressiveness for tailoring a variety of software processes and its usability for real world process engineers.

Acknowledgements. This work is partly funded by Project Fondef GEMS IT13I20010, Conicyt, Chile. The work of Luis Silvestre was supported by PhD Scholarship Program of Conicyt, Chile (CONICYT-PCHA/2013-63130130).

References

1. Balasubramanian, D., Narayanan, A., van Buskirk, C.P., Karsai, G.: The Graph Rewriting and Transformation Language: GReAT. ECEASST 1 (2006)
2. Bastarrica, M.C., Simmonds, J., Silvestre, L.: Using megamodeling to improve industrial adoption of complex MDE solutions. In: Atlee, J.M., Kulkarni, V., Clark, T., France, R.B., Rumpe, B. (eds.) 6th International Workshop on Modeling in Software Engineering, MiSE 2014, Hyderabad, India, 2–3 June 2014, pp. 31–36. ACM (2014)

3. Bendraou, R., Jézéquel, J., Gervais, M., Blanc, X.: A comparison of six UML-based languages for software process modeling. IEEE Trans. Softw. Eng. **36**(5), 662–675 (2010)
4. Bézivin, J., Büttner, F., Gogolla, M., Jouault, F., Kurtev, I., Lindow, A.: Model transformations? Transformation models!. In: Wang, J., Whittle, J., Harel, D., Reggio, G. (eds.) MoDELS 2006. LNCS, vol. 4199, pp. 440–453. Springer, Heidelberg (2006)
5. Costa Silva, G., Rose, L.M., Calinescu, R.: A qualitative study of model transformation development approaches: supporting novice developers. In: Hebig, R., Bendraou, R., Völter, M., Chaudron, M.R.V. (eds.) Proceedings of the 1st International Workshop on Model-Driven Development Processes and Practices Co-located with ACM/IEEE 17th International Conference on Model Driven Engineering Languages and Systems (MoDELS 2014), Valencia, Spain, 28 September 2014, vol. 1249. CEUR Workshop Proceedings, pp. 18–27. CEUR-WS.org (2014)
6. De Oliveira Barros, M., Werner, C.M.L., Travassos, G.H.: A system dynamics metamodel for software process modeling. Softw. Process: Improv. Pract. **7**(3–4), 161–172 (2002)
7. Hurtado Alegría, J.A., Bastarrica, M.C., Quispe, A., Ochoa, S.F.: MDE-based process tailoring strategy. J. Softw.: Evol. Process **26**(4), 386–403 (2014)
8. Irazabal, J., Pons, C., Neil, C.: Model transformation as a mechanism for the implementation of domain specific transformation languages. SADIO Electron. J. Inform. Oper. Res. **9**(1), 49–66 (2010)
9. Cánovas Izquierdo, J.L., Molina, J.G.: A domain specific language for extracting models in software modernization. In: Paige, R.F., Hartman, A., Rensink, A. (eds.) ECMDA-FA 2009. LNCS, vol. 5562, pp. 82–97. Springer, Heidelberg (2009)
10. Kalnins, A., Barzdins, J., Celms, E.: Model transformation language MOLA. In: Aßmann, U., Akşit, M., Rensink, A. (eds.) MDAFA 2003. LNCS, vol. 3599, pp. 62–76. Springer, Heidelberg (2005)
11. Kappel, G., Langer, P., Retschitzegger, W., Schwinger, W., Wimmer, M.: Model transformation by-example: a survey of the first wave. In: Düsterhöft, A., Klettke, M., Schewe, K.-D. (eds.) Conceptual Modelling and Its Theoretical Foundations. LNCS, vol. 7260, pp. 197–215. Springer, Heidelberg (2012)
12. Kleppe, A.G., Warmer, J., Bast, W.: MDA Explained: The Model Driven Architecture: Practice and Promise. Addison-Wesley Longman Publishing Co., Inc., Boston (2003)
13. Mens, T., Czarnecki, K., Gorp, P.V.: 04101 discussion - a taxonomy of model transformations. In: Bézivin, J., Heckel, R. (eds.) Language Engineering for Model-Driven Software Development, 29 February–5. March 2004, volume 04101 of Dagstuhl Seminar Proceedings. Internationales Begegnungs- und Forschungszentrum für Informatik (IBFI), Schloss Dagstuhl, Germany (2004)
14. Object Management Group. Software Process Engineering Metamodel SPEM 2.0 OMG Specification. Technical report ptc/07-11-01, OMG (2008)
15. Oldevik, J., Neple, T., Grønmo, R., Aagedal, J.Ø., Berre, A.-J.: Toward standardised model to text transformations. In: Hartman, A., Kreische, D. (eds.) ECMDA-FA 2005. LNCS, vol. 3748, pp. 239–253. Springer, Heidelberg (2005)
16. Ortega, D., Silvestre, L., Bastarrica, M.C., Ochoa, S.: A tool for modeling software development contexts. In: Alarcón, R., Barceló, P. (eds.) SCCC, Valparaiso, Chile, 2012. IEEE Computer Society (2012)
17. Project, A.E.: Atlas transformation language (2006). http://www.eclipse.org/atl/
18. Rumpe, B., Weisemöller, I.: A Domain Specific Transformation Language. Computing Research Repository (2014). abs/1409.2309

19. Silvestre, L., Bastarrica, M.C., Ochoa, S.F.: Implementing HOTs that generate transformations with two input models. In: XXXII International Conference of the Chilean Computer Science Society SCCC 2013, Temuco, Chile, November 2013
20. Silvestre, L., Bastarrica, M.C., Ochoa, S.F.: A model-based tool for generating software process model tailoring transformations. In: Pires, L.F., Hammoudi, S., Filipe, J., das Neves, R.C. (eds.) MODELSWARD 2014 - Proceedings of the 2nd International Conference on Model-Driven Engineering and Software Development, Lisbon, Portugal, 7–9 January 2014, pp. 533–540. SciTePress (2014)
21. Simmonds, J., Bastarrica, M.C., Silvestre, L., Quispe, A.: Variability in software process models: requirements for adoption in industrial settings. In: 4th International Workshop on Product LinE Approaches in Software Engineering, San Francisco, California, USA, May 2013
22. Sun, Y., White, J., Gray, J.: Model transformation by demonstration. In: Schürr, A., Selic, B. (eds.) MODELS 2009. LNCS, vol. 5795. Springer, Heidelberg (2009)
23. Tisi, M., Cabot, J., Jouault, F.: Improving higher-order transformations support in ATL. In: Tratt, L., Gogolla, M. (eds.) ICMT 2010. LNCS, vol. 6142, pp. 215–229. Springer, Heidelberg (2010)
24. Varró, D., Balogh, Z.: Automating model transformation by example using inductive logic programming. In: Cho, Y., Wainwright, R.L., Haddad, H., Shin, S.Y., Koo, Y.W. (eds.) Proceedings of the 2007 ACM Symposium on Applied Computing (SAC), Seoul, Korea, 11–15 March 2007, pp. 978–984. ACM (2007)
25. Varró, D., Varró, G., Pataricza, A.: Designing the automatic transformation of visual languages. Sci. Comput. Program. **44**(2), 205–227 (2002)
26. Wimmer, M., Strommer, M., Kargl, H, Kramler, G.: Towards model transformation generation by-example. In: 40th Hawaii International Conference on Systems Science (HICSS-40 2007), CD-ROM/Abstracts Proceedings, 3–6 January 2007, Waikoloa, Big Island, HI, USA, p. 285. IEEE Computer Society (2007)

Main Features for MDD Tools: An Exploratory Study

Beatriz Marín[1(✉)], Andrés Salinas[1], Juan Morandé[1], Giovanni Giachetti[2], and Jose Luis de la Vara[3]

[1] Facultad de Ingeniería, Universidad Diego Portales, Av. Ejército 441, Santiago, Chile
{beatriz.marin, andres.salinas, juan.morande}@mail.udp.cl

[2] Facultad de Ingeniería, Universidad Andrés Bello, Sazié 2325, Santiago, Chile
giovanni.giachetti@unab.cl

[3] Certus Centre for Software V&V, Simula Research Laboratory, P.O. Box 134, 1325 Lysaker, Norway
jdelavara@simula.no

Abstract. Software Engineering aims to apply methods and processes for effective and efficient software development. One of the most relevant paradigms for achieving this goal is Model-Driven Development (MDD), which advocates the use of models for automatically generating software products. However, an important issue in the development and selection of MDD technologies is the lack of standardization regarding the features that need to be considered to support the current industry needs. This hinders the comparison of existing technologies since there is no reference point for the creation of new MDD approaches with their corresponding supporting tools. As a solution, this paper proposes a set of main features that MDD tools must support. The set is based on different characteristics that have been acknowledged in the literature, and has been validated by means of an exploratory study with tool vendors. We also present an analysis of how eight industrial MDD tools support these features in order to illustrate the application of our proposal.

Keywords: Model-Driven Development (MDD) · Tools · Features · Exploratory study · Model-Driven Architecture (MDA)

1 Introduction

The goal of Software Engineering is to apply methods for the effective and efficient development of software products [15]. The Model-Driven Development (MDD) paradigm [34] has become a relevant way for achieving this purpose in both academia and industry. Many researchers are working on the development of new MDD approaches for a wide variety of software-related purposes, such as requirements engineering [17], testing [36], and compliance [5]. Practitioners are increasingly adopting MDD [11], which is also reflected in the wide variety of OMG (Object Management Group) standards [24]. MDD approaches typically use technology-independent models at different abstraction levels in order to generate software products by means of model

S. Hammoudi et al. (Eds.): MODELSWARD 2014, CCIS 506, pp. 183–196, 2015.
DOI: 10.1007/978-3-319-25156-1_12

transformations. The software products include source code, documentation, and modeling artifacts.

The MDD paradigm is moving the software development processes to a different dimension, from the solution space (software product) to the problem space (conceptual models). Thus, MDD is focusing on the specification of the real-world phenomena to support instead of on the way to support them. In this journey, the success of MDD solution adoption is directly related to the capability of the available tools to satisfy the needs of different development projects. However, and even though there exists an important amount of MDD tools in the software industry [19], there is a shortage of references that provide a collection of key aspects that need to be considered for selecting or developing a MDD tool. These tools must be properly aligned with industrial MDD processes, needs, and expectations, thus taking this collection of key aspects into account can be essential for MDD tool success.

This paper contributes to mitigating the above issue by proposing a set of main features that MDD tools should possess. This set extends past proposals (see Sect. 2) by compiling several characteristics that have been recently acknowledged by different authors. The set of main features for MDD tools has been validated by means of an exploratory study. A questionnaire was created to ask practitioners about the need for the features, with four people working at tool vendor companies participating in the study. Finally, we show the application of the set of features by analyzing eight MDD tools.

The main contribution of the paper is twofold. Firstly, it presents and analyses a set of main features that a MDD tool must have in order to be successfully adopted in industry. Secondly, it presents which of these features are currently supported by a set of existing MDD tools. This contribution can be very valuable for both researchers and practitioners. Researchers will gain awareness of the features that they need to take into account when proposing new MDD approaches, in order to facilitate their adoption in industry. Practitioners will be able to more easily identify those MDD tools that will be more suitable in practice.

The rest of the paper is organized as follows. Section 2 reviews related work. Section 3 introduces the exploratory study conducted. Section 4 presents the main features for MDD tools and the study results, whereas Sect. 5 presents an analysis of these features in a set of industrial MDD tools. Section 6 presents conclusions and future work.

2 Related Work

Specification of key aspects for software development tools and the application of the corresponding set of features for tool analysis is an area to which significant attention has been paid the last years. Thus, it is easy to find studies that have analyzed and compared software development tools, including tools for requirements engineering [3], collaborative software development [32], and testing [38], among other activities. However, the number of studies proposing sets of key aspects for MDD tools is very limited. We have identified the following ones.

Based on his experience in the development of IBM Rational tools [34], Bran Selic proposed the following success criteria for the development of MDD tools:

- **Standards.** The use of standards is essential to facilitate the adoption of new technologies and reduce the learning curve related to the application of MDD software processes. In this sense, the Model-Driven Architecture (MDA) proposed by the OMG is probably the most well-known implementation schema for MDD tools.
- **Observability and Executability of the Model.** Observability refers to the integration of comparison tools that help in the identification of model versions. Executability refers to the capability to execute the models in early stages of software development, supporting the analysis of system behavior though experimentation and before system deployment.
- **Efficiency of the Generated Code.** The efficiency of the generated code can be decomposed into performance and use of memory. In addition, it is important to take into account the size of the generated system and the compilation time of the models.

In a similar way to Selic's work, Richard Paige and Dániel Varró [28] reported on the knowledge obtained during the development of the Epsilon [8] and VIATRA2 [1] tools. The main conclusions in relation to the features of MDD tools were as follows:

- **Use of Requirement Models for Driving the Development Process.** The use of requirement models in MDD processes help to understand and handle development complexity. Requirements models can drive system construction in terms of development iterations.
- **Flexibility of Architectures and Modeling Tools.** When the MDD paradigm appeared, the flexibility of architectures was promoted instead of the selection of the correct architecture. By having a flexible architecture, it is possible to adapt the generation of the final software products to different architectural patterns in accordance to the needs of the development project.
- **Modeling Technologies.** Modeling technologies refer to the methods used to represent the models (e.g., EMF model representation). The selection of the modeling technology can significantly affect the usability and flexibility of a modeling tool in aspects such as the implementation of model transformations and typing of model elements. In addition, the final user does not necessarily need to know how the representation of the models is implemented; final users just need to know the graphical representation of the models in order to handle the complexity of the modeling technology.

Although the insights provided are useful, the publications above considered a limited set of specific views for the development of MDD tools. Such views were also only based on the authors' experience and opinion. We tackle these issues by considering different publications for the definition of the main features that MDD tools must possess, and by performing an exploratory study with practitioners in order to validate the need for the features. The remaining publications from which we have defined the set of main features, and the motivation for their definition, are presented in Sect. 4.

3 Exploratory Study

In this section, we present an exploratory study on the main features for MDD tools. It corresponds to qualitative research [13], also called flexible research [37], which aims to interpret a phenomenon. The exploratory study has been carried out by means of a survey, which helps to collect information from people that describe, compare and explain knowledge and behavior [37]. This study was carried out by following the guidelines presented in [14].

3.1 Research Question

The aim of this survey is to gain knowledge about the main features that a MDD tool must have from a practitioner's viewpoint. Thus, we have formulated the following research question **RQ:** What features of MDD tools do practitioners regard as the most important ones?

3.2 Survey Design

The survey corresponds to an exploratory study [37], which provides insights for future research. This study consisted in an online questionnaire with 19 questions. The questions were defined by considering the relevant related work presented in Sect. 2. We also added model verification and interoperability as possible features for MDD tools.

Model verification is a relevant feature for ensuring that: (1) all the model information can be transformed into the corresponding software artifacts (syntactic verification) and; (2) the final software product satisfies user requirements (semantic verification) [18]. Model interoperability is a key feature to facilitate (and automate) the interchange of modeling information among tools related to a same domain. For example, it is necessary for interoperability among different UML (Unified Modeling Language) tools, as well as for interoperability among different modeling approaches [29]. Table 1 shows the 19 questions and the related feature for the questionnaire.

Each question was answered using a 5-point Likert scale, which goes from 1 (totally disagree) to 5 (totally agree). Some parts were presented in a randomized way in order to avoid the possible errors in the answers produced by fatigue. Also, some parts were presented using icons that represent the values of the 5-point Likert scale. The respondents had the possibility to add more information in each answer in a text box that was placed in each question. The estimated time for completing the questionnaire was 15 min. The questionnaire can be accessed at https://testmodeproject.typeform.com/to/eUhWIU.

3.3 Instrument Evaluation and Data Collection

Regarding the instrument evaluation, the first and fourth authors screened the questionnaire in order to validate the understandability of each question. From this

Table 1. Questions and related features of the questionnaire.

Id	Question	Feature
Q1	The MDD tool must support the standard UML	Standardization
Q2	The MDD tool must support MDA in terms of CIM, PIM, PSM	Standardization
Q3	The MDD tool must provide extension mechanisms for modeling languages customization to allow the communication with different tools	Interoperability
Q4	The MDD tool must provide extension mechanisms that allow the communication/interoperability with different tools	Interoperability
Q5	It is necessary to have a graphical visualization of a model	Observability
Q6	It is necessary to have a version manager of models	Observability
Q7	It is necessary to have easy human interaction (such as touch screens) to work with models	Efficiency
Q8	The MDD tool must provide verification mechanisms of the models	Verification
Q9	The MDD tool must provide automatic defect detection for the models	Verification
Q10	The MDD tool must provide automatic test case generation of the models	Verification
Q11	The MDD tool must provide simulations of the executability of the model	Executability
Q12	The MDD tool must allow redefinitions of the transformation of the models	Flexibility
Q13	The generated code of an MDD tool must have the same efficiency as the code generated with traditional programming	Flexibility
Q14	The MDD tool must allow the selection of different architectural patterns to generate code	Flexibility
Q15	The MDD tool must be able to generate code reviews	Code generation
Q16	The MDD tool must generate at least the skeleton of the code	Code generation
Q17	The MDD tool must generate totally executable code	Code generation
Q18	The MDD tool must support the specification of all views of a system	Requirements
Q19	The MDD tool must save the traceability from requirements to code	Requirements

evaluation, some minor changes were made in the wording of the questions. Then, a pilot study was performed in order to validate the time for completing the questionnaire. Four undergraduate researchers completed the questionnaire, and the results suggested that it was possible to complete it in less than 15 min.

Regarding data collection, the first and third authors received an e-mail when a respondent finished the questionnaire. Afterwards, a table was created with all the responses for further analysis.

3.4 Subjects Characteristics and Data Analysis

Respondents were selected from our industrial collaboration networks, and four tool vendors completed the online questionnaire. The collected answers are shown in Fig. 1. TV1 to TV4 represent the tool vendors that participated in the survey.

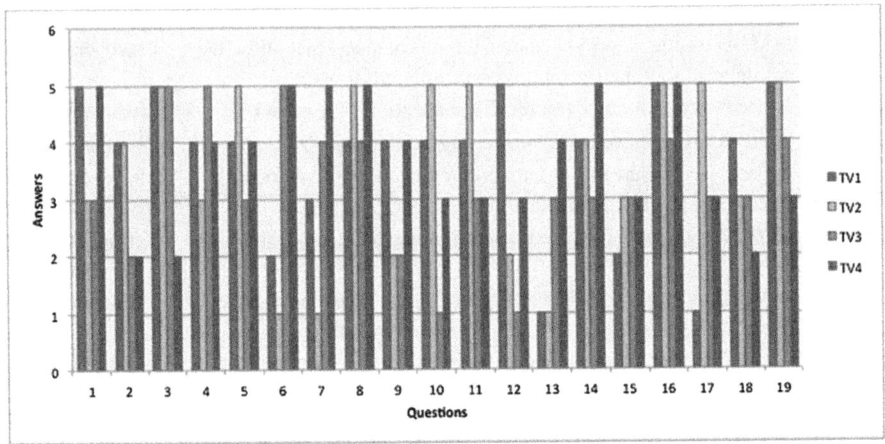

Fig. 1. Study results.

From the results, we can state that the top-three questions (the best results) correspond to Q16, Q8, and Q19, which are related to code generation, verification, and requirements. This indicates that these are important characteristics for MDD tools. By contrast, the worst result is for Q13, related to the efficiency of the generated code, which suggests that in general terms it does not seem necessary that the generated code has the same efficiency as code programmed manually.

Even though there are some threats to the validity of this exploratory study, such as the representativeness of the questions for the different criteria, we consider that it is possible to derive the main features that a MDD tool must have. Repeating the exploratory study with other subjects (e.g., tool vendors or tool users) can give more information about the generalizability of the results obtained.

4 Main Features for MDD Tools

This section presents a set of features that a MDD tool designed to work in industrial projects should offer. The features are based on the literature and on the results of the exploratory study.

4.1 Standardization and Interoperability

Since its inception, the OMG has promoted the standardization of different model-based and object-oriented approaches, such as UML [26] and MDA [21].

Standardization allows establishing an agreement of good practices that facilitate the reuse and interoperability among different tools and modeling approaches, for example by using XMI [27]. For Q1, 50 % of the respondents totally agreed upon MDD tool support to the UML standard, whereas the other 50 % were neutral about this question. For Q2, 50 % of respondents did not agree upon MDD tools support to MDA in terms of CIM, PIM, and PSM, but the other 50 % did. No total agreement or disagreement was indicated for Q2.

Regarding interoperability, 75 % of the respondents totally agreed with Q3, which states that MDD tools must provide extension mechanisms for modeling language customization. For Q4, 75 % of the respondents indicated that MDD tools must provide extension mechanisms for communication or interoperability among different tools.

4.2 Visualization and Management of Models

The main input artifact in a MDD approach is a model, which specifies all the views that represent a system. MDD tools must provide a suitable set of management and visualization features for model definition. The minimum feature to be considered is the possibility of visualizing the models at design time. In particular, it is necessary to provide a graphical user interface that facilitates the management of multiple views that are modeled for a system. In fact, 75 % of the respondents stated in Q5 that it is absolutely necessary to have a graphical visualization of the model.

However, the graphical user interface is not the only concern related to visualization that should be taken into account when a MDD tool is built. Nowadays, more than ever, it is necessary to provide user interfaces that take into account quality characteristics such as usability [12], and new characteristics of hardware devices such as touch panels in desktop and laptop computers [10]. In Q7, we found that 50 % of the respondents agreed upon having an easy human interaction to work with models, and the other 50 % answered that it is not necessary.

Regarding model versioning, in Q6 50 % of the respondents stated that it is absolutely necessary to manage it. They put in the open textbox that this is the only way to work in collaborative industrial projects, where different members of a development team can work over the same model. The remaining 50 % of the respondents indicated that it is not mandatory to have a version manager, but it is a desirable feature.

4.3 Verification

MDD tools use conceptual models as input to generate code. In this context, the generated code becomes black box, rarely reviewed software, in the same way that the machine code generated by a programming language compiler is rarely reviewed because this generation is performed using widely-accepted standards in industry. For this reason, the verification of the model should be a mandatory feature for an industrial MDD tool. In fact, 100 % of the respondents indicated in Q8 that MDD tools must provide verification mechanisms. This implies that the MDD tool is used to find the presence of desirable characteristics and the absence of undesirable characteristics in a model.

Regarding the absence of undesirable characteristics, different researchers have applied reading techniques or heuristics to identify defects in UML models [4, 7, 16, 35]. When asked if it is necessary that a MDD tool provides automatic defect detection in the models (Q9), the respondents indicated that it is desirable, but with a deactivation possibility because some defects depend on the methodology selected in a project. In other words, it would be good to support custom defect detection mechanisms for fulfilling modelers' needs.

4.4 Testing

The most important and most frequently used quality assurance technique applied in the software industry is testing [20]. As a way of performing testing of models, several researchers have proposed model-based testing approaches to generate test cases [6]. These approaches usually create a state transition model to represent the current state of a system and the next state, specifying the events that occur to change the state. In these models, test case design focuses on event execution paths. However, state transition models only provide the behavioral view of the final software system. Thus, after the application of these test cases, it is necessary to manually test the remaining functionality of a system. MDD tools should provide model-based testing approaches that focus on holistic models, in order to reduce the human effort in testing.

In Q10, 50 % of the respondents answered that MDD tools must provide automatic test case generation from models, and the other 50 % answered that it could be good but that it is not essential.

4.5 Code Generation and Simulation

A MDD tool must generate at least the skeleton of the code. The exploratory study supports this assertion in Q16, since all the respondents agreed upon this statement, 75 % of them in full agreement.

Supporting technologies for automating model-based operations such as model transformation, validation, verification, and compilation, are essential for achieving the benefits of MDD. Depending on the tools, code generation can go from the skeleton or code fragments to the complete code of software products. Nevertheless, in Q17 of the study only 25 % of the respondents agreed with the fact that a MDD tool must generate totally executable code, and 50 % of the respondents stated that in some cases the total code generation is adequate. This 50 % of respondents argued that the model needed for generating completely executable code has the same complexity as the code generated.

Regarding simulation, MDD tools should allow the execution of models even though they are incomplete, but valid. The idea is not to wait to finish the model in order to see how the software obtained from the already-specified part of the model looks like. This allows early model correction. In Q11 of the study, 50 % of the respondents agreed that MDD tools must generate simulations of the models created.

4.6 Transformation

A model transformation corresponds to a set of rules and activities such as refactoring, reverse engineering, and application of patterns, among others. Transformations take one or more models as input and, by applying the rules specified, generate one or more output models. This can include the code of the final software product (implementation model). A suitable MDD tool must offer a number of predefined transformations for ensuring a complete model transformation. Features oriented to customize the transformation rules implemented by an MDD tool are supported by only 25 % of the respondents in Q12 of the study.

4.7 Efficiency and Scalability

MDD tools should significantly reduce system development time, effort, and complexity. The productivity gained by using MDD tools can be significant when the code generated is similar to code manually generated in terms of efficiency and scalability. A relevant efficiency measure that can be considered when evaluating a MDD tool performance in relation to the volume of information handled are execution time and the amount of memory used by the generated code. It is expected that the efficiency in execution time of automatically-generated code has a deviation no greater than a 10 % compared to manually programmed code [34]. Results of the study in Q13 reveal that efficiency in the generated code is not a relevant feature for the respondents, taking into account the increase in the productivity of MDD projects.

4.8 Architectures and Maintenance

Since MDD tools work with platform-independent models, the tools must support the transformation to executable code not only to a variety of languages, but also to different architectural design patterns. For example, if a software developer wanted to generate an application in a particular programming language, then the MDD tool should allow the selection between a Client-Server architecture [2] or Model-View-Controller architecture [33]. In Q14 of the exploratory study, 75 % of the respondents agreed that a MDD tool must allow the selection of different architectural patterns for code generation. Regarding the generation of code reviews, 75 % of the respondents are neutral about the ability of MDD tools to perform partial generation of code after model changes when asked in Q15, so that it is not necessary to recompile the whole model if a small change is made. Nonetheless, we believe that this would facilitate software maintenance when small changes or corrections are made during system lifecycle.

4.9 Requirements

Requirements management helps to adequately handle a software development project. To do this, it is desirable that the MDD tool supports the traceability from requirements specifications to the other views of a system. In Q19, 75 % of respondents agreed that is necessary to support the requirements traceability in MDD tools. The remaining 25 % answered that it depends on the usage of the tool since some MDD tools are focused on specific modeling phases.

5 General Analysis of MDD Tools

This section presents a general analysis of the features that existing MDD tools have. To this end, a list of products that are compliant with the MDA approach [22] were considered. This list presents 48 MDA tools. However, many of these tools are no longer available or have not been updated for more than one year. From the 48 MDA tools, only 10 (21 %) are currently in use and have active support. The remaining 79 % have been deprecated or acquired by a larger company.

The 10 available tools provide support for different systems, such as real-time systems or management information systems. We focus the analysis on MDD tools for management information systems since they are more broadly used in industry. Just three tools recognized by the OMG were taken into account in the analysis. Open-source tools that are not included in the OMG site were also included in order to make a more representative analysis. This resulted in the selection of five open-source tools, and thus eight MDD tools were finally analyzed.

First, a characterization of the selected tools was performed regarding the modeling language used, the system views covered by the tool, the language for the specification of the functional view, and the software products generated. This is shown in Table 2.

As Table 2 shows, seven tools support UML [25, 26] and one tool supports OO-Method [30] as modeling language. UML is the de-facto standard, and OO-Method starts from the UML class diagram and adds semantic information to allow the generation of fully-executable code. Using UML or UML-based modeling languages reduces the learning curve of a MDD tool and facilitates the integration with different project management tools.

As a way to avoid or diminish defects and faults in the generated applications, it is very important that a MDD tool provides support to the holistic representation of a system in a conceptual model, including the static, dynamic, functional, and presentation views. More details of these views can be found in [19]. From the eight tools analyzed, and as shown in Table 2:

- One tool (OpenMDX) does not detail the different views supported;
- Two tools (AndroMDA and IBM Rational Rose) support the structural and the dynamic views;
- Three tools (Acceleo, TopCased, and StarUML) support the structural, dynamic and functional views, and;
- Only two tools (Integranova and Blue Age) support structural, dynamic, functional, and presentation views.

Regarding the language for the specification of the functional view, four tools use OCL [23], one tool uses Plain Old Java Objects (POJO) [9], and one tool uses OASIS [31], which is a proprietary scripting language similar to OCL. One tool does not

Table 2. Characterization of the MDD tools analyzed.

MDD tool	Modeling language	System views	Functional view language	Products generated
AndroMDA	UML by using MagicDraw	Structural and dynamic views	–	Structure of the system
OpenMDX	UML	–	POJO	–
Acceleo	UML 2, by using EMF	Structural, dynamic, and functional views	OCL	Code skeleton
TopCased	UML 2, by using EMF	Structural, dynamic, and functional views	OCL	Code skeleton. Documentation. Allows complete code generation by using plugins
StarUML	UML 2.0	Structural, dynamic, and functional views	–	Code skeleton and requirements and implementation documents
Integranova	OO-method	Structural, dynamic, functional, and presentation views	OASIS	Complete, fully working generation code. Documentation. Functional size measurement
IBM rational rose	UML 2.1	Structural and dynamic views	OCL	Complete, fully working generation code
Blu age	UML 2.1	Structural, dynamic, functional, and presentation views	OCL	Complete, fully working generation code

specify the final product generated, four tools generate the skeleton of code, and just three tools generate the code completely. An analysis performed to the features defined in Sect. 4 shows that, in relation to standardization, most of the tools support UML. Only one tool does not support UML, but it supports an extension of UML called OO-Method. However, not all the tools support the same version of UML, which would alleviate the exportation of the models to other formats and promote the interoperability of the tools.

Regarding the visualization of the models, the analyzed tools provide graphical visualization or connections with graphical tools (such as MagicDraw or Eclipse EMF). However, there do not exist any tools that improve the usability by taking advantage of new interaction features provided by current devices such as touch panels [10], which could increase the productivity of software engineers. For model verification, some tools offer verification of syntactical defects in the models and verification of the consistency of the different views supported. Nevertheless, it is also necessary that

MDD tools offer verification of semantic defects in order to prevent faults when the generated system is executed (e.g., appropriate specification of the cardinality involved in the ends of an association between two classes).

With respect to testing and simulation of the models, the analyzed MDD tools do not offer options to generate tests or simulation artifacts in order to facilitate model validation, rather than testing the code once the system is generated. Even though the tools offer refactoring and reverse engineering features, they do not provide facilities to customize transformations in particular situations.

Regarding efficiency and architecture, commercial tools such as Rational or Integranova provide ready-to-use model compilation facilities to generate code and database scripts in different target platforms. In contrast, open-source tools require manual specification of the model-transformation scripts to perform model compilation tasks.

Moreover, none of the eight tools provides support to code optimization.

Finally, regarding requirements traceability, the tools analyzed do not provide mechanisms to ensure the traceability from requirements to code.

6 Conclusion

This paper presents a set of features that a MDD (Model-Driven Development) tool should have for successful application and adoption of the MDD paradigm in industry. An exploratory study was conducted to validate this set of main features for MDD tools.

In addition, an analysis of available MDD tools has been presented to evaluate the support to the features proposed in existing tools. Although the current OMG catalogue of tools was considered for performing this analysis, almost 80 % of these tools are no longer available. This dramatically reduces the set of MDD tools that possess the features proposed and thus are aligned with the needs of software projects.

The remaining tools in the OMG list have reached a level of maturity in which it is possible to generate solutions from a model. However, none of these tools support all the features presented in this paper. An interesting challenge is to collaborate with the existing MDD tool providers to analyze in more depth the features proposed, and to develop a tool (or a suite of tools) more aligned with all these features.

This work is part of a research agenda that aims to develop MDD tools for management information systems. This agenda also include the development of techniques to semantically verify the models and generate test cases automatically from conceptual models as well as empirical studies that validate these techniques. At this respect, the results presented in this paper provide a relevant background for the development of novel model-based technologies that are aligned with industry needs and that cover those features not supported by existing MDD solutions.

Acknowledgements. This work was funded by FONDECYT – CONICYT (Chile) under the projects TESTMODE (Ref. 11121395, 2012–2015), AMODDI (Ref. 11130583, 2013–2017), and from the Research Council of Norway under the project Certus-SFI.

References

1. Balogh, A., Varró, D.: Advanced model transformation language constructs in the VIATRA2 Framework. In: ACM Symposium on Applied Computing – Model Transformation Track (SAC), pp. 1280–1287. ACM Press (2006)
2. Berson, A.: Client/Server Architecture. McGraw-Hill, New York (1996). ISBN 0-07-005664-1
3. Carrillo-de-Gea, J.M., Nicolás, J., Fernández Alemán, J.L., Toval, A., Ebert, C., Vizcaíno, A.: Requirements engineering tools: capabilities, survey and assessment. Inf. Softw. Technol. **54**(10), 1142–1157 (2012)
4. Conradi, R., Mohagheghi, P., Arif, T., Hegde, L.C., Bunde, G.A., Pedersen, A.: Object-oriented reading techniques for inspection of uml models – an industrial experiment. In: Cardelli, L. (ed.) 17th ECOOP, vol. 2749, pp. 483–501. Springer (2003)
5. de la Vara, J.L., Panesar-Walawege, R.K.: SafetyMet: a metamodel for safety standards. In: Moreira, A., Schätz, B., Gray, J., Vallecillo, A., Clarke, P. (eds.) MODELS 2013. LNCS, vol. 8107, pp. 69–86. Springer, Heidelberg (2013)
6. Dias Neto, A.C., Subramanyan, R., Vieira, M., Travassos, G.H.: A survey on model-based testing approaches: a systematic review. In: 1st ACM International Workshop on Empirical Assessment of Software Engineering Languages and Technologies (WEASELTech 2007), pp. 31–36. ACM (2007)
7. Egyed, A.: Instant consistency checking for the UML. In: 28th ICSE, pp. 381–390. ACM (2006)
8. Epsilon. http://www.eclipse.org/gmt/epsilon
9. Fowler, M., Parsons, R., MacKenzie, J.: Pojo, an acronym for: plain old java object. http://www.martinfowler.com/bliki/POJO.html
10. Garber, L.: Tangible user interfaces: technology you can touch. IEEE Comput. **45**(6), 15–18 (2012)
11. Hutchinson, J., Whittle, J., Rouncefield, M., Kristoffersen, S.: Empirical assessment of MDE in industry. In: ICSE 2011, pp. 471–480 (2011)
12. ISO/IEC: ISO/IEC 9126-1, software engineering – product quality – part 1: quality model (2001)
13. Juristo, N., Moreno, A.: Basics of Software Engineering Experimentation. Springer, Berlin (2001)
14. Kitchenham, B., Pfleeger, S.: Personal opinion surveys. In: Shull, F, Singer, J., Sjøberg, D.I. K. (eds.) Guide to Advanced Empirical Software Engineering. Springer, 63–92 (2008)
15. Kitchenham, B., Pfleeger, S.: Software quality: the elusive target. IEEE Softw. **13**(1), 12–21 (1996)
16. Lange, C., Chaudron, M.: An empirical assessment of completeness in UML designs. In: 8th Conference on Empirical Assessment in Software Engineering (EASE), pp. 111–121. IEEE (2004)
17. Loniewski, G., Insfran, E., Abrahão, S.: A systematic review of the use of requirements engineering techniques in model-driven development. In: Petriu, D.C., Rouquette, N., Haugen, Ø. (eds.) MODELS 2010, Part II. LNCS, vol. 6395, pp. 213–227. Springer, Heidelberg (2010)
18. Marín, B., Giachetti, G., Pastor, O., Vos, T.E.J., Abran, A.: Using a functional size measurement procedure to evaluate the quality of models in MDD environments. ACM Trans. Software Eng. Methodol. **22**(3), Article 26, 1–31 (2013)

19. Marín, B., Pereira, J., Giachetti, G., Hermosilla, F., Serral, E.: A general framework for the development of MDD projects. In: 1st International Conference on Model-Driven Engineering and Software Development - MODELSWARD 2013, pp. 257–260. SciTePress (2013)
20. Marín, B., Vos, T., Giachetti, G., Baars, A., Tonella, P.: Towards testing future web applications. In: 5th International Conference on Research Challenges in Information Science (RCIS 2011), pp. 226–237. IEEE Computer Society (2011)
21. OMG: MDA guide version 1.0.1 (2003). http://www.omg.org/mda/mda_files/MDA_Guide_Version1-0.pdf (last visited September 2015)
22. OMG: MDA products and companies. http://www.omg.org/mda/committed-products.htm
23. OMG: Object constraint language 2.0 specification (2006). http://www.omg.org/spec/OCL/2.0 (last visited September 2015)
24. OMG: Object management group web site. http://www.omg.org/
25. OMG: UML 2.1.2 infrastructure specification (2007). http://www.omg.org/spec/UML/2.1.2/Infrastructure/PDF (last visited September 2015)
26. OMG: UML 2.3 superstructure specification (2010). http://www.omg.org/spec/UML/2.3/Superstructure/PDF (last visited September 2015)
27. OMG: XMI 2.1.1 specification (2007). http://www.omg.org/spec/XMI/2.1.1 (last visited September 2015)
28. Paige, R.F., Varró, D.: Lessons learned from building model-driven development tools. Softw. Syst. Model. **11**(4), 527–539 (2012)
29. Pastor, O., Giachetti, G., Marín, B., Valverde, F.: Automating the interoperability of conceptual models in specific development domains. In: Reinhartz-Berger, I., Sturm, A., Clark, T., Cohen, S., Bettin, J. (eds.) Domain Engineering: Product Lines, Languages, and Conceptual Models, pp. 349–374. Springer, Berlin (2013)
30. Pastor, O., Gómez, J., Insfrán, E., Pelechano, V.: The OO-method approach for information systems modelling: from object-oriented conceptual modeling to automated programming. Inf. Syst. **26**(7), 507–534 (2001)
31. Pastor, O., Hayes, F., Bear, S.: OASIS: an object-oriented specification language. In: International Conference on Advanced Information Systems Engineering (CAiSE), pp. 348–363 (1992)
32. Prikladnicki, R., Marczak, S., Carmel, E., Ebert, C.: Technologies to support collaboration across time zones. IEEE Softw. **29**(3), 10–13 (2012)
33. Reenskaug, T.: The model-view-controller (MVC), its past and present. University of Oslo (2003)
34. Selic, B.: The pragmatics of model-driven development. IEEE Softw. **20**(5), 19–25 (2003)
35. Travassos, G., Shull, F., Fredericks, M., Basili, V.: Detecting defects in object-oriented designs: using reading techniques to increase software quality. In: OOPSLA 1999, pp. 47–56 (1999)
36. Utting, M., Pretschner, A., Legeard, B.: A taxonomy of model-based testing approaches. Softw. Test. Verification Reliab. **22**(5), 297–312 (2012)
37. Wohlin, C., Runeson, P., Host, M., Ohlsson, M., Regnell, B., Wesslén, A.: Experimentation in Software Engineering - An Introduction. Kluwer Academic Publishers, Dordrecht (2000)
38. Yang, Q., Li, J.J., Weiss, D.M.: A survey of coverage-based testing tools. Comput. J. **52**(5), 589–597 (2009)

Author Index

Printed in the United States
By Bookmasters